20TH-CENTURY COMPOSERS

The Beatles

PLEASE
USE THE
LITTER
BINS

The Beatles

by Allan Kozinn

Phaidon Press Limited
Regent's Wharf
All Saints Street
London N1 9PA

First published 1995

ISBN 0 7148 3203 0

A CIP catalogue record for this book is
available from the British Library

Printed in Singapore

Frontispiece, the Beatles
in 1962, poised to
revolutionize popular music.
They are, from left to right,
Paul McCartney, Ringo
Starr, John Lennon and
George Harrison.

Contents

Preface

I was nine years old when 'I Want to Hold Your Hand' and 'She Loves You' began to be heard ceaselessly on American radio, but unlike most of my friends, I was not immediately swept up in the madness. Naturally, I was among the tens of millions who watched the Beatles' first appearance on the Ed Sullivan Show, eager to see what all the fuss was about. I remember collecting Beatles gum cards that year, and spending afternoons with friends who had Beatles records and Beatles wigs, and who liked to while away the hours miming Beatles' songs using brooms as surrogate guitars.

Still, I had reservations. I was devoting my own musical energies to classical music, and was studying the piano with a woman whose father had been a pupil of Liszt – and who kept a collection of Liszt's cigar butts, framed in her studio. It was after one of those piano lessons, though, that I began to see the light, or at least part of it. On a warm spring afternoon, as I waited outside my teacher's house for my father to collect me, a car full of teenagers cruised past. It was a convertible, with the top down. 'She Loves You' was blasting from the radio, and everyone was singing along. To a nine-year-old, that was the life: cars, girls, music, fun. To hell with Liszt's cigar butts!

I did not give up my studies of classical music, but from that day in 1964 I stopped thinking of the Beatles' work as a lesser musical sub-species. On some level, as that convertible drove past and as the strains of 'She Loves You' disappeared into the distance, I began wondering what it was that made the Beatles' music so energizing and infectious. I listened closely from then on, and the more I did, the more ingenious the music seemed. Yet whenever I thought I had discovered what made the music tick, a new Beatles record would be released and I would have to start over again, since the Beatles seemed inclined to rewrite their own rules every time they walked into the recording studio.

More than three decades later, the music of many of the Beatles' contemporaries seems quaint and time-bound – great fun for nostalgic moments, and as a snapshot of an exciting time, but not much more. The Beatles' music has worn well by comparison. Their melodies and lyrics, their approach to instrumental textures and vocal harmonies, still seem remarkably fresh. And after listening to each of their songs what must be thousands of times, I can still find twists and subtleties that had not been apparent before. The ability to yield new secrets after many listenings is, of course, one of the hallmarks of great art.

I have tried, in this book, to uncover some of the mechanisms that drive the Beatles' music, and to show how these intuitive but unschooled musicians from Liverpool evolved into some of the most original and inventive musicians the world of popular music has produced. I have given an overview of each of the Beatles' albums and singles, and instead of a song-by-song survey, I have focused on the recordings in which the Beatles made their most significant leaps. It may seem odd, for example, that in my discussion of *Abbey Road*, I give greater attention to John Lennon's quirky, often overlooked, 'I Want You (She's So Heavy)' than to George Harrison's far more popular 'Here Comes the Sun'. My reason for doing so is that 'Here Comes the Sun', for all its beauty, is a relatively straightforward song, whereas 'I Want You (She's So Heavy)' is full of novel and experimental touches.

Of course, the Beatles did not create their music in a vacuum, so although the music is the main focus here, it was also necessary to step back and take a broader view of their development as performers, the details of their public career and, particularly in the final years of their collaboration, the ways in which their changing private concerns were played out in their musical lives.

I would not have written this were it not for the conspiratorial efforts of Ginny Macbeth and Norman Lebrecht, and could not have written it without the advice and encouragement of many friends. I am extremely grateful to Mark Lewisohn, who revolutionized Beatles scholarship and who provided a great deal of information and helpful criticism in an exchange of ideas that has kept our fax machines humming for the last six years. And I cannot sufficiently thank my wife Johanna, who proof-read with a poet's eye and listened to a great deal of arcane information ('listen – there's an extra woo before the guitar solo in the mono mix') with extraordinary patience and support.

I am indebted to the generosity of Eddie Fennell and Eddie Suarez for many particularly interesting, unusual and useful materials; to Marvin Siegel, for agreeing that the *New York Times* needed a Beatles Desk within its classical music department during his years as the paper's culture editor, thereby making it legitimate for me to indulge in occasional Beatling during business hours; to Bill and Leslie King of *Beatlefan* magazine for keeping me up to date and providing an open forum; to Beatles-obsessed friends at various cyber-outposts on the Internet, particularly Martin C. Babicz, Joseph C. Self, D. L. MacLaughlan, Doug Sulpy, Steve Shorten, Steve Marinucci, Kevin O'Hare and Mike Edsall; and to James R. Oestreich, Gene Santoro, Tim Page and Peter G. Davis, decidedly non-Beatles-obsessed friends and colleagues who listened indulgently and offered wise counsel.

Last but certainly not least, I owe an incalculable debt to my father, Richard Kozinn, who taught me a great deal about organizing ideas and turning unruly sheaves of information into reasoned discourse. This book is dedicated to his memory.

Allan Kozinn
New York, 1995

Introduction

Consider these two images of the Beatles, captured on film at key moments in their career:

The first – the earliest performance footage of the group – shows them on stage at the Cavern, a crowded basement club in Liverpool, on 22 August 1962. They are not quite at their most primal: nearly a year earlier, their manager, Brian Epstein, had persuaded them to abandon leather outfits in favour of jackets and ties, and to tone down their raucous stage act. And having clocked countless hours playing local dances and eight-hour shifts in Hamburg nightclubs, they produce a tight, unified sound. They had recently joined the roster of Parlophone Records, a subsidiary of EMI, and in less than two weeks they would make their first record, an original song called 'Love Me Do'.

They are seen here, however, playing someone else's music, a song called 'Some Other Guy', which had recently been a hit for Ritchie Barrett. The music could hardly be simpler: its chord progression is a slightly embellished blues pattern, its beat is steady and danceable, and its lyrics are basic: my girlfriend ran off with someone else, and now I'm sad and lonely.

Leap forward to 25 June 1967. Twenty-four days earlier, the Beatles had released *Sgt. Pepper's Lonely Hearts Club Band*, a remarkably colourful album, with songs that ran the gamut from pure fantasy to treatises on inner spirituality. Its instrumental textures embraced not only the electric guitars, bass and drums they are seen playing in the 'Some Other Guy' clip, but Indian instruments, keyboards of various kinds, electronic tape loops and a chamber orchestra. Now, with *Pepper* topping the charts, they were fulfilling a commitment to the producers of *Our World*, a global satellite broadcast that would reach 400 million people. Invited to supply a brand new song for the broadcast, they produced 'All You Need Is Love' – the perfect song for such a multinational occasion, and for the summer of 1967, which quickly entered pop culture mythology as the Summer of Love.

In the clip, the Beatles are shown perched on high stools, wearing headphones and dressed in the flowery, rich-textured style of the day. Balloons, posters, streamers and a crowd of celebrity onlookers complete an almost carnival atmosphere. A thirteen-piece ensemble – strings, winds, brass and accordion – accompanies the foursome. And the heart of the instrumentation was not the energetic guitar playing of the Cavern performance, but a delicate harpsichord.

By this point the Beatles were playing only their own music, songs composed mostly by John Lennon, the rhythm guitarist – 'All You Need Is Love' was one of his – and Paul McCartney, the bassist. The lead guitarist, George Harrison, had also been contributing songs steadily, and Ringo Starr, the drummer, would soon be writing too.

The song begins with a cosmopolitan touch, a brass setting of the opening bars of 'La Marseillaise'. And then something odd happens. A seemingly simple, sweetly harmonized vocal section creates the illusion of a smooth natural flow, but actually moves back and forth between three and four beats to the bar. These metre shifts continue through the rest of the song, as if Lennon, unhindered by the strictures of pop song structure, had decided to make the music follow the contours of his lyrics instead of bending the words to suit the musical form.

The lyrics reinforce this notion. 'There's nothing you can do that can't be done,' Lennon calmly intones, adding, 'nothing you can sing that can't be sung.' And as the song winds to a close, a string of musical quotations drift past – a trumpet figure from Bach's Brandenburg Concerto No. 2, a string version of the old English lute song 'Greensleeves', a touch of the jazz standard 'In the Mood', and a bit of an early Beatles hit, 'She Loves You'. Surely no one watching the Beatles at the Cavern in August 1962 could have envisaged the Beatles playing so complex and colourful a song, let alone composing it.

The Beatles' metamorphosis from the tough, provincial rock band of the 1962 clip to the sophisticated musicians shown on *Our World* in just under five years is an astonishing story of musical development. Yet music is only one element of the story.

The Beatles' career paralleled the rise of the post-war youth culture, which came to be a potent force in the world economy just as the Beatles were making their earliest records. The Beatles quickly dominated this emerging culture, first as conventional teen idols, as Frank Sinatra and Elvis Presley had been before them, but eventually as political and even quasi-religious figureheads. Along with their generation, they adopted flamboyant fashions and political positions that challenged the established norms, and they celebrated a kind of hedonism most directly expressed in a pervasive experimentation with drugs, either in pursuit of spiritual revelation or merely for the thrill of it.

Yet the Beatles themselves were the first to admit that although they seemed to be the leaders of this new youth culture, they were by no means its architects. Rather, they had an unfailing ability to detect trends early, and when those trends matched their own impulses, they adopted and amplified them, making them instantly chic for the millions of fans who looked to the Beatles for guidance.

There is a paradoxical aspect to their ability to tap the *Zeitgeist* so successfully as to always seem a step ahead of their audience. On one hand, they were able to produce music that so thoroughly filled their listeners' expectations that it could almost be taken for granted that their records would dominate the hit parade. Yet they never stood still. Particularly in the years between 1963, when they were fresh and eager, and 1968, when they began to fragment, every one of their records explored new ground and either tested or redrew the limits of pop sensibility.

But experimentation aside, the group's songs are so durable because they are good. The lyrics are unusually articulate (if some-times deliberately cryptic) and Lennon, McCartney and later Harrison proved to be not only inventive, original melodists, but skilled manipulators of song structures. In any case, the music has survived the rebellious Anglo-American 1960s' youth culture that spawned it, and has flourished outside its original context.

In fact, the music's adoption outside the youth culture was fairly immediate. Leonard Bernstein, the composer of *West Side Story* and then the music director of the New York Philharmonic, became a champion of the Beatles' music as early as 1964, and sometimes used Beatles songs to illustrate his televised 'Young People's Concerts'. His admiration for their music never faded. He referred to them (and other rock groups) when he delivered the Charles Eliot Norton Lectures at Harvard University in 1973. And in an interview shortly before his death in 1990, he restated his opinion that the Beatles were the Schuberts of our time.

Other 'serious' composers, performers and critics championed the Beatles with equal zeal. The critic William Mann, in a famous review in *The Times* of London at the end of 1963, stunned the classical music world – and the Beatles themselves – when he called Lennon and McCartney the outstanding composers of 1963, and compared a chord sequence in their 'Not a Second Time' to the conclusion of Mahler's *Das Lied von der Erde.*

In 1966, the Italian avant-garde composer Luciano Berio arranged an album's worth of Beatles tunes to be sung by Cathy Berberian, his wife and an expert performer of contemporary concert music. The same year, Joshua Rifkin, then a fledgling record company arranger, now a renowned Baroque music scholar and conductor, recorded *The Baroque Beatles Book,* an amusing LP on which Beatles melodies became the themes of trio sonatas, cantatas, orchestral suites and the like.

Sgt. Pepper convinced other doubters that the Beatles' music was not merely pop ephemera. By the end of 1967, Aaron Copland, regarded as the dean of American composers, had pronounced Beatles songs to be music of quality, as had the musicologists Wilfrid Mellers, Hans Keller and Deryck Cooke. And Ned Rorem, an American composer known for his graceful art songs, responded to a rock critic's lukewarm appraisal of *Sgt. Pepper* with a lengthy appreciation in which he cast the Beatles virtually as the saviours of music from post-1950 academic modernism.

A fascination with the Beatles can still be detected in parts of the classical music world. By the 1970s composers as diverse as Leo Brouwer in Cuba, Toru Takemitsu in Japan, and Peter Maxwell Davies in Great Britain, had published arrangements of Beatles songs. In the late 1980s, Aki Takahashi, a Japanese pianist who specializes in new music, commissioned dozens of composers from around the world to set Beatles tunes. Among the results were a fantasy on Lennon's 'Give Peace a Chance' by Frederic Rzewski; *The Beatles 1962–1970* by John Cage; *Nothing Is Real (Strawberry Fields Forever)* by Alvin Lucier; and *The Walrus In Memoriam (I Am the Walrus)* by Terry Riley.

There is also, of course, the appeal the Beatles' music had in various pop realms outside mainstream hit-parade rock. The Beatles often cited American performers – particularly those who recorded for the Detroit-based Motown record label – as primary influences. By the mid-1960s, quite a few of the Motown artists whose music the Beatles used to play were recording their own takes on Lennon and McCartney songs. Ray Charles, Elvis Presley, Frank Sinatra and Ella Fitzgerald recorded Beatles songs as well. The most successful of those songs, of course, was McCartney's 'Yesterday'. More than 2,000 performers of all stripes have recorded it, and Broadcast Music Incorporated, the American performing rights organization, has estimated that it was played on the radio more than five million times between 1965 and the early 1990s. But virtually every song the Beatles wrote has been covered (or reinterpreted) by someone – even Lennon's quirky, unreproducible electronic music piece, 'Revolution 9'. And the music has been reconfigured by performers of all kinds, from pops orchestras to jazz bands, from country and western singers to 1950s' retro-rockers.

Yet for all the interpretive ingenuity that has been applied to the Beatles' music, there is also a degree to which the songs and the group's own recordings are inseparable. From a pop perspective, this is an unconventional view. But it is a crucial point, for particularly after 1964, they used the recording studio not simply as a place to document their compositions, but as the workshop in which the songs took form. In much the same way a classical composer might sit at his desk with a piano sketch and turn it into a symphony, the Beatles experimented in the studio, trying and discarding sounds, altering them electronically and tinkering with balances until they were satisfied. Their recordings are, in effect, electronic music, as carefully crafted as, say, Karlheinz Stockhausen's electronic works. And in that sense, the Beatles' recordings of these songs, rather than their representation in printed sheet music, are the definitive original versions.

A related and equally unusual aspect of the group's work is the sometimes cloudy issue of compositional credit. Lennon and McCartney agreed early on that they would be considered a team, like Rodgers and Hammerstein; yet they never adhered to the standard configuration in which one collaborator wrote the words and the other wrote the music. When they composed together, both contributed lyrics and musical ideas. Sometimes one would bring an incomplete song to the studio and the other would put on the finishing touches. But more often than not, they composed separately.

There were other kinds of collaborations too. One cannot overlook the contributions and influence of George Martin, the producer who oversaw their sessions from the start, and who was one of the few outsiders whose judgement they trusted. Martin's suggestions were often decisive. When Lennon and McCartney first played him 'Please Please Me', it was in a slow version, influenced by Roy Orbison. Martin told them it was dreary and needed a jolt. When they brought it back as an upbeat rocker, Martin let them record it, and at the end of the session, he proclaimed his belief that it would be their first number one record, as indeed it was.

It was Martin, too, who persuaded McCartney to record 'Yesterday' with a string quartet, against McCartney's initial resistance. Once McCartney agreed, he took a hand in the arrangement: Martin has pointed out that the distinctive cello line, which moves in lovely counterpoint to the melody, was McCartney's. At other times, Martin was left to his own devices. During the sessions for Lennon's 'Strawberry Fields Forever', in November 1966, the group recorded several arrangements and although Lennon was displeased with them all, he asked Martin to make a composite of two very different versions. Because the performances were in different keys and tempos, this was a daunting task, but Martin found a way, and deserves a good share of the credit for what turned out to be one of the Beatles' most brilliant recordings.

During their years together, the Beatles released roughly ten hours of music, with scarcely a loser in the lot. They raised the stature of rock music, and forged a high artistic path from which other rock composers (Pete Townshend of the Who, Ray Davies of the Kinks, Mark Knopfler of Dire Straits, David Bowie and Elvis Costello, to cite only a few) could set out in different directions.

Yet not one of the Beatles studied music formally, and none of them could read musical notation. They achieved what they did entirely by instinct, and on the effervescence generated in a perfectly balanced, freakishly rare form of musical and personal chemistry. And the world has seen nothing like them since.

I

From Quarry Men to Beatles 1957–61

With fans looking on, the Beatles pose for an early publicity photo at the docks in their native city of Liverpool

There was nothing big in Liverpool. It was very poor, a very poor city, and tough. But people have a sense of humour because they are in so much pain ... It is cosmopolitan, and it's where the sailors would come home with the blues records from America on ships.

John Lennon, 1970 (*Rolling Stone*)

From Quarry Men to Beatles 1957–61

Liverpool may never escape its reputation for post-industrial hopelessness, but as a place that might spawn a peculiarly English musical group, it had everything going for it in the years after World War II. Like any port city, it was a place where diverse musical influences converged. Sounds from distant places would arrive there first, and at the time, the most interesting sounds were coming from America – soul, rhythm and blues and country records, in particular. The city also had a more colourful ethnic make-up than many other English cities at the time. There was a large Irish population, as well as sizeable Jamaican, Indian, Chinese, Slavic and Jewish communities, making Liverpool the kind of cultural melting-pot that New York was and London was not.

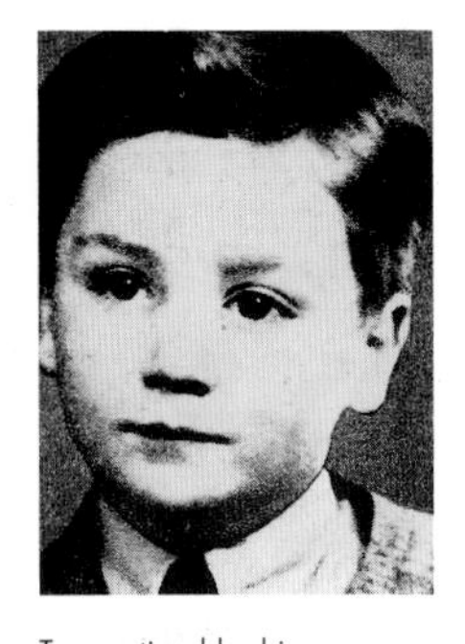

Traumatized by his parents' breakup, but not yet smitten by rock and roll, John Lennon looked deceptively like an angelic schoolboy, c. 1945.

These influences, both individually and in their mixture, can be heard tellingly in the Beatles' early work. Listen closely to 'Love Me Do', for example, and a peculiar hybrid comes into focus. The song was meant to be bluesy, and it is to a degree. But would an authentic blues band embellish its plaint with vocal harmonies in thirds, fifths and octaves, harmonies that in this context have an almost medieval sound?

The founder of the group, John Winston Lennon, was born during a German bombing raid on 9 October 1940, to Julia Stanley and Alfred Lennon. They had married in 1938, but Alfred, a merchant seaman, was absent for long stretches during Lennon's early years. Julia was described as a free if somewhat flighty spirit. It was decided in the spring of 1941 that John would have the greatest chance of a stable home life if he were brought up by Julia's childless sister Mary Elizabeth, known as Mimi, and her husband George Smith, in Woolton, a Liverpool suburb.

Thus Lennon was insulated from the breakup of his parents' marriage in 1942. He saw his father occasionally until he was five, whereupon Alfred disappeared until 1965, when a London newspaper reported that while his son was making millions, Alfred Lennon was a dishwasher in a hotel. They maintained an odd, rocky relationship thereafter. Julia, on the other hand, took up the role of the affectionate, eccentric aunt, who countered the strict upbringing Mimi was giving John by indulging and encouraging his earliest bohemian instincts including his interest in music.

One trait emerged early: a penchant for twisting the language. From the time he was a somewhat mischievous seven-year-old at Dovedale Primary School through his years at Quarry Bank High School and the Liverpool College of Art, he entertained his friends by writing booklets of parodies and nonsense verse, illustrated with cartoons and caricatures. This talent came to full flower not only in his song lyrics, but in the two books he published during the Beatles years, *In His Own Write* in 1964 and *A Spaniard in the Works* in 1965, and in the posthumous compilation, *Skywriting by Word of Mouth*, published in 1986.

In 1955 and 1956, rock and roll, a high-energy pop form based on rhythm and blues, was revitalizing American popular music and had found its way to Britain via the film *Blackboard Jungle*, which featured Bill Haley and the Comets singing 'Rock Around the Clock'. Elvis Presley records soon followed, and Presley quickly gained a hold on Lennon's imagination.

Presley was essentially a blues singer with a heavy country and western accent – or was it the other way around? He drew his repertory from both sides of the track, but his vocal style struck listeners of the time as a black sound. He was also a very physical performer: his hip-swivelling drew ecstatic screams from his female fans. The qualities that made Elvis so appealing to people of Lennon's age struck their parents as cause for grave concern. Just when their kids seemed to be turning out right, wearing crew cuts and dancing to saccharine ballads, here was a Southern truck driver with jet black hair stacked elaborately but with a touch of waywardness, gyrating behind a guitar and growling 'you ain' not'n but a hound dog'.

In truth, parental concern was not wholly unwarranted. There was, after all, a decidedly anti-authoritarian undercurrent in early rock, an attitude that teenagers seized upon immediately. And Presley was only the tip of the iceberg. Jerry Lee Lewis, a wildman who was wont to play the piano with his feet, came from the same Memphis, Tennessee milieu as Presley and offered a similar musical admixture. Carl Perkins's brand of rock leaned closer to country, and sounded civilized by contrast, yet it was funky enough to make its appeal. Over in Texas, Buddy Holly took all those elements and moulded a somewhat more refined style. And then there was the wave of black performers who came to reclaim rock and roll from Presley and company, the most notable being the spectacularly uninhibited Little Richard and a sly guitar master from St Louis, Chuck Berry.

All these musicians made a profound impression on Lennon and the other Beatles-to-be. Several of their songs remained in the group's performing repertory; in fact, their final public concert, at Candlestick Park in San Francisco, on 29 August 1966, began with Berry's 'Rock and Roll Music' and ended with Little Richard's 'Long Tall Sally'. More immediately, though, the tide of American rockers created a boom market for guitars in Liverpool, England. One eager customer was John Lennon. Julia, who played the banjo, taught him his first chords.

In a middle-class home in Allerton, not far from Lennon's home in Woolton, Paul McCartney was also fascinated by Elvis Presley. Born James Paul McCartney on 18 June 1942, he was the most musically inquisitive of the Beatles, probably because a rather more advanced musical culture flourished in his home. Lennon's parents were amateurs: Julia could sing to her own banjo accompaniment, and Alfred fancied himself a singer too. But McCartney's father, a self-taught pianist, actually led his own Jim Mac Jazz Band in the 1920s. In 1941 he married Mary Mohin, a nurse and midwife. The McCartneys had a piano in their house, although Paul seems to have ignored it after a few lessons. He also took up the trumpet briefly, and taught himself to pick out a few tunes. But what really excited him was the music he was hearing on Radio Luxembourg, which played some of the American pop records that were making their way across the Atlantic.

Imported rock was not the only music to engage young Lennon and McCartney. In January 1956, just a few months before Elvis's 'Heartbreak Hotel' began to electrify the airwaves, a skiffle craze broke out all over England, instigated by Lonnie Donegan's hit recording of 'Rock Island Line'. The song was another American import, an old tune made famous by the blues singer Huddie Ledbetter, better known as Lead Belly. Skiffle was based on country blues, and its attraction was that anybody could join in. The guitar, or sometimes the banjo, was the central instrument in a skiffle band,

Liverpool, the northern port city from which, London music world executives insisted, nothing great would come

which might also include a percussionist who used a thimble to scrape away on a washboard, and a bassist who played an instrument made from a tea-chest, a single string and a broomstick.

Like Lennon, McCartney clamoured for a guitar. When he got one, there was a problem: being left-handed, he had trouble coaxing his fingers to make the chord shapes he was trying to learn. His solution was to restring the guitar backwards, so that he could play it upside down. Thereafter, he spent night and day alternately picking at the instrument and perfecting an imitation of Little Richard's screaming vocal style.

Once he heard Elvis, Lennon disdained crooning and soft pop. But McCartney was not so immune to it. He later cited 'White Christmas' and 'Over the Rainbow' as early favourites. And from the middle ground between light pop and Elvis, he was particularly fond of the Everly Brothers, an American duo whose close, beautifully worked-out harmonies would serve as a model for the early Beatles.

But apart from an attempt to form a duo with his younger brother in 1957, his musical development was fairly solitary. Lennon, by contrast, saw music as a social avocation from the start, and in March 1957, soon after he got his first guitar, he gathered some friends and formed his own skiffle band. For a week, the band was known as the Black Jacks; thereafter it was Quarry Men, in honour of the Quarry Bank High School for Boys, where Lennon was an increasingly indifferent student.

The Quarry Men had a fairly fluid line-up and performed at parties and contests in the spring of 1957 with Lennon as its lead guitarist and singer. Correctly assuming that Mimi would object to his fronting a band, Lennon and his friends rehearsed at Julia's house. It was entirely by accident that Mimi discovered her nephew's secret life. On 6 July 1957 she attended the summer fête at St Peter's Parish Church, and was horrified to discover that what she later described as

The Quarry Men – John Lennon at the microphone, flanked by Eric Griffiths (guitar), Rod Davis (behind Lennon, also a guitarist), Pete Shotton (washboardist) and Len Garry (washtub bassist) – at St Peter's Church, Woolton, just hours before Lennon was introduced to Paul McCartney.

an 'eruption of noise' was produced by Lennon and the Quarry Men. A recording of Lennon singing two songs that day – Arthur Gunter's 'Baby, Let's Play House', which he knew from an Elvis Presley record, and 'Puttin' on the Style', a Lonnie Donegan hit – turned up in a private collection in 1994. There are also photographs of the band in action on that date. And a local newspaper referred briefly to the Quarry Men performance.

It is extraordinary that a performance by a band of teenagers in Liverpool suburb in the late 1950s should have been so well documented – and all the more so because the date turned out to be a milestone in the Beatles' history. It was at this church fête, between Quarry Men sets, that John Lennon met Paul McCartney. Ivan Vaughan, one of several tea-chest bassists in the group, was a classmate of McCartney's at the Liverpool Institute Grammar School, and knew McCartney to be a better guitarist than anyone in the band.

McCartney was intrigued by Lennon, who played the guitar using banjo chords, and whose haphazard knowledge of song lyrics led him to make up the verses he didn't know. And Lennon could see that McCartney knew a thing or two. For one thing, he could tune a guitar, a skill none of the Quarry Men had mastered; and perhaps even more crucially, he proved his knowledge of rock and roll by writing out the lyrics to Eddie Cochran's 'Twenty Flight Rock' and Gene Vincent's 'Be-Bop-a-Lula', and by singing 'Long Tall Sally' in his best Little Richard voice. A week passed before McCartney was invited to join the group. Lennon had no doubt that in purely musical matters, McCartney would be an asset. But the Quarry Men was not only Lennon's band: it was his gang, and it was important that he be perceived as its leader. Having someone better than himself in the group might mean sharing the spotlight. He decided to put the band first.

McCartney made his first appearance with the Quarry Men on 18 October 1957, and apparently had designs on the lead guitar spot, an ambition he dropped after botching his solo moment. He was, on the other hand, not shy about pointing out musical weaknesses elsewhere in the band. Virtually from the start, his criticisms were a source of tension that the group had not known when the sole controlling voice was Lennon's. This was an important difference between Lennon and McCartney, one that would remain in high relief through the Beatles years. Lennon knew what he wanted, and he was usually able to persuade his bandmates to at least approximate the sound he had in mind. But he was also something of a bohemian, and when perfection seemed out of reach, he settled for the attempt. McCartney was a perfectionist, and was loath to abandon ideas that he knew could be achieved. That his collaborators might consider his demands unreasonable did not faze him: the result was all that mattered.

By early 1958 the Quarry Men's personnel had stabilized, with Lennon, McCartney and Eric Griffiths on guitars, Colin Hanton on drums, Len Garry on bass, and John 'Duff' Lowe as occasional pianist. As the skiffle boom faded, Lennon and McCartney were pushing the band's repertory toward Elvis and Little Richard, a taste their bandmates did not all share. Within months, Griffiths and Garry left, and McCartney brought in a guitarist he knew from the Liverpool Institute, George Harrison. Harrison was a year younger than McCartney but was obsessed with the guitar and was making quick headway. When he turned up at a performance on 6 February 1958, a few weeks short of his fifteenth birthday, he struck Lennon as a child, and a sullen one at that. But Harrison found his way into the band the same way McCartney did: by showing that he could play things that Lennon could not. With McCartney's encouragement, he tagged along with the band to a few engagements, and by mid-year, he was a member.

Harrison was born on 25 February 1943, the youngest of the four children of Harold Harrison and Louise French, who married in 1930. His father drove the bus that brought both Harrison and Paul McCartney to the Liverpool Institute. Harrison was generally disenchanted by school, but until he took up the guitar his main outlet for rebellion was dressing in the flamboyant Teddy Boy style – tight trousers, elaborate coats, long greased-back hair – that parents found menacing, or at least irritating. Unlike Lennon and McCartney, who approached the guitar as something to accompany their singing, Harrison was drawn to the solos on early rock records. He did have some band experience before the Quarry Men: he and his older brother, Peter, had a band called the Rebels. He also made it a practice to bring his guitar to dances in the hope that one of the bands would let him sit in or even join. Even after he joined the Quarry

Men – whose performing dates were few – he continued playing with other groups.

The Quarry Men's performing fortunes were at low ebb by mid-1958, but there were compensations. In late 1957, Lennon and McCartney began composing songs, sometimes together and sometimes in competition. McCartney initiated the collaboration by playing Lennon his first song, 'I Lost My Little Girl', a simple, three chord number with a melody that would not have been out of place on an Everly Brothers album. Lennon, though impressed that McCartney had written a song, was not uncritical. When McCartney revived the song for a television performance in 1991, he said that Lennon used to rib him about some of the lyrics, particularly the lines: 'Her clothes were not expensive, Her hair didn't always curl'. Sillier lyrics were doing perfectly well on the pop charts, but Lennon's verbal sensitivity was one of the most important things he brought to the collaboration. His other response was to write a song of his own,

Obsessed with the guitar from the age of thirteen, George Harrison practised until his fingers bled. In one of the first photographs to capture this fascination, he navigates the fretboard of his first guitar, a second-hand steel-string acoustic model, purchased for £3.

'Hello Little Girl'. Although the Beatles dropped it well before they became famous, two early performances survive – one on a 1960 rehearsal tape, in which they sing it with Everly Brothers style tandem harmonies; the other a harder-edged version, performed during a 1962 audition for Decca Records.

Curiously, in light of McCartney's later reputation as the more musically astute composer, Lennon's song shows greater sophistication. The melody of 'I Lost My Little Girl' is as simple as can be: an ascending motif based on the first four steps of the major scale. 'Hello Little Girl' is far prettier and considerably more complicated. But Lennon used a different sort of model – a half-remembered 1940s' pop song his mother used to sing him, though later he was unable to recall the title. Using older songs as templates was one of Lennon's modes of composing. Other examples come easily to mind: 'Please Please Me', in its early slow incarnation, was patterned after Roy Orbison's 'Only the Lonely'. The opening lines of 'Do You Want to Know a Secret' are taken from a song in Walt Disney's 'Snow White and the Seven Dwarfs', and the opening line of 'Run for Your Life' is lifted from 'Baby, Let's Play House', one of the songs heard on the 1957 Quarry Men tape.

Not that Lennon worked this way all the time. Many of his best songs are entirely without precedent or model. Still, using an earlier piece of music as either a source of ideas or as the foundation for a new work is a time-honoured practice. In the fifteenth and sixteenth centuries, church composers like Guillaume Dufay and Josquin Després routinely based their Masses on popular melodies, tunes that any listener of the time would have known. But these composers did not have copyright lawyers looking over their shoulders. Lennon knew that if he were going to use existing works as models, he had to disguise them, but occasionally he let a clue slip through. In 1969 he patterned 'Come Together' after Chuck Berry's 'You Can't Catch Me'. Lennon's song was original enough that the melodic similarities would not have been apparent had he not retained a line of Berry's lyric. Berry's publisher sued, and in 1975, as part of the settlement, Lennon recorded 'You Can't Catch Me' for his *Rock 'n' Roll* oldies collection.

Early in their collaboration, Lennon and McCartney agreed to work as a team, like George and Ira Gershwin, Jerry Lieber and Mike

Stoller or Gerry Goffin and Carole King. All their songs would bear both names, whether they were written together (as many were) or individually (as most were). By 1959, they had filled a notebook with songs, a few of which – 'Love Me Do', 'One After 909' and 'When I'm 64' – eventually found their way onto Beatles records. Apparently, there was a brief collaboration between McCartney and Harrison as well. In mid-1958, Lennon, McCartney, Harrison, and John Lowe recorded two songs in the home studio of Percy Phillips. One side was Buddy Holly's 'That'll Be the Day', with Lennon singing lead. The other, 'In Spite of All the Danger', was credited McCartney–Harrison, although McCartney, recalling the collaboration in 1989, said that the song was essentially his and that Harrison shared the credit because he devised the guitar solo.

Just as Lennon's musical life was getting into gear, his personal life was falling apart. As a teenager and fledgling musician, he had found a supportive ally in his mother, Julia. But on 15 July 1958, she was struck and killed by a car. Her death had a profound effect on Lennon: not having seen his father in a dozen years, he now felt that his parental abandonment was complete – a theme he explored on his pained, intensely autobiographical *Plastic Ono Band* album in 1970. More immediately, Lennon's sense of loss intensified his 'them against us' approach to the world. He had long been a loud-mouth and a class clown; now he adopted an aggressive front as well.

Julia's death also gave Lennon and McCartney something else in common: McCartney's mother had died of breast cancer on 31 October 1956. McCartney's response was notably different from Lennon's. Whether out of practicality or shock, he wondered aloud what the family would do without her income. He then took on an extra share of family responsibilities. And he threw himself more fully into mastering the guitar.

By late 1958, work had virtually dried up for the the Quarry Men, and the group essentially disbanded except for occasional performances into early 1959. Lennon and McCartney continued to compose, and Harrison moved on to steadier work with the Les Stewart Quartet. They reconvened that August to work as the house band in the Casbah Coffee Club, but quit after a pay dispute. That October, they renamed themselves Johnny and the Moondogs, and made it to the finals of a Carol Levis talent contest. Lennon was by then enrolled at the Liverpool College of Art, where he was supposed to be studying lettering. But with Harrison and McCartney next door at the Liverpool Institute, the temptation to find an empty classroom at the college and spend the day jamming was impossible to resist. Lennon did attend some classes: it was at the college that he met Cynthia Powell, whom he would marry in 1962. He also became friendly with Stuart Fergusson Victor Sutcliffe, a Scottish-born art student whose Abstract Expressionist paintings showed great promise. One of Sutcliffe's paintings was included in the second biennial John Moores Exhibition at the Walker Art Gallery late in 1959, and when the exhibition ended, Moores bought the painting

A prize-winning artist but a woefully amateurish bassist, Stu Sutcliffe joined the band at Lennon's insistence in 1960, was a member for less than a year and died in 1962; nevertheless, he influenced the group's attitude and look, and suggested the name Beatles.

for £65, which Lennon persuaded Sutcliffe to spend on an electric bass guitar.

Sutcliffe's talents were not musical, and he never did master the instrument. But for Lennon to bring him in showed that even in light of the band's professional ambitions he still thought of it partly as a social club, and he wanted his friends to be in it, musical abilities notwithstanding. Sutcliffe was in the group for less than a year, but he made a few notable contributions. He suggested, for example, renaming the group the Beatles (although his original spelling was Beatals), a play on the name of Buddy Holly's band, the Crickets, with a pun on 'beat'. From May to July, the band played in dance halls all over Liverpool under the names Silver Beats and Silver Beetles before Lennon definitively adopted Sutcliffe's idea.

At the end of 1960, after the Beatles played their first season in Hamburg, Sutcliffe bailed out of the band to remain in Germany with his fiancée, Astrid Kirchherr. But his influence in non-musical areas continued. He adopted the forward-brushed hairstyle favoured by the Existentialist student crowd with which Astrid mixed in Hamburg. The Beatles, then still Elvis clones, were derisive at first, but soon embraced what came to be known in the early 1960s as the Beatle haircut. He also introduced another early Beatles visual trademark, the collarless jacket, while the band was still in leather. Beyond these superficial contributions, he seems to have brought out the intellectual curiosity that Lennon was hiding under a tough veneer. Sutcliffe was more passionate about art and literature than about music, and Lennon wanted to understand what Sutcliffe saw in them. The letters the two exchanged after the band left Hamburg are full of anquished philosophizing and serious, if self-conscious, poetry, not quite what one would expect of a musician with the cocky rock-guitarist persona that Lennon presented publicly.

A tape of the group from mid-1960 exists, and although it is clearly an informal rehearsal, it runs for over two hours and includes both songs and extended jams, thereby giving an impression of the then drummerless quartet's abilities. Sutcliffe is inaudible much of the time; when he can be heard, his basslines are of a simple one-note-to-the-bar variety. In the long jams, there seem to be two distinct lead guitarists, one comparatively fluent and bluesy, the other awkward

The Beatles as they were in 1960, posing before a Hamburg ruin in a famous portrait by Astrid Kirchherr. From left to right: Pete Best (drummer), the three-guitar nucleus of Harrison, Lennon and McCartney, and Sutcliffe with his bass.

HANNOVER
20km

and fumbling, though intent on playing quick scale-like runs. One, obviously, was Harrison; the other might have been McCartney.

The are some engaging moments. Most striking are a handful of Lennon-McCartney numbers. Besides 'Hello Little Girl', there are two versions of 'One After 909' that wonderfully illuminate the band's skiffle roots. Shotten's washboard is of course long gone, but one can almost hear the echo of it in the chunky, off-the-beat chordal accompaniment. One hears the locomotive chugging along far more clearly here than in the version the Beatles recorded for the *Let It Be* album in 1969. Otherwise, the song did not change much. But 'I'll Follow the Sun' changed considerably between its appearance here and the version recorded for *Beatles for Sale* in late 1964. The finished version begins with a graceful walk through the song's chord progression, then right into the lyrics. The 1960 account starts with a twangy, Buddy Holly-ish lead guitar introduction. The melody and the lyrics of the first two verses are already there, although the accompaniment is a blend of skiffle and vaudeville, a far cry from the supple support of the 1964 recording. But the song's bridge section was entirely revised between the two recordings. In 1960 it was a simple, brief country and western pastiche with the Holly-style solo leading back into the verse. The 1964 bridge, more spacious and with new lyrics, moves from the bright major key feeling of the verse into a bittersweet minor mode digression.

The tape also gives an impression of the band's taste in cover versions, which are split between blues numbers (Fats Domino's 'I Will Always Be in Love With You'), brighter rhythm and blues songs (Ray Charles's 'Hallelujah! I Love Her So'), country and western tunes (Carl Perkins's 'Matchbox'), and sizzling rockers (Duane Eddy's 'Moovin' 'n' Groovin'' in a version that replaces Eddy's slinkiness with direct aggression).

Soon after Sutcliffe joined, the Beatles took on a manager of sorts. Allan Williams ran a club called the Jacaranda, and undertook various freelance promotions that brought rock stars like Gene Vincent and Billy Fury to Liverpool, with local bands filling out the bill. He was not, at first, impressed with the Beatles: they had no drummer, and were less accomplished than Cass and the Cassanovas, Rory Storm and the Hurricanes and Gerry and the Pacemakers, all local bands with plenty of experience. Still, Williams enlisted the group to play at his New Cabaret Artistes, an illegal strip club, backing a dancer who insisted on the accompaniment of a live band. Actually, she had hoped to strip to the music of Beethoven and Khachaturian, and distributed scores to Lennon, McCartney, Harrison and Sutcliffe. But since they were unable to read these, she had to settle for 'Summertime', 'The Third Man Theme', 'Begin the Beguine' and other standards. According to the account in Williams's autobiography, *The Man Who Gave the Beatles Away*, McCartney filled in on drums.

They did need a permanent drummer though, and Williams found one for them – Tommy Moore, a 36-year old fork-lift operator. Moore accompanied the Silver Beetles on a short tour of Scotland as a backup band for the singer Johnny Gentle, and for a few engagements in Liverpool, but left the band when his girlfriend persuaded him to devote his energies more fully to his day job at the Garston Bottle Works. Another drummer, Norman Chapman, was enlisted when they heard him practising in a building across the street from Williams's Jacaranda; but soon after he joined the group, he was conscripted.

In the summer of 1960, Williams made a connection with Bruno Koschmider, the owner of several clubs on the Reeperbahn, the red light district in Hamburg. Koschmider was in the market for English rock bands, and had contracted several Liverpool groups from Williams. But the Beatles were not held in high regard by their peers, and when Williams wrote to tell his other musicians that the Beatles would arrive in mid-August, he received a letter of protest, warning him that sending a group as bad as the Beatles would ruin the scene for everyone. Williams ignored the letter, but two weeks before their planned departure date, the Beatles were still searching for a drummer. Their quest brought them back to Mona Best's Casbah, where the proprietress's son, Randolph Peter Best, was playing drums in his own band, the Blackjacks. Best had his heart set on becoming a professional drummer, and with the other Blackjacks about to leave for college, he was easily induced to throw in his lot with Lennon, McCartney, Harrison and Sutcliffe.

In Hamburg, the group's daily sets at the Indra and then at the Kaiserkeller lasted late into the night, and to maintain the energy they needed, they began to consume amphetamines prodigiously. The

Pete Best, who joined the Beatles on the eve of their first Hamburg trip in 1960 and was unceremoniously booted out on the eve of their success in 1962

ambience was entirely decadent, and living conditions were dismal: Koschmider gave the group poorly-lit quarters behind the screen at the Bambi, a decrepit cinema. On the other hand, they fell in with a crowd of German students who were interested in contemporary art and Existentialist literature, and whose dress, depending on the occasion, varied from straight black to the almost costumed look that became current in London seven years later. One of the students, Klaus Voorman, maintained his ties with the group: he designed the cover for their *Revolver* album in 1966, and was the bassist on a few of Lennon's early solo recordings. And Astrid Kirchherr and Jurgen Vollmer, photographers with a sense of the unusual, took what became the classic early photographs of the group, pictures that capture something of their ambition and defiance.

Sutcliffe in particular was drawn to this crowd, and especially to Astrid, to whom he became engaged. His immersion in Astrid's sophisticated world reminded him that he had put his own artistic destiny on hold. And although he enjoyed playing in the band, his mediocre musicianship gave rise to increasing tensions. McCartney was particularly critical, but Lennon later told interviewers that they all gave Sutcliffe a hard time, so that in the autumn of 1960 he resolved to remain in Hamburg and was accepted for further studies

Opposite, Lennon was always nostalgic for the tough Bohemian days this 1961 Hamburg portrait evokes; in 1975 he used it as the cover photo for *Rock 'n' Roll*, an album of songs by the musicians who influenced him.

with Eduardo Paolozzi, the Scottish-born sculptor and pioneer in pop art.

For the rest of the group, the three and a half months the Beatles performed in Hamburg were decisive in their transition from musical hobbyists to full-time musicians. If hints of the Beatles style are evident on the mid-1960 tape, their sound was truly crystalized by some 500 hours of all-night performing. They had to keep current by working up versions of the latest hits, both rockers and crooners, songs they added to their backlist of personal favourites from late 1950s' America. And with these examples in mind they were churning out songs of their own with increasing confidence.

Just as life in Hamburg was taking shape, the band's luck changed. In October, when Koschmider discovered that the Beatles were

In Hamburg, 1961, the Beatles abandoned their Elvis-clone hairstyles in favour of the brushed-forward look popular with Sutcliffe's art student friends. It was another six months before they traded in their leather jackets for stage suits.

Collaborating with Tony Sheridan (right) at the Top Ten Club in Hamburg got the Beatles fired from their own job at the competing Kaiserkeller in 1960, but led to their first professional recordings, as Sheridan's backup band the following spring.

spending their breaks at the competing Top Ten club, and sometimes performing there with the singer Tony Sheridan, he cancelled their contract. Harrison, then seventeen, was suddenly discovered to be under age, and was deported. And when McCartney and Best gathered their belongings from the Bambi in order to move to the Top Ten, they set a condom afire to provide light, leaving burn marks on the wall. Koschmider had them arrested for arson, and they too were deported.

Sutcliffe remained in Hamburg, effectively resigning from the band, although he sat in with them occasionally during their Hamburg stint in 1961. And Lennon returned to Liverpool in December, ten days after McCartney and Harrison. He did not get in touch with the others immediately: rather, he spent a week wondering whether the band was worth continuing. On reflection he had no choice. Although he had talents for drawing and writing, his heart was in music, and the Beatles were too good a resource to squander. He called the group together, with Chas Newby (the bassist from Best's Blackjacks) temporarily taking up Sutcliffe's role during his college holiday, and their performances in the final days of 1960 reinforced his decision. Musically, the Beatles were far better than they had been when they left Liverpool, and the combination of beer, amphetamines and the encouragement of boisterous German audiences had led them to develop a kinetic, electrifying stage show. Suddenly, their Liverpool audiences were responding with signs of the ecstatic frenzy that, three years later, would be called Beatlemania.

2

Liverpool Dance Halls 1961–2

This advertisement for an April 1962 concert at the Cavern appeared well after Brian Epstein put the Beatles in spiffy stage suits, but their old informal image still appealed to their Liverpool fans. Some of those fans would protest four months later, when drummer Pete Best, on the right, was replaced by Ringo Starr.

I had never seen anything like the Beatles on any stage. They smoked as they played and they ate and talked and pretended to hit each other. They turned their backs on the audience and shouted at them and laughed at private jokes. But they gave a captivating and honest show and they had very considerable magnetism. I loved their ad libs and I was fascinated by this, to me, new music with its pounding bass beat and its vast engulfing sound.

Brian Epstein, in *A Cellarfull of Noise*, 1964

Liverpool Dance Halls 1961–2

It would be several years before composition eclipsed performing as the Beatles' principal concern. And although they returned from Germany in magnificent musical shape, there were still changes in store for the band. The chemistry would not be entirely right until August 1962.

The most pressing question facing them at the beginning of 1961 was what to do about a bassist, now that Sutcliffe was out. Lennon tried to persuade Harrison to take the job, but he declined, having worked so hard to perfect his rock and country style solo spots. That left McCartney, whose decision to take up the bass proved more momentous than it could have seemed at the time. Its immediate effect was to thin the group's texture from three guitars to two, sharpening the distinction between the chordal bed provided by Lennon's rhythm guitar and Harrison's embellishments. More significantly, the switch to bass gave McCartney an opportunity to distinguish himself instrumentally in a way not available to him as one of three guitarists.

Bass lines on early 1960s' rock records were typically simple: depending on the style and context, a bassist would pummel away at the root of the chord being played, or would trace the notes of the chords in an unassuming blues pattern. McCartney did not eschew these traditions entirely. As late as 1968, a sped-up version of one standard blues pattern became the spine of the song 'Birthday'. And when a song demanded simplicity, McCartney's lines were direct and unadorned. But the exceptions prove the rule, which is that for McCartney, the bass was almost an alternate form of lead guitar. His bass lines are active and exploratory, and often have the same sort of centrality within the Beatles' recordings as Johann Sebastian Bach's bass lines have in his contrapuntal keyboard, chamber and choral works. Especially in the period from *Rubber Soul* to *Sgt. Pepper*, the bass lines are so intricate that they can stand alone as melodies. Yet they are also propulsive, an essential part of the band's rhythm section.

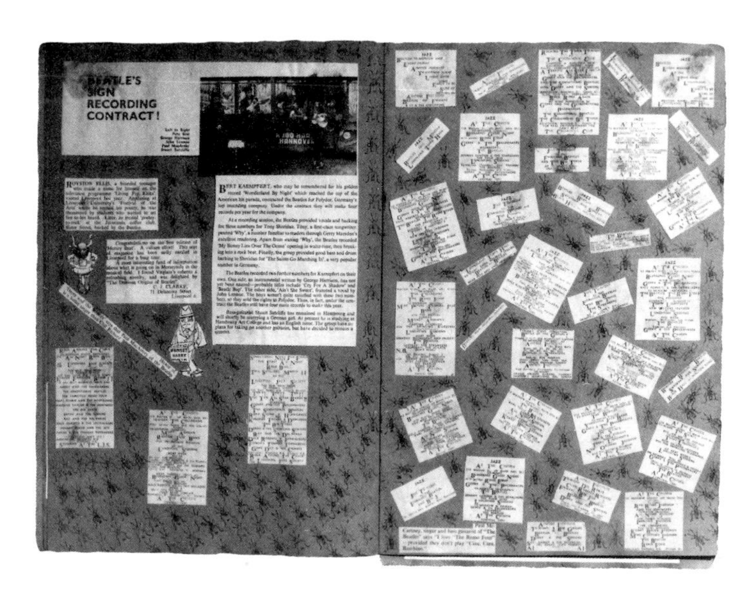

As a sideline to his work as the Beatles' drummer, Pete Best saw to some of the management chores, not only arranging for performing dates but keeping a fastidious scrapbook of clippings about the group. This early volume includes advertisements for several gigs as well as a *Mersey Beat* article about the group's 1961 Hamburg recordings with Tony Sheridan.

That McCartney's ability on the instrument developed quickly is evident from the recordings the Beatles made in Hamburg in June 1961, as the backing band for the British singer Tony Sheridan. Six months after he took up the instrument, he was adding fancy turn-around figures between verses, keeping performances moving and drawing the ear to the bass at the same time.

By the end of 1963, McCartney's inventiveness could be stunning once one focused on it, although part of its beauty was its sense of inevitability within the musical texture. In 'All My Loving', a McCartney song that figured prominently in the group's stage sets and is included on the *With the Beatles* album, the first thing that strikes the ear is the sweetly floating melody. The next is the texture, specifically the rapid electric guitar chording, in triplets, played by Lennon. Pressed to cite a third element, a listener might focus on Harrison's mildly jazz guitar solo. But the bass line, heard almost subliminally, is absolutely crucial. In a way, it is the picture of simplicity: with an unvaried rhythm, McCartney puts a single note under every beat. He begins his bass line on the root of the opening chord, and then steadily walks his way down the scale, ending each phrase with a graceful punctuating figure that hops back to the top of the

CAVERN

Left, freshly back from Hamburg, the scruffy young Beatles come up for fresh air between sets at the Cavern on Matthew Street, the dank cellar club where they gave nearly 300 lunchtime and evening performances between February 1961 and August 1963.

progression. Harmonically, the line makes a great effect, particularly in combination with the song's other textural elements.

Later his lines were more overtly sophisticated, and he began to lavish greater care on them. By the time of *Sgt. Pepper*, he had taken to first recording a simple, provisional bass line, and then, as the song took shape, replacing the original version with something more fully worked out. This level of detail was a far cry from the comparatively quick-and-dirty approach to recording pop music in the early 1960s, although in fairness, the more traditional approach – heard on the Sheridan recordings and on the Beatles' own début album – was meant to capture the energy and spontaneity of a band's live sound.

In 1961 the Beatles performed most nights in the dance halls and social clubs in Liverpool and environs. They had also found something of a headquarters: the Cavern Club, a crowded, unventilated, poorly lit cellar that had once been a vegetable warehouse, remained their principal haunt until August 1963. In its intimate confines, they cultivated a loyal local audience.

A second visit to Hamburg kept the Beatles out of Liverpool from 27 March to 2 July. This time they played at the Top Ten, alternating sets with Tony Sheridan, and working until two or three in the morning. They seem to have thrived under these conditions, and they particularly enjoyed their reunion with Sheridan, who from their point of view was already a star, having made recordings and performed on British television. It was towards the end of this visit that they recorded a handful of ballads and rocked-up standards with Sheridan, two of which – 'My Bonnie' and 'When the Saints Go Marching In' – were released as a single a few months later.

At the Sheridan sessions, the Beatles also taped two songs on their own: a version of 'Ain't She Sweet', with Lennon singing, and more notably, an original instrumental, 'Cry for a Shadow'. The only Beatles song credited as a collaboration between Lennon and Harrison, 'Cry for a Shadow' parodied the twangy style of the Shadows, the most popular British guitar-based band of the early 1960s, and the backing group for Cliff Richard, a squeaky-clean teenage heart-throb, modelled after Elvis. The Beatles loathed the Shadows, but the song – which was also, at one point, called 'Beatle Bop' – does not show it, except to the extent that its wildness and energy reveals the typical Shadows' instrumental as sterile and contrived. Lennon's guitar churns out the chords, McCartney provides a characteristically active bass line, Best drums along speedily, and Harrison plays a lead guitar line in which the lazily bending notes of the verse melody are contrasted against the more fiery twists of the song's bridge. His playing shows more than a hint of Duane Eddy's influence, although he had not quite mastered Eddy's cool proficiency.

Although the Beatles' Liverpool and Hamburg repertory included several instrumentals, 'Cry for a Shadow' is the only early one to survive in a professional recording. Another, 'Catswalk', was captured on a 1962 Cavern rehearsal tape, but was never attempted in the studio; instead, McCartney tucked the tune away until 1967, when he gave it to the Chris Barber Band, a brass-based group better equipped than the Beatles to explore the song's jazzy implications.

The Beatles themselves did not take another instrumental into the recording studio until the *Rubber Soul* sessions in the autumn of 1965. The song, '12-Bar Original', is a rambling piece that bears an uncanny resemblance to the sound heard typically on the American Stax-Volt soul label, and particularly to the music of Booker T. and the MG's. After a single complete take, the Beatles abondoned it. It was not until *Magical Mystery Tour*, in 1967, that they released a second instrumental. That song, 'Flying', was credited to all four Beatles, and was essentially a functional piece, used as incidental music for a fantasy scene in a psychedelic travelogue.

However far they had come in 1961, the end of the year left the Beatles feeling that they were in a rut. They had two Hamburg stints behind them, as well as formal recording experience. They were now considered a hot band locally, but they knew that if they were going to make an impact, they had to perform beyond Merseyside and they had to make records. And these goals were beyond their grasp. A reasonable observer might have concluded that such goals were also beyond the grasp of Brian Epstein, a former drama student who, after a run of early academic failures, worked for his parents' furniture store and had lately made a success of the family record shop, the North End Music Stores on Whitechapel Street, not far from The Cavern. Epstein's interest was in classical music, not rock and roll. He attended the Liverpool Philharmonic's concerts, and had become friendly with its conductor, John Pritchard. Judging from the items he singled out in his weekly record news column in *Mersey Beat*, he also had a fondness for Frank Sinatra, Anthony Newly, Beatrice Lilly and show tunes.

In his autobiography, *A Cellarful of Noise*, Epstein wrote that he knew nothing of the Beatles until customers began ordering 'My Bonnie', then available only on the German Polydor label. It may seem odd that he was entirely oblivious; after all, the same *Mersey Beat* that carried his record column was full of news of the Beatles, and had reported on their German recording sessions in some detail. But it is likely that Epstein's interest in *Mersey Beat* was confined to its utility as an advertising vehicle, and that since he had neither a personal nor a commercial interest in the local beat scene, he simply did not read the articles about it. As it turned out, Epstein was unable to find a British distributor for the record. But he made it a point of pride not to turn customers away unsatisfied, and when he learned that the group played regular lunchtime sessions at a club ten

The dapper Brian Epstein had neither managerial experience nor a particular interest in rock and roll, but was captivated by the Beatles at first hearing and worked tirelessly to get them a hearing beyond Liverpool.

The Beatles performing under the trademark arch of their *de facto* Liverpool headquarters, the Cavern.

minutes' walk from his shop, he decided to seek them out. His search brought him to the Cavern for the Beatles' lunchtime set on 9 November 1961.

Nothing could have been farther from the regular milieu of this dapper, upper-middle-class 27-year-old businessman, but he was captivated by what he saw and heard. The initial attraction, undoubtedly, was extra-musical. Epstein, a homosexual who had a particular fondness for low-class ruffians, found himself in a dank, crowded club, with sweat dripping from the walls, watching a band of leather-clad rock and rollers stomping their way through American hits and songs of their own. They were, in Epstein's eyes, thoroughly unprofessional, even a bit uncouth. They smoked and ate on stage, shouted at their audience and indulged in private jokes. But he found the energy of their performance irresistible; indeed he later admitted that he felt a strong attraction to the most aggressive of them, Lennon.

Epstein returned to the Cavern several times over the next three weeks, slowly persuading himself that he could successfully manage a rock band. When he met with the Beatles in early December, he promised to improve the quality of their bookings, get them higher fees, arrange performances outside Liverpool, and get them a contract with a major British record label. Epstein believed, however, that he could not accomplish this with the Beatles as they were. Henceforth they were to cleanse their stage patter of obscenities and private jokes. There would be no more smoking, eating or drinking on stage. Their sets would be organized, their time on stage would be strictly limited, and their leather jackets would be exchanged for matching suits and ties.

Lennon later described these changes as a Faustian bargain, and as a whole, the group adopted these new work rules unenthusiastically. But they clearly trusted that Epstein could deliver on his promises, and one thing the new regimen did was get them to focus more fully on the shape of their stage show, and more to the point, how their own music would figure into it. Cover versions remained necessary staples, but Lennon and McCartney were increasingly interested in showing off their material, and by 1962, several of the songs that found their way onto their first two albums were being tested on the stage.

Epstein quickly discovered that he had underestimated the difficulty of getting the London-based record labels to consider recording a rock band from Liverpool. He did, however, get them a hearing at Decca Records. Mike Smith, a young assistant producer, was sent to Liverpool to hear the band at the Cavern on 13 December and returned with a favourable report. The next step was a formal audition in Decca's studios on 1 January 1962. The conditions weighed heavily against success: the Beatles had spent the night travelling from Liverpool to London through heavy snowstorms, and when Smith arrived, he insisted that the band use studio equipment rather than their own battered but familiar amplifiers. Seasoned performers though they were, the high stakes made them nervous, something clearly audible on the fifteen-song tape that the sixty-minute session produced.

There may have been another factor weighing against them: Epstein had tailored the set list to show off the group's versatility, but it could be, as Lennon later argued, that the material was not their best. Their versions of 'The Sheik of Araby', 'Searchin'' and 'Three Cool Cats' sound uncharacteristically goofy. One can hear that their account of 'September in the Rain' was meant to swing, but here it sounded wooden. Meredith Willson's 'Till There Was You', from *The Music Man*, was by then a McCartney show-stopper, but you would not have known it from his vocally tense performance. Only three originals were included: Lennon's songwriting debut, 'Hello Little Girl', and two McCartney songs that had been in the band's repertory for a few years, 'Like Dreamers Do' and 'Love of the Loved'. None came off especially well, and after mulling over the decision for more than a month, Decca turned down the Beatles.

The wisdom of hindsight makes the Decca tape fascinating listening. Their novelty numbers may have been looser and funnier live, but this part of their repertory was otherwise undocumented. It also offers a glimpse of their early songwriting efforts. In any case, the session yielded a professionally recorded tape, which Epstein carried with him on his rounds of the London record label offices. The rejections were unanimous. Within two months of taking on the Beatles as his first management client, he seemed to have hit a brick wall. The first nibble, actually, came not from a record label but from a publisher – Sid Colman of Ardmore and Beechwood, an EMI subsidiary – who liked the sound of the three Lennon–McCartney songs. Upon Epstein's insistence that recordings were more important to the group than a publishing contract, Colman arranged for a mid-February meeting with George Martin, the head of Parlophone, an EMI subsidiary.

Martin, born in 1926, came to the record world with a solid musical training, and when he became head of Parlophone in 1955, he was twenty-eight years old and the youngest producer ever to be put in charge of an EMI label. Martin was a talented pianist as a child, and during his school years he led a dance band, George Martin and the Four Tune Tellers. As a flyer in the Navy's Fleet Air Arm during World War II, his off-duty piano playing attracted the attention of a BBC producer, who arranged for him to perform one of his own compositions on the 'Navy Mixture' radio programme. After the war he attended the Guildhall School of Music as a student of composition, conducting, orchestration and music theory, with piano as his principal instrument. He also took up the oboe, which he played as an orchestral freelancer before taking a job in the BBC's music library. In 1950, EMI lured Martin away from the BBC, hiring him as second in command at Parlophone. His first jobs were classical orchestral and choral sessions, but he soon took on light music (Sidney Torch and the Queen's Hall Light Orchestra) and jazz (Humphrey Lyttelton and John Dankworth). His experience with rock was slim, but not non-existent. To EMI's chagrin, he turned down Tommy Steele, who went on to become one of Britain's big pre-Beatles stars. He was, however, impressed with Steele's band, the Vipers, and signed them.

Where Martin really made his mark was in comedy records. In 1952 he produced Peter Ustinov's 'Mock Mozart', an opera parody in which the actor supplied all the voices. He also recorded Peter Sellers, both as a soloist and with Spike Milligan as the Goons – favourites of Lennon's – as well as Flanders and Swann and 'Beyond the Fringe'.

Martin liked what he heard on Epstein's tapes, and drew up a provisional contract that covered their formal audition session, on 6 June 1962. The Beatles were in Hamburg when they received the heartening news that Parlophone would give them a listen. They were near the end of the forty-eight-night stint at the Star-Club, Hamburg's newest and biggest club, where they were the main attraction. The visit had begun tragically: upon their arrival in Hamburg on 11 April they learned from Astrid that Sutcliffe had died of a brain haemorrhage the previous day. He was twenty-one years old.

Back in England, they carted their tattered gear to EMI's recording studios in Abbey Road for the test session. As at Decca, the technical staff shook their heads in dismay at the sight and sound of their equipment, and one of the engineers borrowed a speaker from an echo chamber to provide heft to McCartney's bass sound. Martin was immediately taken with the group's charm and humour; what he thought needed attention was their musicianship.

Four songs were recorded that day, three of them Lennon–McCartney compositions: 'Love Me Do', 'P.S. I Love You' and 'Ask Me Why'. The fourth was 'Besame Mucho', a rocked-up Latin standard that the group had played at the Decca session. Martin was satisfied enough to commit Parlophone to the group, but he felt that the recordings themselves were not suitable for release. He was not, for one thing, convinced that their original material was chartworthy, so he gave them 'How Do You Do It', a song by Mitch Murray, to learn for the next session, scheduled for 4 September. He also disliked Pete Best's drumming, which he described as not regular enough and not the right kind of sound. He did not recommend replacing Best, who he considered the best looking and likely to be a focus of their visual image. But he told Epstein that he intended to bring in a session drummer.

Lennon, McCartney and Harrison had their own doubts about Best. In Hamburg they had become friendly with Ringo Starr, the drummer for Rory Storm and the Hurricanes, another Liverpool group. Musically and temperamentally, he fitted into the group better than Best. And when he joined, the constellation was complete: Lennon, McCartney, Harrison and Starr out front, Epstein and Martin working behind the scenes.

Starr, whose real name is Richard Starkey, was born in Liverpool on 7 July 1940 to Elsie Gleave and Richard Starkey, who divorced in 1943. He was a sickly child: at six, appendicitis, peritonitis and a string of mishaps kept him hospitalized for more than a year. Seven years later he was hospitalized with pleurisy, which kept him off the streets until he was fifteen. His schooling was virtually non-existent, and his work experience in a variety of short-term jobs was limited. His main enthusiasm was for playing drums, starting on a kit bought for him by his stepfather, Harry Graves, who had married Elsie in 1953. In 1957, when he was an apprentice joiner, he joined the Eddie Clayton Skiffle Band, and got a fancier trap set. Two years later he joined the Raving Texans, which later became Rory Storm and the Hurricanes. His penchant for wearing an inordinate number of rings earned him his nickname, which also appealed to him because of its cowboy aura. And Starr seemed a better stage name than Starkey. He joined the Beatles on 18 August 1962.

The firing of Best was handled with what the Beatles later admitted was shameful cowardice. They told him nothing of their displeasure with his work, nor did they pass along Martin's comments. He

Above, Richard Starkey – better known as Ringo Starr – crouching as a member of Rory Storm and the Hurricanes, the band for which he drummed until the Beatles lured him away in August 1962
Right, onstage clowning was part of the Beatles' act before Brian Epstein persuaded them of the benefits of professional decorum. Here Harrison, McCartney, Best and Lennon enjoy a rave up at the Cavern.

Richard Starkey (Ringo Starr), with George Harrison at the Tower Ballroom, New Brighton, in November 1961. Still a member of Rory Storm and the Hurricanes, Starr sported a beard and had a grey streak in his slicked back hair, both of which he would lose when he joined the Beatles nine months later.

was effectively out of the picture soon after the Parlophone audition. When he heard rumours of his imminent dismissal, in mid-June, Epstein offered only reassurance. So it was with no sense of insecurity that he arrived for a meeting with Epstein on the morning of 16 August only to hear Epstein blurt out, 'the boys want you out and Ringo in'.

There is only a limited degree to which Best's drumming with the Beatles can be assessed now. His playing on the Decca tapes and the Parlophone version of 'Besame Mucho' (the only surviving recording from the 6 June session) is proficient but not inspired. Best could fill out a texture with an efficient pattern of quick rolls, rapid, light-handed tapping, and sensible use of the cymbals. His playing on the Sheridan recordings is considerably more lusty. The few BBC broadcasts on which Best performed survive in recordings so fuzzy that the drumming is hardly audible, but what can be heard sounds straightforward, dutiful and sometimes energetic. What his playing lacks, in these examples, is the variety and personality that Ringo

John Lennon's first wife Cynthia (née Powell), looking very much like Brigitte Bardot, Lennon's notion, in the early 1960s, of the ideal woman.

Starr's drumming added to the group's performances. But Best had a following in Liverpool, and his firing was controversial. When Granada Television filmed the Beatles in action at the Cavern on 22 August, it caught a hint of the dissension: as the Beatles finish their version of 'Some Other Guy', a voice from audience can be heard calling out, 'We want Pete'.

The Beatles would scarely have had time to reconsider even if they had been so inclined. In addition to daily performances, they were rehearsing material for the 4 September session. And amid all this, Lennon discovered that Cynthia Powell, his girlfriend since art college, was pregnant. John and Cynthia were married on 23 August, the day after the Granada filming; their son, Julian, was born on 8 April 1962.

Martin, informed that the Beatles had a new drummer, did not bring in a studio player on 4 September. They recorded 'How Do You Do It' but persuaded Martin to shelve it and reconsider one of their own songs as a first single. Then they turned their attention to 'Love Me Do', lavishing considerable effort – fifteen takes plus overdubs – on what must be the simplest Lennon–McCartney composition the Beatles ever recorded.

As it turned out, Martin was not much more impressed with Starr's drumming than he had been with Best's. He booked another session for 11 September, this time hiring Andy White, an experienced session drummer. 'Love Me Do' was tackled again, this time with White on drums and Starr playing tambourine. White also drummed (with Starr on maracas) on 'P.S. I Love You', a McCartney ballad with the trace of a Latin beat. Somehow, the Beatles persuaded Martin that Starr would be able to handle the job once he settled in; this was the only session for which Martin employed a stand-in drummer. At the end of the session, Martin settled on 'Love Me Do' and 'P.S. I Love You' as the first single. It did not set the British charts on fire when it was released, on 5 October, but it reached Number 17, not bad for a first release by an unknown provincial band. And with its laconic harmonica introduction, played by Lennon, its gently bluesy tune and its distinctive vocal harmonies, it served notice that there was something a bit different going on in Liverpool.

It was the Beatles' second single, 'Please Please Me' that galavanized the pop world, and with good reason. When the Beatles first

George Martin, a schoolmasterish overseer of the Beatles' recording sessions in the early days, listens as McCartney and Lennon play him one of their songs during an early visit to EMI's studios in Abbey Road.

played it for Martin, it was a slow ballad, meant to sound like a Roy Orbison song. Martin liked the song but hated the way they played it, and told them to spice it up. When they returned to Abbey Road on 26 November, they had quickened the tempo and brightened the arrangement, and Martin cobbled together an introduction using the opening melody line. On stage, Harrison played this introduction on guitar. But Martin felt that the harmonica had been a useful signature sound on 'Love Me Do', so on the recording, Lennon doubles Harrison's guitar line. Martin also came up with the brisk chord sequence that ends the song.

'Please Please Me' lasts just under two minutes, but an extraordinary density of musical detail is packed into it. The vocal harmony, to begin with, is different from anything the Beatles had attempted until then, and unusual for a pop song. Each verse has only two lines and a refrain, and on each of the lines, Lennon and McCartney begin in unison, then move gradually apart as McCartney repeats his opening note and Lennon takes the descending main melody.

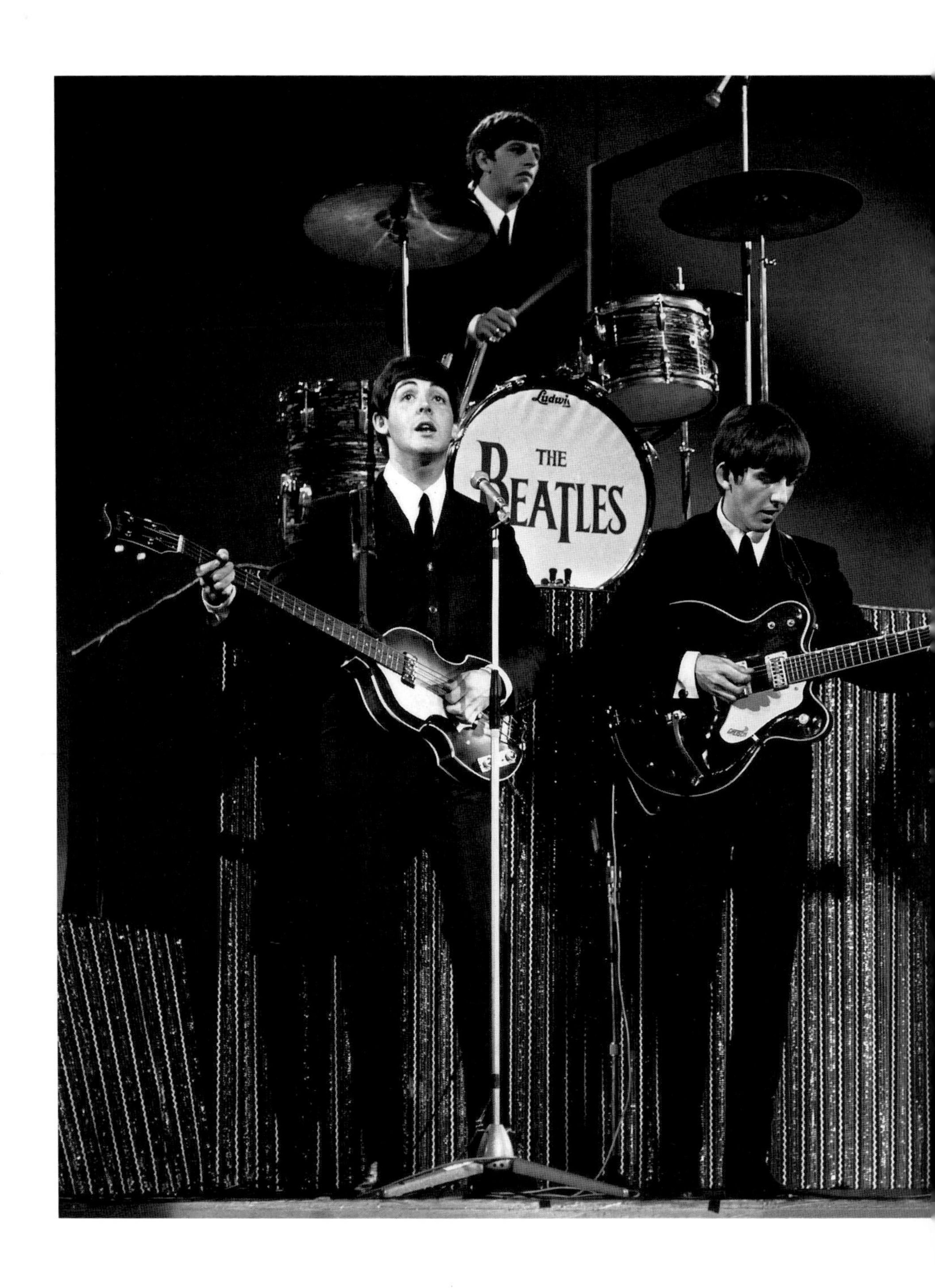
Ludwig
THE
BEATLES

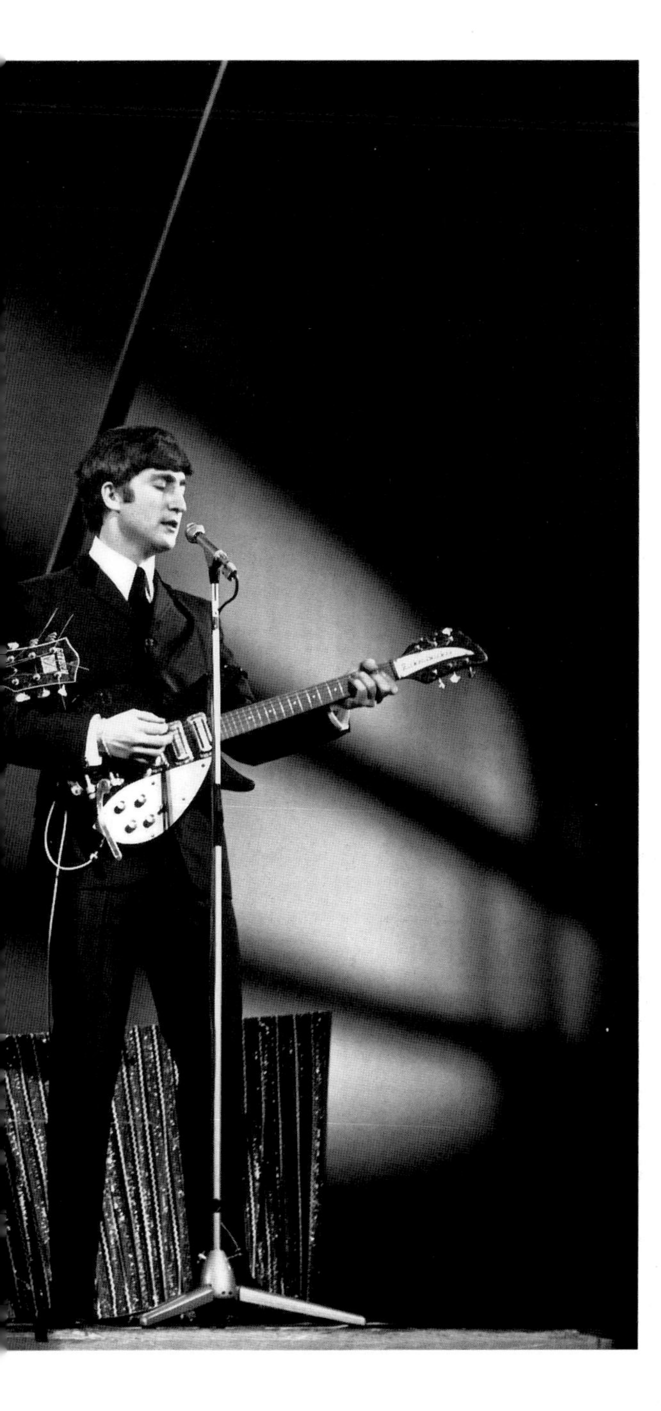

A far cry from the scruffy, leather-clad rockers Epstein discovered at the Cavern, the freshly-scrubbed, carefully tailored Beatles perform on British television in 1963.

A quickly ascending series of guitar chords and a rapid-fire burst from Starr links the first and second verse lines, and a single line guitar figure leads into the pleading (and suggestive) refrain, 'come on, please please me, oh yeah, like I please you'. Lennon repeats 'come on' four times, with each of his solo invocations followed by a harmonized version by McCartney and Harrison. The solo plea rises gradually in pitch, and the harmonized responses, rise, fall and rise. The tension created by this seemingly simple figure, which lasts seven seconds, is magical.

Underpinning the verse melody is an atypically monotonous yet remarkably effective bass line from McCartney, who simply plays the chord roots in a pneumatic repeating eighth-note figure (that is, two notes to the beat), adorned only by occasional grace notes, executed as quick slides from below. It is only at the 'come on' section that McCartney's bass playing steps into character, with a line that seems to sing on its own, playing off the rhythm of the solo 'come on'

Though they would eventually play in big concert halls and stadiums, in the Beatles' early years cinemas were the traditional venues for rock concerts. These theatres could scarcely keep up with the demand for tickets; here a few fans brandish theirs.

figure. And in the two bars that lead from that section back to the start of the verse melody, McCartney's bass line positively dances. Starr, too, is at his finest, accompanying the verses solidly, filling in gaps between vocal lines – and supporting the 'come on' section – with rapid fills, and driving home the chordal finale with a chain of sharp, machine-gun-like bursts.

The bridge section – the secondary melody and chord progression, which the Beatles usually called 'the middle eight', regardless of the actual number of bars required – adds another picturesque element. Lennon sings here that he doesn't want to complain; yet the melody, built of repeating figures on two adjacent note, is a musical evocation of whining, softened somewhat by the harmonized 'ah' sung by McCartney and Harrison. But in the end, it explodes in frustration, leaping up an octave, into falsetto on the final word of the line, 'it's so hard to reason with you'. The bridge ends with the equivalent of a resigned sigh, the line, 'why do you make me blue?'

Most listeners at the time would not have concerned themselves with the song's harmonic touches, instrumental felicities or even the ways in which the music mirrored (or, in the bridge, belied) the lyrics. More immediately relevant was that it was a great tune, and you could dance to it – in fact, you could hardly help dancing to it. Martin was so confident that the revamped 'Please Please Me' worked that when the Beatles finished recording it, he announced over the studio intercom, 'you've just made your first number one.' It did not go there immediately, as later Beatles releases would. Released on 11 January 1963, it cruised up the charts for six weeks before hitting number one on 22 February.

It had some help. EMI, which had typically ignored Parlophone's productions, quickly got behind Martin's new discovery. The BBC took a shine to the Beatles as well. They had made their first radio appearance on a *Teenager's Turn* show on 8 March 1962, and made a handful more appearances that year. By mid-1963, they were regulars on the BBC's pop programmes, and even had a series in their own name, *Pop Go the Beatles*. Epstein was getting them television appearances too. Suddenly, they seemed to be everywhere. Looking at Epstein's neatly typed, detailed schedules, they saw themselves committed to one, two or three performances every day, sometimes punctuated by as many as three BBC sessions and a television date.

The radio programmes, which typically included brief interviews, offered hints of the Beatles' cheeky pun-driven humour, a quality the press picked up on quickly.

As 1962 ended, it seemed that the Beatles were working as hard as a band could work. But throughout 1963, with the fame they sought finally at hand, they stepped up the pace and intensity of their assault on the world.

3

Beatlemania in England 1963

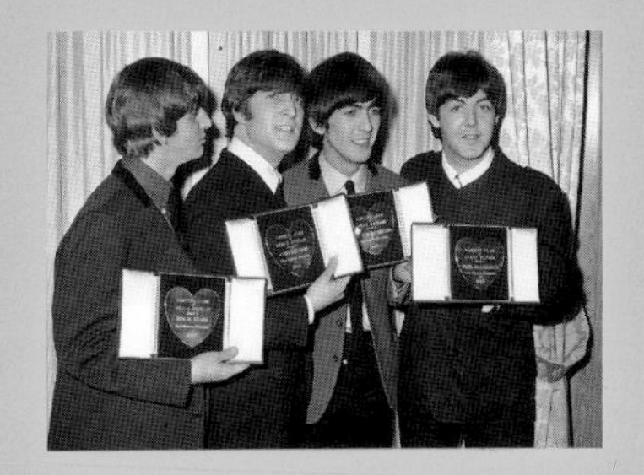

When the Beatles were presented the Variety Club of Great Britain's Show Business Personalities of 1963 award by Harold Wilson, then the opposition leader, John Lennon quipped, 'thanks for the Purple Hearts,' referring to a US military medal awarded to soldiers wounded in action.

They learned so quickly. But when I first met them, I had absolutely no idea at all they would write decent material. They wrote songs that were pretty awful – 'One After 909' and 'P.S. I Love You' and 'Love Me Do' were the best of them. It was pretty rough stuff. I didn't really blame the guy who had turned them down.

George Martin, 1993

Beatlemania in England 1963

Just before the sessions for 'Please Please Me' and its flipside – a slightly Latin-flavoured Lennon–McCartney collaboration called 'Ask Me Why' – the Beatles had spent two weeks at the Star-Club in Hamburg, sharing a bill with one of their heroes, Little Richard, and they returned to the Star-Club one last time in mid-December, staying until New Year's Eve. On that final night, one of their Liverpool colleagues taped their performance on amateur equipment. The tapes languished in Liverpool until 1972, when Allan Williams found them and approached Harrison and Starr with a proposal to release them and split the profits. They declined, but Williams eventually found a buyer, and the tapes were released over the Beatles' objections in 1977.

In their original state, the recordings are quite raw: the performances are imperfect, and without Epstein there to oversee them, the Beatles slip back into the profane stage patter that had been their pre-Epstein style. But before the tapes were released, they underwent an ambitious editing and sonic restoration job, the result of which was an idealized thirty-song set that offers a fascinating glimpse of the Beatles at a turning-point in their career. It captures them in the milieu that shaped them, playing rock favourites, covers of recent hits, and new songs of their own. But they were already on their way out of that world.

When they returned to the studio on 11 February, 'Please Please Me' was making steady progress up the *New Musical Express* chart, and though not yet number one, it was a certified hit. The conventional strategy called for the quick release of an album to capitalize on these successes. Martin had already broken the mould by presenting the Beatles as a cohesive group rather than as a singer with backup, and by favouring their own songs over those of professional songwriters. Now there would be another innovation. Typically, a pop album would present the hits, padded out with lightly cooked filler. Martin followed this formula only to the extent that he included the four songs released on singles. Another producer might have increased his quotient of available material by using the file recordings of 'How Do You Do It' and 'Besame Mucho'. But Martin and the Beatles decided to begin the album sessions fresh, and to treat every song as if it were a potential single.

The session for this début album, *Please Please Me*, was amazingly productive. In just under ten hours of session time, the Beatles recorded eleven new songs – five originals and six covers. Of those, one of the originals, 'Hold Me Tight', was temporarily shelved, to be attempted again, more successfully, seven months later during the sessions for the second album, *With the Beatles*. The model for *Please Please Me* was the Beatles' stage set. Like their concerts, the album begins and ends with upbeat rockers. Between those book-ends, the group's versatility is displayed almost in variety show style. Each of the Beatles has an image-establishing moment in the spotlight. McCartney, already identified as the band's balladeer in 'P.S. I Love You', takes that further with his cover of a waltzy show tune, 'A Taste of Honey'. Yet he opens the album in his rock voice, singing his own 'I Saw Her Standing There'. Lennon also takes up a few ballads, Arthur Alexander's 'Anna (Go To Him)' and the Shirelles' 'Baby, It's You', but his renderings show something of his aggressive edge, with a slight current of bitterness. As McCartney opens the album, Lennon closes it, singing the Isley Brothers' 'Twist and Shout' with an explosive vocal grittiness. Starr applies his distinctively nasal tone to another Shirelles tune, 'Boys'. And Harrison, who retained a heavy scouse accent in his singing voice, gave slightly fragile performances of a Goffin-King classic, 'Chains', and a lively Lennon–McCartney song, 'Do You Want to Know a Secret'.

The covers show the presence of new influences, again from America. One is Motown, a Detroit-based style (also the name of the most prominent label specializing in the music) in which black vocal groups melded rhythm and blues with aspects of gospel and top-forty pop styles. Both within and on the periphery of this new style was another genre new to rock, though familiar in the 1940s: girl groups. Three of the six covers on *Please Please Me* were first recorded by American girl groups – 'Boys' and 'Baby It's You' were Shirelles songs, and 'Chains' was a hit for the Cookies. On *With the Beatles* the group would add the Marvellettes' 'Please Mister Postman' and the Donays'

Left, Paul McCartney, the most personable of the Beatles, was often the most eager to discuss the group's work with interviewers.

'Devil in Her Heart'. And their concert sets still included the Teddy Bears' 'To Know Him is to Love Him', with the gender changed.

The Motown and girl group songs did not pass through the Beatles repertory without leaving traces on Lennon's and McCartney's compositional styles. Both genres made prominent use of gospel's call and response gesture, in which a solo vocal line is repeated by a backing chorus. The effect is heard in the 'come on' section of 'Please Please Me', and its mirror image – the chorus singing the main melody and the solo vocalist responding with free-floating, improvisatory amplifications – is heard near the end of 'P.S. I Love You'. A variation of this move was to have the lead singer's lines punctuated by nonsense syllables, 'sha la la,' or 'doo wah doo.' This too became part of the Beatles arsenal, starting with 'Do You Want to Know a Secret'. And it may be that the Beatles' interest in Motown and girl groups led them to expand their harmonic style from the pure duet sound of the Everly Brothers to a richer texture, often with a bluesy cast.

Of course, as much as the cover versions tell us about the wells the Beatles' were drawing from, the real points of interest on *Please Please Me* are the originals. Some show the signs of continuing apprenticeship. 'Ask Me Why', for example, has an underlying cha-cha beat that even in 1963 was on the border of sounding dated. 'Misery' and 'There's a Place', by contrast, present a new kind of vocal and instrumental texture, something different from 'Love Me Do' and 'Please Please Me', and a precursor of the sound the group would explore throughout 1963. Both have Lennon and McCartney singing tandem lines, in unison for stretches but with ear-catching divergences at key points. And both feature a tightly compressed lead and rhythm guitar sound, energetic, efficient drumming, an active bass line, and brief patches of extraneous but effective colour – Martin's brief punctuating piano figure in 'Misery', Lennon's harmonica on 'There's a Place'.

As songs, they are not timeless masterpieces. But they capture something of the adolescent spirit of 1963. 'There's a Place', for instance, argues that the best escape from the heartache and sorrow of unrequited love is to turn inward, to a world of introspective fantasy. It was not an uncommon conceit. Five months later and half a world away, the Beach Boys recorded Brian Wilson's 'In My Room', a somewhat more sophisticated exploration of comparable sentiments.

Wilson is unlikely to have heard the Beatles song, which was not yet released in the USA. Yet the songs are uncannily similar and in fact begin with the same line, 'There's a place where I can go'.

'There's a Place' and 'Misery' are period pieces. But 'I Saw Her Standing There' has a vitality that time has not tarnished. The song is essentially McCartney's, but Lennon added some useful touches. In its original form, it began: 'She was just seventeen, never been a beauty queen'. Lennon replaced the second line with 'and you know what I mean' – hardly profound, and less picturesque than McCartney's line, yet wonderfully suggestive and exactly the right line for that moment in the song. The arrangement evolved too. A Cavern Club rehearsal tape recorded sometime after mid-August 1962 includes an embryonic version of the song with an awkward harmonica accompaniment, square phrasing and seemingly unfinished bridge lyrics. By the time they played the song at the Star Club in December, the harmonica was dropped, and the song was in its finished form.

Melodically, it could not begin more simply: the first two lines are really just inflected speech. But just as expectations drop, McCartney provides a beautifully arching line, a short rhapsody on the lyric, 'and the way she looked was way beyond compare'. On the verse's final couplet, Lennon sings a lower harmony in thirds, fourths and sixths, and the active bass line keeps the song moving while betraying its roots: it is similar in shape and spirit to the bass line of Chuck Berry's 'I'm Talking About You', a song the Beatles performed at the time.

Several sonic gimmicks on their way to becoming Beatles signatures are found here too. An octave leap to a falsetto 'oooh', first heard in 'Please Please Me', would return in most of their hits of 1963. Its roots are in the songs of the Isley Brothers and Little Richard, but the Beatles made it their own by incorporating it in the amalgam of English and American styles that yielded their identifiably Beatlesque sound. They also found it a useful effect in their stage shows. The days of screaming girls was upon them, and when they stepped up to the microphone, shook their heads and delivered that falsetto 'oooh', the audiences went even wilder.

However, the Beatles disliked literal repetition. So when they repeated an effect, even something as seemingly inconsequential as a falsetto 'oooh', they tried to find a different use for it the second time. When they returned to Abbey Road to record their third single on

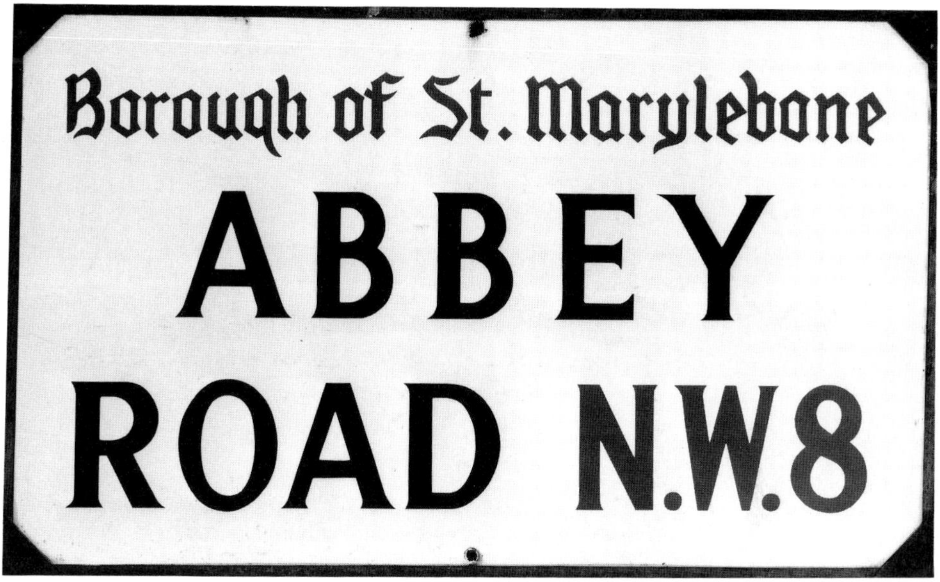

A component of Beatlemania was a desire to own anything associated with the Beatles, however peripherally. Once it became known that the Beatles recorded at EMI's studios in Abbey Road, street signs vanished regularly. This one turned up at auction years later.

5 March, they brought 'From Me to You', a song that uses that 'oooh' again. But where the effect had been merely an ornament in 'I Saw Her Standing There', it found its way into the lyrics of 'From Me to You', giving the song's second line, 'if there's anything I can do' a burst of energy on its final word. In fact, the effect is expanded here. Lennon and McCartney sing the first three words of that line in unison, but on the last three words McCartney leaps up an octave and sings in a falsetto with a slight vibrato that suggests the head-shaking of the stage show.

Lennon and McCartney were also testing a new theory here, the notion that songs in which 'me' and 'you' were used prominently and repeated frequently would strike listeners as personal, and would have a special appeal. It may seem quaint that the Beatles, who would soon rule the pop charts and spawn countless imitators, were so intent on discovering the key to audience appeal. But as they composed 'From Me to You', they were savouring the success of their first number one record, then in its second week at the top. However confident they may have been, they had no reason to assume that everything they touched would turn to gold, and at this point they were intent on discovering the mechanics of hitmaking.

Long after the shrill obbligato of screaming fans rendered acoustic guitars impractical for stage use, the Beatles sometimes used them in the recording studio and, as Lennon demonstrates here, in their television appearances.

Once 'From Me to You' followed 'Please Please Me' to the top of the British charts, Lennon and McCartney tweaked their compositional formula once again. On 1 July, they bounded into Abbey Road with 'She Loves You', a song they had written only four days earlier in a hotel room in Newcastle upon Tyne. The recording they made that day had the quintessential early Beatles sound: vocals lines that begin in unison and end in harmony, jangly guitars, an assertive bass line linked to a steady drum beat with plenty of cymbals, and that head-shaking falsetto 'oooh', here placed strategically before the song's most ear-catching element, the joyously cathartic 'yeah, yeah, yeah' refrain. It would be their first million seller.

Without question, 'She Loves You' is a masterpiece of pop song construction, yet it breaks a number of rules. There is, for example, no bridge. Structurally, it is nothing but an introduction, three verses, all of which lead back to the refrain, plus an ending that ties up all those 'yeahs' in a sixth chord – a G major chord with an added E (the sixth degree of the scale) that makes the chord slightly ambiguous and unstable. Martin objected to this ending, a common trick in the 1940s, but archaic in 1963. But Lennon and McCartney insisted, and Martin came to realize that the chord was a final, delicious touch in a song full of great hooks.

The lyric was also something new for the Beatles. Until now, the 'you' in their songs was a prospective, current or former girlfriend. Typically in pop songs, when men sing to other men, they do so either to moon about their woman, or to deliver blustery warnings about encroaching on their turf. But in 'She Loves You', the singer has listened to the lament of his friend's paramour, apparently in some detail, and is urging his friend to patch things up. Two years later, in 'You're Going to Lose That Girl', they took this approach again, but with a twist: if you don't treat the lady right, I'll steal her away.

'She Loves You' was clearly composed for the Beatles' own immediate use, but by now Lennon and McCartney were also beginning to think of composing as an endeavour separate from performing. They had a ready market. Epstein, convinced that he had found his calling in musical management, expanded his business to include other groups and singers, mostly from Liverpool, and several benefited from access to Lennon–McCartney songs that the Beatles either wrote specifically for them, or found unsuitable for their own use. 'Hello Little Girl' became a hit for the Fourmost. Cilla Black, a former hat-check girl at the Cavern, had an early hit with 'Love of the Loved' and was later given other McCartney songs, 'It's for You' and 'Step Inside Love'. And 'Bad to Me' was written for Billy J. Kramer and the Dakotas.

Performers outside the Epstein circle tapped the Beatles' golden songwriting machine as well. In 1963, the Beatles became friendly with the Rolling Stones, a blues band making its way in London, and still without a number one record. Lennon and McCartney cobbled together 'I Wanna Be Your Man', a riffy, basic song that suited the Stones' early style. When the Stones' recording hit the top of the charts, the group's singer, Mick Jagger, and its rhythm guitarist, Keith Richards, decided that if Lennon and McCartney could write their own songs, so could they. They were not alone in this realization, and by 1964, rock bands that composed their own music – rather than recording songs handed to them by their record producers – became the rule rather than the exception.

Between visits to Abbey Road, the Beatles undertook a non-stop touring schedule. By August 1963, Epstein took them entirely off the

The Rolling Stones were the Beatles' strongest rivals among British bands, but the two groups maintained a competitive friendship. Lennon and McCartney wrote the Stones' first number one hit, 'I Wanna Be Your Man' in 1963; later, members of the Stones appeared in the Beatles 'All You Need Is Love' telecast, and the Beatles' faces are scattered on the cover of the Stones' album *Their Satanic Majesties Request*.

ballroom circuit: now they were playing only in proper theatres, on raised stages. And by the end of the year, the length of their stage set was reduced from an hour to thirty minutes. They were also becoming increasingly regular visitors to the radio studios of the BBC, where they were not only guests on shows like *Saturday Club*, *Here We Go* and *Side by Side*, but also had their own showcase, *Pop Go the Beatles*. Another Beatles-centred show, *From Us to You*, was broadcast on bank holidays between December 1963 and August 1964, and in June 1965 they were the stars of *The Beatles Invite You to Take a Ticket to Ride*.

For these programmes – fifty-three of them, broadcast between 8 March 1962 and 7 June 1965 – they performed live or with minimal overdubbing in the BBC's studios. Their sheer productivity was amazing: they recorded 88 songs at these sessions, some in as many as a dozen versions, for a total of more than 280 recordings. Of the 88 songs, 36 were numbers from their early stage repertory that they never committed to tape at EMI. Of those, only one – the lovely 'I'll Be On My Way', another hit for Billy J. Kramer – was a Lennon–McCartney original.

The BBC recordings of songs by Little Richard, Chuck Berry, Carl Perkins and Arthur Alexander (as well as more arcane numbers like Mikis Theodorakis's 'Honeymoon Song') are an important source of information about the Beatles' early repertory. And the songs that the Beatles did record for EMI show how the group performed their hits without the benefit of studio trickery and unencumbered by the shrill obbligato of high-pitched screaming that pervades recordings of their concerts. They demonstrate that the group's performances were not quite as calcified as the Beatles themselves often claimed they were. Harrison's solo in 'Till There Was You', for example, grew increasingly florid between July 1963, when they recorded the song at Abbey Road, and June 1964, when they dropped it from their concert repertory.

At the end of 1963 they were not yet making a firm distinction between their recording and performing careers, but that was clearly in the cards. Their second album, *With the Beatles*, took longer to make than its predecessor, and by then the Beatles had adopted the view that singles and albums should be treated as separate projects. There would be exceptions later in their career, but for the moment they argued that if their fans had bought their singles, they should not have to buy the same tracks again on albums. In immediate practical term, this meant that the four songs released on singles since *Please Please Me* could not be considered for the new album.

In its broad outline, *With the Beatles* follows the pattern established on *Please Please Me.* The opener, Lennon's Motown-inspired 'It Won't Be Long', immediately grabs the listener's attention with its call and response refrain – a back and forth on the word 'yeah'. And an aggressive cover, Barrett Strong's 'Money', closes the set. As on the first outing, the band supplied eight originals and performed six covers. But this time one of the originals was a Harrison song, 'Don't Bother Me', his first composing credit since 'Cry for a Shadow'. Harrison devoted the rest of his microphone time to Chuck Berry's 'Roll Over Beethoven' and the Donays' 'Devil in Her Heart'. Stuck for something for Starr to sing, Lennon and McCartney gave him 'I Wanna Be Your Man', the rave-up they had written for the Rolling Stones. McCartney's facility as a crooner is again tapped for a show tune, 'Till There Was You', but he also sings his own somewhat punchier 'Hold Me Tight' and the magnificent 'All My Loving', certainly the most memorable of the originals.

It is Lennon, however, who dominates the album. He sings lead on most of the originals (an indication, usually, of which collaborator was the principal composer), as well as on three Motown covers, all hard driving songs that showcase his remarkably communicative voice. All told, the album has a tougher edge than *Please Please Me.* Yet ironically, it also sounds more leisurely, more carefully considered, more settled.

This time the sessions were staggered, with stretches of work in July and September, and touch-up sessions in October. The Beatles were learning that even if their albums documented their concert sets, they need not be limited by the instrumentation of their stage arrangements. They raised no objection to Martin adding piano parts to 'Money' and 'You Really Got a Hold on Me', or Hammond organ to 'I Wanna Be Your Man'. They even gave him the solo in 'Not a Second Time', a graceful, single-line piano part. Martin encouraged them to experiment with textures. On 'Till There Was You', Harrison plays a seemingly un-Beatlesque nylon-stringed Spanish guitar, and Starr, lured away from his trap set, plays bongos. Lennon, McCartney and Starr add mildly exotic percussion – tambourine, claves and an African bongo – to 'Don't Bother Me'. And all four show their enthusiasm for a studio trick Martin showed them: strengthening the lead vocals by double-tracking them.

Musically, the album is a decisive step forward. Harrison, in particular, seems to have been listening to some jazz guitar. It had been his idea to end 'She Loves You' with that sixth chord, a standard jazz move, and his solos in 'All My Loving' and 'Till There Was You' have a decidedly jazzy accent. More blatantly, he opens Lennon's 'All I've Got to Do' with a chord fully at home in jazz and entirely foreign to rock, an E augmented, with an added ninth and eleventh. The chord stands entirely outside the song: it rings out at the start and does not return. Yet it sets the song's slightly bluesy, Motown-inspired mood perfectly, and it lingers in the memory, even as Harrison goes on to play a more commonplace progression of major and minor chords.

Towards the end of the sessions, EMI installed four-track recording equipment at Abbey Road, new tape machines that allowed much greater flexibility than the two-track recorders Martin had used until then. Two-track was fine for orchestral recording: with good microphone placement and sensible mixing, it yields a realistic stereo image. But the recordings Martin was making with the Beatles were more complex. In order to retain full control over the balances, he was recording instruments on one track and vocals on the other. Overdubbing meant copying to a second tape, which entailed a loss in quality.

The upgrade was long overdue; indeed, it had not been lost on Martin that EMI in England was invariably the last among the major labels to adopt new technology. During a visit to the USA in 1958, Martin attended Frank Sinatra's recording sessions at Capitol, EMI's American affiliate, and was astonished to see that the company used three-track recorders, which allowed for stereo orchestral backing tracks as well as a separate vocal track that could be centred during the mixing process. Upon his return to London he tried to persuade EMI to install similar equipment, but his requests were ignored.

Martin's use of the old two-track system was adequate for making monaural recordings, but militated against properly balanced stereo mixes. Although stereo was not yet a major concern, particularly in England, EMI released its recordings in both mono and stereo formats, and Martin had little choice but to provide stereo versions in which the extreme separation of the raw tapes was modified only slightly. Still, exactly because the early stereo is so primitive, these recordings offer a bird's eye view of the group's instrumental and vocal arrangements, and reveal details that are lost in the compressed mono mixes.

Four-track recording solved the problem. Now the instruments could take two or more tracks. Lead and backing vocals could be recorded separately, and the stereo mixing sessions would yield more artfully balanced recordings. Most crucially, the expanded facilities gave the Beatles greater leeway for experimentation, a freedom they would exercise as they learned more about studio technology. But their first recordings on the new equipment remained fairly basic. On 17 October, near the end of the *With the Beatles* sessions, they brought in the songs they had in mind for their next single, 'I Want to Hold Your Hand' and 'This Boy'.

'This Boy' was something new for the Beatles, and for Lennon in particular: a slow ballad, based on a chord progression native to 1950s' doo-wop, performed entirely in close three-part harmony. Even the bridge, in which Lennon steps out for a full-throttle solo vocal, has a wordless harmony backing from Harrison and McCartney. Appealing but not earthshaking, it is nevertheless the progenitor of a long line of lushly harmonized Beatles songs, from 'If I Fell' and 'Yes It Is' to 'Sun King' and 'Because'.

'I Want to Hold Your Hand', a Lennon–McCartney collaboration, reprises the celebratory sound of 'She Loves You', but is more conventionally structured. The Beatles had opened 'She Loves You' with a tom tom roll that tumbled immediately into the introductory chorus. In 'I Want to Hold Your Hand', the introduction is more ambitious: guitar chords become a springboard, catapulting the listener into the verse. The song is actually quite subversive. The innocent declaration of the title was exactly the sort of thing that would reassure parents that the Beatles were safe and wholesome; yet for anyone listening closely, the music tells a different story. That eager octave leap ('you'll let me hold your hand') that leads into the refrain expressed undisguised sexual tension, and the bridge amplifies the image of false restraint: the studied calmness of its opening line, 'and when I touch you I feel happy inside', is belied in the building energy and rising melody of its conclusion, 'it's such a feeling that my love I can't hide, I can't hide, I can't hide'.

Seeing a sexual undercurrent in such a seemingly naïve song is not merely analytical fantasy. In the manuscript of the song's lyrics (now in the British Museum), McCartney jokingly noted the second verse refrain as 'you'll let me hold your thing', and in some of his more unbuttoned interviews, Lennon referred to the song as 'I want to hold your head' – which is what he often seems to be singing on tapes of the group's concerts.

The importance of texture in this recording is evident from the first line. McCartney and Lennon sing it in unison, but when Harrison fills in the pauses in the lyric with a winding guitar line set in the same register as the voices, his playing seems less an embellishment than an integral part of the melody. There are also small but effective touches – the stray twangs of a solo guitar that dot the texture like sighs, and the overdubbed handclapping that supports the rhythm and brightens the record's sound. Starr's drumming is also an important element. When Lennon and McCartney take their octave leap on the word 'hand', Starr plays a cascading fill. And in the bridge, he taps along with patient steadiness until 'I can't hide', and then mirrors the tension of the vocal line with a steady, driving bash at the floor tom tom and open high hat.

If anyone had the idea at the beginning of 1963 that the Beatles were a flash in the pan, 'I Want to Hold Your Hand' made them think again. Released on 29 November (a week after *With the Beatles*), it sold 1.5 million copies within six weeks in Great Britain alone, and when it replaced 'She Loves You' at the top of the hit parade, it was the Beatles' fourth number one record of the year. The albums were doing equally well. *Please Please Me* topped the album chart for thirty weeks, until *With the Beatles* replaced it. According to a report in the British trade publication *Record Retailer*, the group's record sales for 1963 totalled some £6,250,000.

Their ascendancy was reflected outside the pop charts as well. On 9 October they were featured in *The Mersey Sound*, a television documentary about the Liverpool rock scene. And on 13 October, four days before they recorded 'I Want to Hold Your Hand', the Beatles topped the bill on *Sunday Night at the London Palladium*, seen by an estimated fifteen million television viewers. It was after

'The Beatles? I thought they were wonderful – who doesn't?' asked the German film and cabaret star Marlene Dietrich, who appeared on the same bill as the Beatles at the Royal Variety Show in 1963.

this performance, with its accompanying screams from the audience, that the British press began reporting on what it called Beatlemania. On 4 November, Beatlemania went upmarket when the Beatles played in the Royal Command Variety Performance at the Prince of Wales Theatre in London. Their contribution was a fairly sedate performance of four not particularly sedate songs, 'From Me to You', 'She Loves You', 'Till There Was You' and 'Twist and Shout'. Before the last, Lennon delivered his oft-quoted introduction, 'Would the people in the cheaper seats clap your hands? And the rest of you, if you'll just rattle your jewelry.'

Newspapers and magazines went wild over the Beatles, filling their pages with pictures and stories. And manufacturers of trinkets – Beatle wigs, handbags, buttons and even wallpaper – cashed in on the phenomenon. Yet amid all the madness, one serious, respected critic, William Mann of *The Times* of London, published an end-of-

By late 1963 a merchandising principle had evolved: put the Beatles' names or likenesses on trinkets of all kinds – clothing, glasses, jewelry, pins, posters, wallpaper, ice cream wrappers, toys, dolls, wigs, and hundreds of other items – and people will buy them. The ephemera shown here now sells for premium prices at collectors' conventions around the world.

year review that argued that there was more to Beatlemania than head-shaking, screaming girls and pop culture ephemera. What he found most fascinating, he wrote on 27 December, was the music. In a music theorist's rhapsody, Mann celebrated what he heard as pandiatonic clusters in 'This Boy', Mahleresque Aeolian cadences at the end of 'Not a Second Time', and the major tonic sevenths and ninths and flat-submediant key switches he heard in several other songs. The musicologist Deryck Cooke, writing about the Beatles five years later, poked fun at what he called Mann's 'dovecot–fluttering', arguing that a harmonic analysis is misleading (but conceding that Mann's was accurate). The Beatles, untutored in music theory, did not have a clue what Mann was talking about, and did not particularly care, although it tickled them to be taken so seriously.

With their first hits behind them, and America and *A Hard Day's Night* just ahead, the Beatles sang for 3,000 members of their British fan club at the Wimbledon Palais, London, on 14 December 1963.

They were making headway outside England too. Australian radio had adopted them enthusiastically. They were taking off in Europe as well, although television and radio recordings from their Scandinavian tour in October show that audiences there were considerably more sedate than those at home. Their greatest frustration,

LES!

though, was that until the final weeks of 1963, they had failed to crack the American market. There had been some television coverage, mostly condescending, which presented the Beatles and their fans as the latest examples of British eccentricity. But Capitol Records, EMI's American arm, had turned down each of their singles and albums. And when EMI licensed the material to the smaller Swan and Vee Jay labels, they scarcely made a ripple on the charts. And so America, the world's largest record market and the source of their early inspiration, remained closed to them.

That was about to change.

4

The Beatles Conquer America 1964

The British newspapers were saying, well, what's left to do, you've conquered everything, and we'd say America. *We got the Number One, did Ed Sullivan. By then we'd distilled our stuff down to an essence, so we weren't coming on just as any old band.*

Paul McCartney, 1980

In April 1964, only days after finishing their first film, *A Hard Day's Night*, the Fab Four taped a Rediffusion television special, *Around the Beatles*. They are shown here performing a round-robin version of the Isley Brother's 'Shout', a song they never recorded commercially.

The Beatles Conquer America 1964

In the rich mythology that has sprung up around the Beatles' story, events that were impressive enough in reality have been magnified in the retelling. One myth started by Epstein and carried on by the Beatles themselves, is that the group refused to visit the USA until they had a number one record in the American charts. America had been notoriously inhospitable to British pop singers and groups, and as the story goes, the Beatles were disinclined to cap their astonishing British successes with failure in the USA.

As it turned out, 'I Want to Hold Your Hand' was indeed riding the top of the charts when the Beatles arrived at the newly renamed Kennedy International Airport on 7 February 1964. But the arrangements to bring them over were finalized early in November, weeks before 'I Want to Hold Your Hand' was released in Britain, and nearly two months before its American release in the last days of December.

The catalyst for the trip was Sid Bernstein, a fledgling New York concert promoter who had been reading about Beatlemania in British newspapers. In the autumn of 1963, he enterprisingly telephoned Epstein and offered him nearly double the Beatles' usual fee for two shows at Carnegie Hall. Epstein accepted, and Bernstein booked Carnegie Hall for afternoon and evening shows on 12 February. Epstein, however, did not want to bring the Beatles to the USA just for concerts. What he wanted was an important television appearance, something that would have the national reach that *Sunday Night at the London Palladium* had in England. The nearest equivalent was the Ed Sullivan Show, an hour-long variety show broadcast by CBS on Sunday evenings. As it turned out, Sullivan also knew about the Beatles. He had been at London Airport on 31 October, when a mass of screaming fans greeted them on their return from Sweden.

When Epstein visited New York in November, he and Sullivan struck a bargain: the Beatles would have top billing on three

Opposite, inclement weather during the Beatles' first visit to the United States, in February 1964, forced them to travel from New York to Washington by train. In those early days they were amused and even a little surprised by the crush of fans who attended their arrivals and departures.

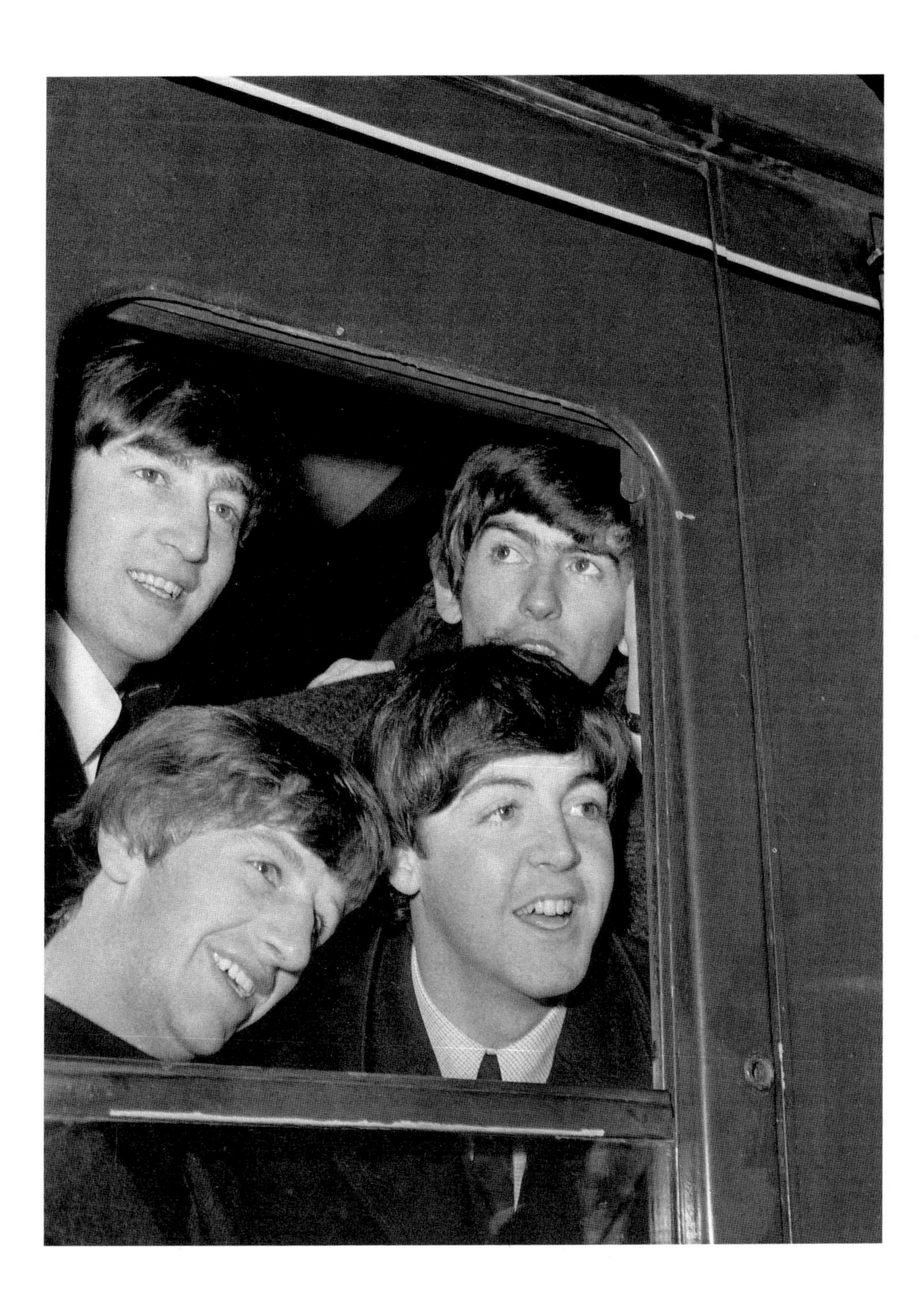

consecutive shows, on 9, 16 and 23 February 1964; but they would perform for a reduced fee. Epstein also met with executives at Capitol Records, who had reconsidered their initial reluctance to issue the group's recordings. They may still have harboured doubts, but Epstein was hard to resist: urbane, polished, convinced that making the right impression was everything, and focusing on the most minute details of how that impression should be made, he now had the inarguable track record of having turned a provincial band into the British pop music success story of the decade.

Sociologists searching for ways to explain the Beatles' impact at this time have made much of a presumed psychological need for non-threatening, escapist entertainment in both Britain and the USA in 1964. In Britain, a government sex scandal involving the Secretary of State for War, John Profumo, monopolized the headlines during the summer of 1963; and just as John Le Carré was beginning to make his mark as an author of cold war spy novels, Kim Philby, a British journalist, was revealed as a Soviet spy. In the USA, the Civil Rights movement was meeting violent resistance in the South. The American government was sending aid to Vietnam without much of a clue what it was getting into. And on 22 November 1963 – the day *With the Beatles* was released in Britain – John F. Kennedy, the popular young President, was assassinated, abruptly ending what had promised to be a rejuvenation of American politics.

The major political scandal involving a Cabinet Minister, John Profumo (*right*) and his relationship to a call-girl, Christine Keeler (*above*) in 1963 did much to undermine the authority of the British establishment and promote attitudes that popular music began to reflect.

A moment that shocked and stunned the United States: aided by a Secret Service agent in the tense confused seconds after John F. Kennedy is assassinated in Dallas on 22 November 1963, Jacqueline Kennedy escapes from the limousine.

According to the psychological-need theory, all this bad news produced a craving for a lightweight, happy obsession, and the story of the four young moptops and their screaming teenage fans fitted the bill perfectly. Yet, the need for diversion cannot seriously be advanced as a factor in the Beatles' success. Conditions, after all, have not improved greatly since 1963. War, government corruption, racial injustice, inner-city violence, financial disarray and environmental disasters have continued to dominate the news; if a need for diversion lay at the heart of Beatlemania, why have the equally troubled 1970s and 1980s produced nothing like the hysteria that attended the Beatles' early years?

That said, there is no denying the Beatles' extramusical appeal to teenagers of the time, who saw in their musical, sartorial and tonsorial style a clear break from the expectations of their parents and teachers. The Beatles were something of their own, and the pudding-basin haircuts in particular, though pixieish by today's standards, seemed scandalous in 1964 and made for comparatively harmless intergenerational friction.

More crucially, they revitalized popular music at a time when it reached one its periodic troughs. By 1963 the overt sexuality of early Elvis had been largely banished from mainstream pop. Crooners like Steve Lawrence (with 'Go Away Little Girl') and Bobby Vinton (with 'Blue Velvet' and 'There I've Said it Again') topped the charts. Broadway show tunes still registered, as did novelties along the lines of the Singing Nun's 'Dominique', which was the number one record in the USA for most of December 1963.

There were signs suggesting that a revival of rock would be welcome. The Four Seasons, a group with a sound that thrived on vocal harmonies and the soaring falsetto of its lead singer, Frankie Valli, were a fairly hot chart group. The Chiffons and Stevie Wonder had number one hits in 1963. There was teenage *angst* (in Lesley Gore's 'It's My Party'), sassiness (in the Angels' 'My Boyfriend's Back') and even some early surf music from Jan and Dean and the Beach Boys in the hit parade.

There was also a growing alternative audience. Bob Dylan, Joan Baez, Phil Ochs and an army of acoustic guitar-wielding folk-singers were setting socially-conscious poetry to simple, folkish melodies, and were playing to college students and sophisticates. And the genres that appealed to the Beatles in their formative years – Motown, rhythm and blues, soul – had a predominantly black audience in the USA, although the style was making enough crossover headway to propel occasional records into the upper reaches of the charts. The Beatles would help make both these genres more mainstream. When they played Chuck Berry, Little Richard and Motown songs, and expressed their preferences in interviews, young white record buyers who were either too young to have heard the originals or who were not interested at the time, suddenly had reason to investigate them.

Connections with the folk camp were forged later in 1964, when Bob Dylan visited the Beatles during their second North American tour. His attraction was based on a misunderstanding: he thought the line 'I can't hide', in 'I Want to Hold Your Hand' was 'I get high', and was amazed that the Beatles got this apparent drug reference into the pop charts. The Beatles were not complete innocents in the drug culture, having lived on amphetamines in Hamburg. But they had never smoked marijuana until Dylan's visit. There was a musical give and take between the Beatles and Dylan as well. By the end of 1964, Lennon was including Dylan-like harmonica figures in his songs and was thinking more carefully about the literary merit of his lyrics. Dylan's approach was suddenly accessible to pop fans who had been

First captivated by the Beatles because he thought they were singing 'I get high' in 'I Want to Hold Your Hand' (the actual line is 'I can't hide'), the American folksinger Bob Dylan gave the foursome its first taste of marijuana, influenced Lennon's approach to lyric writing, and was himself influenced by the Beatles to switch from acoustic to electric instruments.

disinclined to follow him directly, and in 1965 he met them more than half way, abandoning his folk guitar for an electric rock band.

It was almost by accident that 'I Want to Hold Your Hand' was injected into the confused musical milieu of the USA late in 1963. In much the same way as the Beatles kept tabs on American music by listening to the records brought back to Liverpool by sailors, Carroll James, a Washington DC disk jockey, had asked a British Airways stewardess to bring him some British pop music. It was only natural that 'I Want to Hold Your Hand' was in the stack she gave him in December 1963. When James played the record on the air, the response was tremendous.

Capitol reconfigured the single, replacing the British B-side, 'This Boy', with the much earlier 'I Saw Her Standing There'. An album, *Meet the Beatles,* was assembled, using both sides of the American single, plus 'This Boy' and nine of the fourteen tracks on *With the Beatles.* Capitol had planned to issue 'I Want to Hold Your Hand' in mid-January and the album just before the Sullivan appearances. But by mid-December disk jockeys around the country were playing advance copies, and Swan and Vee Jay, sensing that their investments in the Beatles' early recordings might at last pay off, reissued their versions. Capitol moved legally against Swan and Vee Jay, reacquiring its rights to the early material it had rejected, and moved up its own release dates.

In the calm before the storm, the Beatles take a break after setting up for a London performance in the spring of 1964

As the ground was being prepared for them in the USA, the Beatles turned their attention to Paris, where for eighteen days they shared a bill at the Olympia Theatre with Sylvie Vartan and Trini Lopez. The French audience was more reserved than the Beatles were then used to. But there were compensations. On their first day in Paris, they received word that 'I Want to Hold Your Hand' was number one on the weekly chart published by Cashbox, having sold more than a million copies in only two weeks. Meanwhile they were thinking about another project that was quietly getting underway. Film executives at United Artists had noted the Beatles' sales potential in late 1963, and approached Epstein with a contract offer. Their plan was to exploit the Beatles' fame – to their mutual benefit – with a quick, inexpensive, black-and-white film, specifically for the British market.

The pop exploitation film has long been a dead form, but in the early 1960s there was a natural symbiosis between pop music and film. Elvis had been cranking out movies like sausages, and in England Cliff Richard followed suit. Chuck Berry, Little Richard and other early rockers had made at least cameo appearances in films for the teen market; and of course, Bill Haley's performance of 'Rock Around the Clock' in *Blackboard Jungle* was a clarion call in the early days of rock. Plot lines and acting ability were not great concerns; the main thing was that the soundtrack be peppered with potential hits. United Artists' principal interest, in fact, was less in the film itself than in the rights to a soundtrack album.

Not long after the deal was signed, however, it began to dawn on United Artists that perhaps the Beatles might yield something better than the standard pop film. And the Beatles, who were feeling their own commercial clout, had ideas about the film as well. Mainly, they did not want to be made to look foolish. That was fine with Dick Lester, the young American expatriate director who was hired for the project.

Lester was ideal for the Beatles: he had directed Peter Sellers in *The Running, Jumping and Standing Still Film*, a manic eleven-minute featurette starring Peter Sellers, Spike Milligan and Leo McKern. The Beatles loved it; its offbeat comedy suggested that Lester could handle their own humour. The Beatles and Lester agreed that the best approach would be to show the group as what it was: a band of distinct but complementary personalities who were both buoyed and trapped by their success. And at the Beatles' insistance, the Liverpool writer Alun Owen was hired to write the script, gathering his material by following the Beatles briefly. He completed his work by January, and when Lester visited the Beatles in Paris, he brought a draft with him.

Besides looking over the script, the Beatles were committed to some recording in Paris. Electrola, EMI's West German arm, had insisted that the Beatles would not be a hit in Germany unless they sang in German. The plan was to record their two biggest hits, 'She Loves You' and 'I Want to Hold Your Hand', with German lyrics, as 'Sie liebt dich' and 'Komm, gib mir deine Hand.' The Beatles were not keen on the idea. They agreed only reluctantly, and then in a test of wills, they decided not to show up at the Pathé–Marconi studio, and not to take Martin's call when he telephoned to find out where they were. A livid Martin arrived at their hotel a few minutes later, and insisted that they make the recordings. Once in the studio, they worked so efficiently that in addition to the German recordings, they taped the basic tracks for their next single – and their first contribution to their film soundtrack – 'Can't Buy Me Love'.

The song, by McCartney, was not remarkable: its verses are set to a standard blues progression, its bright, bouncy arrangement offsetting its mildly bluesy melody and a minor key bridge. The lyrics could conceivably have been a response to the words Lennon sang (but did not write) in 'Money', the closing track of *With the Beatles.* There, love was all very well, but money was the thing to have. Now, even as the royalty cheques were pouring in, McCartney proposed a more idealistic sentiment, 'I don't care too much for money, money can't buy me love'.

The session tapes show a working method that would become increasingly typical, which is that the Beatles began taping the song without having worked up a finished arrangement. At first, they seemed intent on highlighting the song's blues character, partly by using a call and response approach. In the first two takes, Lennon and Harrison responded to McCartney's lead vocal with harmonized repetitions of the lyrics. And through take three, Harrison punctuated McCartney's vocal lines with a descending guitar figure in the style of Carl Perkins. There is an interesting touch in the second take. McCartney, after botching the vocal, began scat singing in the style of Ella Fitzgerald. Perhaps he saw the possibilities in the song: Fitgerald eventually recorded her own version.

After three unsuccessful tries, they stopped to rethink the arrangement. Lennon's and Harrison's responsive vocals and Harrison's guitar punctuation were dropped, and the basic tracks were completed in a single take. Still, there was work to be done. It was clear from the early takes that Harrison hadn't figured out what to do in the verse left open for a guitar solo. That, along with some cosmetic overdubbing, was deferred until a London session just after the American trip.

The Beatles spent only two weeks in the USA, but the visit had profound consequences, not only for the Beatles and their immediate audience, but for the emerging international popular culture and its institutions, particularly the record business. From the moment they arrived in New York on 7 February, until their departure on 22 February, Epstein balanced their schedule so they seemed both ubiquitous and scarce. No newspaper or magazine let their presence go unremarked, and they were all over the airwaves. But Epstein limited the number of writers granted personal audiences with his charges. And although thousands of ticket-seekers had been turned away from Carnegie Hall and the Ed Sullivan Show, he declined offers for extra concerts, including Sid Bernstein's proposal for shows at Madison Square Garden.

The Beatles' own manipulation of the press began moments after they landed at Kennedy Airport, where they were greeted by some 3,000 screaming fans. The entourage was ushered into the Pan American lounge to be quizzed by a press corps that was used to teen fads and did not expect much. But with snappy answers, wisecracks and ad-libs, the Beatles turned what could have been a desultory affair into great copy. Elvis Presley's press conferences were all deference: he even called reporters sir and ma'am. The Beatles were not that way. Asked to sing, they refused. Pressed by a reporter who said there was doubt that they *could* sing, Lennon said drily, 'we need money first'. Asked why their music excited teenagers, McCartney deadpanned, 'we don't know, really', to which Lennon added, 'if we did we'd form another group and be managers.'

Musically, the agenda was continued proselytization. At their first American concert, at the Washington Coliseum on 11 February, and at Carnegie Hall the next day, they were preaching largely to the converted. But their first appearance on Sullivan's show brought them into the homes not only of the already smitten, but of the undecided and even the openly hostile. The show was seen by seventy-three million people, a record for the time. Some sixty per cent of American televisions were tuned in, and newspapers made much of reports that for that one hour, crime statistics plummeted.

The atmosphere of the show on 9 February was electrifying. Sullivan, now free of any doubt that he had a hit on his hands, revelled in the sense of occasion. He gave the Beatles a good deal more screen time than most musical guests – five songs, rather then the usual two. A week later, the Beatles followed Sullivan to the Deauville Hotel in Miami Beach, Florida, this time playing six songs. They were back in England by the time of their third contracted appearance on 23 February, but left Sullivan three songs on tape.

The visit was extraordinarily well documented. Albert and David Maysles, a young team of documentary filmmakers, trailed the Beatles in New York and Washington, capturing both the

Following page, for a scene in *Around the Beatles*, an army of fans was enlisted to carry portraits and placards and sing 'We Love You Beatles', a rewrite of the adulatory hit from the film *Bye Bye Birdie*.

BEATL
WE LOVE Y
WE LO
JO

pandemonium that attended their public movements, and more private footage from the eye of the hurricane, their suites at the Plaza Hotel. At the Washington Coliseum, a second crew filmed the thirty-minute show for a closed-circuit theatre broadcast in March. Missing, alas, is documentation of the Carnegie Hall concerts. Surviving correspondence and contracts show that Capitol intended to record the performances. But objections from the American Federation of Musicians prevented the taping at the last moment. The Maysles' cameras were not allowed inside either: after the Washington segment, their footage skips to Florida.

Their documentary, *What's Happening! The Beatles in the USA*, was re-edited in 1990, and released on videotape as *The Beatles: The First U.S. Visit*. This revised version includes a curiosity left out of the original. Lennon, sitting in his room at the Plaza, is shown playing with a toy instrument, a hybrid keyboard and harmonica. The chord progression he plays bears an uncanny resemblance to the introduction of 'Strawberry Fields Forever', a song nearly three years, thousands of touring miles and several stylistic changes in his future.

The Beatles' visit created a voracious market for British bands. The Dave Clark Five, Herman's Hermits, the Rolling Stones, the Animals, the Yardbirds, the Hollies, Freddie and the Dreamers, Gerry and the Pacemakers and a dozen others crossed the water and received a welcome not hitherto extended to British pop groups. Capitol Records suddenly found itself in the ideal position to both stoke the fires of Beatlemania and exploit the demand. While EMI awaited new material, Capitol Records could draw on a backlog of early Beatles recordings, which it released in the most parsimonious way, on albums that generally had only eleven or twelve songs, compared with the fourteen on British Beatles albums. Capitol also considered songs released as singles to be fair game for album compilations, something the Beatles themselves deliberately avoided. To the Beatles' chagrin, Capitol did not buy their notion that albums and singles should be kept separate; nor did they regard the Beatles' albums as integral statements. Thus, every two British Beatles albums, and related singles, yielded three albums from Capitol. There was a slight silver lining for American fans. To help Capitol pad out its releases, EMI sometimes supplied tracks from works-in-progress. Thus, on hodgepodge collections like *The Beatles Second Album*, *Beatles VI* and

Opposite, McCartney tuning the left-handed Hofner bass that was his trademark instrument from the start of the Beatles right through to the end.

Yesterday and Today, American fans actually got to hear new material several months before their counterparts abroad. Nevertheless, Capitol's reconfiguration, which persisted until *Sgt. Pepper's Lonely Hearts Club Band* in 1967, distorted the purposeful sequences the Beatles and Martin had devised. When EMI transferred the Beatles catalogue to compact disc in 1987, the British originals were adopted as the global standard.

However much the Beatles objected to Capitol's tampering with their releases, they could take pride in some interesting statistics made possible by the American label's freehanded policy. In April 1964, when they had released only six singles in England, they held no fewer than fourteen places on the Hot 100 singles chart published by the American trade magazine *Billboard*. And in May they held three of the top four places on *Billboard*'s album chart, even though by their own reckoning, they had made only two.

5

Hard Days For Sale 1964

The Beatles in a portrait by Astrid Kirchherr, who came to England to photograph them during the filming of *A Hard Day's Night* in the spring of 1964.

They were rather war-weary during Beatles For Sale. *One must remember that they'd been battered like mad throughout 1964, and much of 1963. Success is a wonderful thing but it is very, very tiring.*

George Martin, 1988

Hard Days For Sale 1964

Having broken the USA's resistance to British pop, the Beatles were given a hero's welcome upon their return to London on 22 February 1964. Airport interviews, spiced with footage of the huge, vocal crowd awaiting the group, were filmed for both television and for Pathé News, which had already devoted several of its theatrical newsreels to the Beatles. And the group, energized by the success of its American visit, returned immediately to work, performing and participating in comedy sketches during a *Big Night Out* television appearance. On 25 February, they returned to the Abbey Road studios to finish off 'Can't Buy Me Love' and record its companion, Lennon's bluesy 'You Can't Do That'.

Now the Beatles had more irons in the fire than ever. Lennon, whose *Daily Howl* pseudo-newspapers used to keep his school classmates in stitches, had continued writing pun-filled nonsense verse in

The Beatles, followed by Brian Epstein, return to England triumphant on 22 February1964, after two weeks of utter pandemonium in America. They had hoped to storm the bastion of pop music on that first visit to the USA, and encountered little resistance.

Lennon's first collection of nonsense verse and idiosyncratic drawings, *In His Own Write*, was published in March 1964; the Beatles, in the velvet-collared jackets they sported during their winter and spring 1964 tours, help him promote it.

the style of Edward Lear and Lewis Carroll, and short prose full of Joycean wordplay. He also continued filling scraps of paper with peculiar line drawings of people with multiple heads, human–animal hybrids, and deformed fantasy creatures of all sorts. During the band's early years he had published some of his stories in *Mersey Beat*, and he occasionally read them to interviewers. In March, he published a seventy-nine-page collection, *In His Own Write*, which met with virtually unanimous critical admiration on both sides of the Atlantic.

For the most part, the weeks following the American trip were devoted to their film, *A Hard Day's Night*. Lennon, in deconstructing the Beatles myth years later, complained that Alun Owen's script was too reductive. But Owen did what was demanded of him. Although there was undoubtedly both exaggeration and over-simplification in his characterizations, he drew on the traits the Beatles projected publicly. Lennon was cast as the rebellious, cutting wit. McCartney was the engaging, diplomatic cutie. Harrison was shy but cheeky. And Starr was the slightly sulky last among equals, the comic foil for the others. Owen's script follows the Beatles as they prepare for a television appearance, and is leavened by fictional devices: Paul's troublesome grandfather tags along, and Ringo deserts the group for a few hours, imperiling the performance. Along the way, the Beatles run for their lives to avoid being torn to pieces by their adoring fans, and chafe against being held prisoner by those charged with keeping them safe. Naturally, they also play some of their newest songs.

Filming took seven and a half weeks, from 2 March to 24 April. The band had a respite from concerts during this period; but they taped several television and radio appearances, and there was work to be done on the soundtrack album, which would include both film songs and new material not used in the film. They had written most of the new songs in Paris, and as it turned out, they managed to record all the film songs except the title track (which was composed near the end of filming) in the week between their return from the USA and their first day before the cameras. The non-film songs were recorded later in the spring, and when the sessions ended in early June the Beatles had seventeen new songs, fourteen of them by Lennon and McCartney.

Thirteen of the originals were included on the album of *A Hard Day's Night*, the first collection devoted entirely to the Beatles' own compositions. The remaining original, 'I Call Your Name', had been written for Billy J. Kramer, and was included with the session's three covers – Little Richard's 'Long Tall Sally', Carl Perkins' 'Matchbox' and Larry Williams' 'Slow Down' – on an extended play single, called *Long Tall Sally*. The *A Hard Day's Night* album is unquestionably the peak of the band's early period, a collection of songs full of energy and assurance. A transitional trough would follow in late 1964 and early 1965, but for the moment there was no sign of the weariness that could be heard on their *Beatles For Sale* and *Help!* albums.

'A Hard Day's Night', the title track of both the album and the film, begins with a perfect attention-grabbing flourish, a stark, bright-edged, slightly dissonant guitar chord that lingers defiantly for a few seconds before the song begins. It took several tries to find the right chord, and the right coloration: they tried it distorted and plain, more dissonant and less, and even with tremolo. In the end, Lennon and Harrison settled on an intriguingly ambiguous configuration. Harrison, playing a twelve-string guitar, and Lennon playing a six-string standard instrument, played different voicings of a G suspended fourth chord – G major with an added C – while McCartney played a D on his bass. The bright, open sound they settled on was perfect for the gesture.

The song posed a compositional challenge for Lennon and McCartney. Until early April, the film had been called, variously, *Beatles No. 1* or *Beatlemania*, pending a better title. It was Starr who came up with the title *A Hard Day's Night*, although there are several versions of how that happened. Lester has said that Starr tended to come out with amusing malapropisms when he was drunk, so they simply waited for the right moment. Another version has it that Starr, emerging from the studio after a long session, noted that 'it's been a hard day', and then noting that it was dark, added 'night'. But Starr must have used the phrase well before the filming began, because Lennon included it in 'Sad Michael', one of the pieces in *In His Own Write*, published in March.

Whatever the origin, it was left to Lennon and McCartney to come up with a song that would make prominent use of the phrase, and could be used to begin and end the film. A day after Lester and the producer, Walter Shenson, approved the title, Lennon and McCartney turned up with the lyrics and chords written on a matchbook. It is a good model of the Lennon–McCartney collaborative process, such as it was: Lennon wrote (and sang) the verses, which tell of long, hard days at work, made bearable by the woman he comes home to, while McCartney contributed the bridge, a paean to domestic bliss. The contrasts between these sections show certain classic traits.

Lennon's verse melody is mildly exotic, and slightly bluesy. It appears, at first, to be in plain G major; but in the third bar, when the ear expects the melody to move up to an F sharp, it hits an F natural instead. Lennon lingers on the F, giving the melody a temporarily bluesy cast, but then restores the F sharp, both in the melody and the accompanying chords, as the verse ends. And as a final twist, in the closing line ('you know I feel alright') Lennon brings in a sultry blue note, a flatted third, on the word 'feel'. The minor key accompaniment to McCartney's bridge melody gives it a bitter-sweet quality, but McCartney ends the section with a burst of unequivocal joy – a rising melody for the line, 'feeling you holding me tight, tight, yeah'. Harrison's use of a twelve-string guitar gives the song an effervescent quality, particularly in the arpeggiated fade-out and in a quirkily elegant solo (doubled by Martin on the piano) distinguished by a rolling figure that hammers home that mixolydian F natural.

McCartney composed only a few of the album's songs, but his contributions are notably durable. Besides 'Can't Buy Me Love', there is the tuneful, up-tempo 'Things We Said Today', which projects a love affair so solid and long-lasting that the participants will eventually look back at the present in a haze of loving nostalgia. And there was 'And I Love Her', the first in a line of gentle ballads, models of symmetry and directness, with lyrics that are sweetly poetic. Love, here, is idyllic. There is, in fact, an appealing fragility in the song, which dictated an instrumental texture similar to that of their 'Till There Was You' recording. Starr, ordered away from his drums, was given bongos and claves, and both Lennon and Harrison use nylon-string guitars. In his solo, Harrison merely restates the melody. But during the verses, he provides a lovely, arpeggiated accompaniment that plays nicely off Lennon's straightforward strumming.

Lennon's songs dominate the collection, and generally paint more three-dimensional pictures than McCartney's. In 'I Should Have Known Better', his melody is bright and eager, and so is his harmonica-dominated texture; yet his lyrics suggest some reluctance about letting a flirtation blossom into something grander. The object of his attentions, in fact, sounds frustratingly dim: 'And when I tell you that I love you,' Lennon sings, 'you're gonna say you love me too. And when I ask you to be mine, you're gonna say you love me too.' Lennon urges her on: 'If this is love you've got to give me more, give me more, hey, hey, hey, give me more.' But when the bridge comes around again, her response is just the same as the first time.

In 'If I Fell' – a gorgeous ballad in the style of 'This Boy', but with a decidedly more sophisticated chord progression and sleeker vocal harmonies – Lennon describes a delicate situation in which the protagonist has a girlfriend, but is attracted to another. He is disinclined to proceed, partly because he does not want to cause his current girlfriend pain, but mainly because he wants an assurance that the new relationship will be an improvement on the old one.

'When I Get Home,' a soul-tinged rocker, has the singer impatient for a reunion with his sweetheart – yet there is also a faint undercurrent of extracurricular activity in the lyrics. 'I've got no business being here with you,' he sings, and after a telling pause he adds, 'this way.' In 'Any Time at All', Lennon offers his services as a lover, or if not that, than as a shoulder to cry on. And since Harrison had not

A scene from *A Hard Day's Night* which, like the rest of the movie, offered a reasonably realistic view of the Beatles' lives on tour. In this scene they are stuck in a hotel room, set to the task of answering fan mail.

produced a follow-up to 'Don't Bother Me', Lennon gave him 'I'm Happy Just to Dance With You', an attractive but inconsequential cousin to 'I Want to Hold Your Hand'.

These were Lennon's cheerier love songs. Others had a rougher edge. 'Tell Me Why', for example, is a peculiar combination of accusation and grovelling beneath its ebullient surface. The first thing we learn is that the woman the song is being sung to has lied to the singer, treated him badly and left him. His response, sung in the magnificently pressured voice Lennon used on rockers, is: 'If it's something that I've said or done, tell me what and I'll apologize.' As that is obviously insufficient, he begs and pleads on bended knee, until finally, thoroughly emasculated, he sings a line in falsetto: 'Is there anything I can do?'

In 'I'll Cry Instead', he is not so accommodating. The circumstances are similar – his girlfriend has left him – but this time he is angry and is plotting indirect retaliation. Specifically, he intends to break the hearts of other women. Or at least, so he threatens. When it comes down to it, he confesses that all he can manage to do for the moment is cry. For all its macho posturing, the wronged lover here is as pathetic as the one in 'Tell Me Why'.

Another warning song in this collection is 'You Can't Do That', a burst of jealousy in a modified blues form. Lennon here warns that if his woman continues to flirt, he will leave her. In fact, the lyric goes on, it is not only the flirtation that irritates him, but the thought of being ridiculed as a cuckold. The exasperation is captured in the music: Lennon plays the lead guitar solo, and instead of the smooth lines Harrison favoured, he came up with a constricted, sputtering sequence of bent notes and rapid-fire seventh chords – a concise expression of pure rage.

One more Lennon song, 'I'll Be Back', closes the album. After the posturing of 'You Can't Do That', which immediately precedes it, 'I'll Be Back' is a bitter-sweet admission that threats of abandonment are actually meaningless. Singing in close harmony with McCartney, to a lush backing of acoustic guitars and a simple, lightly syncopated bass-line, he not only admits that if he leaves, he will be back, but also confides that there has already been a pattern of punitive but clearly ineffective departures. But rather than begging, as in 'Tell Me Why',

Richard Lester, centre, explains his requirements to a small army of film and sound technicians as he prepares to film the group's performance of 'If I Fell'. All the Beatles are assembled except Lennon, who was off getting the acoustic guitar he used in this sequence.

he offers a touch of sarcasm: 'You could find better things to do than to break my heart again.'

All told, the Beatles continued to function as a self-contained unit on *A Hard Day's Night*, but their sense of texture continued to evolve. The fascination with double-tracked vocals, evident on *With the Beatles*, continued here. So did the group's interest in expanding the percussion battery. The main addition to this was the cowbell, prominent in the bridge of 'A Hard Day's Night' and throughout 'You Can't Do That' and 'I Call Your Name'.

The piano, played by both Martin and McCartney, had an increased if subtle role. Often it was buried so deep in the texture that listeners tended to sense it without quite hearing it; and often it was used to play single, unharmonized lines, as if it were an oboe. Its appearance in 'Any Time at All' is a case in point. A series of descending whole notes, played in the bass register under the frothy guitar chords of the verses, creates a peculiar resonance. But it is only clear that there is a piano in the mix when it joins Harrison's twelve-string guitar in the brief instrumental solo section.

The electric twelve-string guitar also adds significantly to this album's distinctive coloration, and was something rock bands elsewhere immediately adopted. Most notably, the Byrds, based in California, added a twelve-string guitar to their arsenal, and when they came to prominence early in 1965, it was with Beatlesque arrangements of early Dylan songs. The Byrds' guitarist, Jim (who later changed his name to Roger) McGuinn, used the instrument more aggressively than Harrison did, making bright-toned arpeggiations the centrepieces of his arrangements. Harrison, clearly influenced by McGuinn, adopted that approach for his own 'If I Needed Someone' in 1965.

A Hard Day's Night also pointed up the efficiency with which the group had absorbed the various rock, rhythm and blues and country styles in which they had performed in their early years, and the ease with which they applied classic moves to their own material. Harrison's lead guitar line, which ambles through 'I'll Cry Instead', would have sounded entirely at home on a Carl Perkins or Buck Owens record, just as Lennon's lead in 'You Can't Do That' owed something to the guitarists who backed the soul singers Wilson Pickett and James Brown. The Beatles' real achievement here, as in

Lennon warms up during a chat with Harrison backstage at the Scala Theatre in London as the Beatles wait to film one of the performance sequences in *A Hard Day's Night*.

Ringed by policemen whose duty it was to prevent teenage girls from hurling themselves at the group during performances, the Beatles play a concert during their first fully fledged North American tour in the summer of 1964.

most of their songs from 'Love Me Do' on, is in the way they wove these influences, along with their own melodic and harmonic gifts, into a style that was identifiably their own. And although perceptible links can be found between the worlds of *Please Please Me* and *A Hard Day's Night*, far more striking is the considerable degree to which the Beatles have moved forward.

After they had finished filming *A Hard Day's Night*, the Beatles played a handful of British concerts, recorded some television and radio performances, and took a brief holiday, reconvening on 1 June for the three days of recording required to finish the album and the *Long Tall Sally* EP. Two days after the sessions ended they were on stage in Copenhagen, the first stop in a twenty-six-day tour that proceeded to the Netherlands, Hong Kong, Australia and New Zealand. For part of the tour, Starr was sidelined with tonsillitis; until 15 June, a studio drummer named Jimmy Nicol filled in for him.

Their schedule would not let up all summer. July saw more British concerts, as well as tumultuous London and Liverpool openings of *A Hard Day's Night*, and attendant radio and television appearances. And on 11 August, they returned to the Abbey Road studios to start work on their next album, which EMI wanted in the shops in time for the holidays. They had time for only two sessions (during which they started work on four songs) before it was time to leave for a month-long tour of the USA and Canada.

Though it was not yet clear to the Beatles, concerts were already irrelevant to their creative process. In fact, they were living a triple life, musically: in the recording studio they bolted forward, perfecting new songs and experimenting with new sounds and textures. At the BBC's studios they glanced backwards, reviving songs that they had not performed on stage since 1962 and were apparently uninterested in bringing to Abbey Road. But in concert they were merely treading water, playing the same dozen songs show after show. The rigidity of the set list meant that there was a growing catalogue of songs that the Beatles never performed on stage. The concerts were also increasingly frustrating for four musicians who thought of themselves as more than teen idols. Early on, they had told interviewers that they liked their fans to scream during their performances, and indeed, they were disappointed by the restraint of their first Paris concerts. But as the venues grew larger, from theatres to concert halls to stadiums,

Following page, all the madness the Beatles had witnessed until then was eclipsed by the scene in Melbourne, Australia, where thousands of fans came to the Town Hall to catch a glimpse of the Fab Four waving from a balcony.

NO CENTRE TURN

HELANCA
A.N.Z. CENTRE

the volume of the screaming killed any possibility of the Beatles being heard.

Offstage, too, the Beatles found themselves the focus of unfathomable madness. In Australia, crowds estimated at between 250,000 and 300,000 gathered outside their hotel, hoping for nothing more than a glimpse. Security concerns meant that they were confined to their hotels rooms between shows. And although they continued to project an image of innocence, their backstage life was a non-stop orgy. Lennon, looking back at the endless parade of backstage groupies, said in 1970 that the Beatles 'were like Satyricon on tour'.

The press did not report on this aspect of touring life, except in the relatively few cases where local police made a point of dragging young girls out of the Beatles' hotel rooms. Yet the constant presence of reporters contributed to the feeling that they were living in a fishbowl. Lennon found himself regularly denying reports that he and Cynthia had split up. McCartney regularly denied rumours that he was about to marry his longtime flame, the actress Jane Asher. Similar fascination attended Starr's courtship of a Liverpool hairdresser, Maureen Cox, and Harrison's romance with Pattie Boyd, an actress he met on the set of *A Hard Day's Night*.

The evidence that all this was taking its toll can be heard on the group's fourth album, *Beatles For Sale*, a collection that sounds dark and autumnal after the radiant energy of *A Hard Day's Night*. Started before the North American tour, the sessions resumed in late September, but were again interrupted for concerts in Britain. The final sessions, in October, were sandwiched between concerts. Being good craftsmen and knowing the taste of their market, they included a few rosy love songs, like 'Eight Days a Week' and 'Every Little Thing', both Lennon–McCartney collaborations. But the songs that dominate the record are about disconnection, self-doubt and even self-pity. Mostly they are Lennon's. Having turned twenty-four during the recording of the album, he seems to have begun a process of self examination and he was not happy with his findings.

In all, they recorded seventeen songs, ten originals, seven covers. For the fourteen songs included on the album, they reverted to the balance of eight originals and six covers that had worked on *Please Please Me* and *With the Beatles*. Two more originals, Lennon's 'I Feel Fine' – notable for its controlled use of guitar feedback as an introduction – and McCartney's 'She's a Woman', were released as a single. That left one recording, a cover of Little Willie John's 'Leave My Kitten Alone', sung with stunning power by Lennon, unaccountably not released.

Contrasting the *Beatles For Sale* sessions with the burst of creativity that yielded the all-original *A Hard Day's Night*, it is difficult not to regard the group's revival of its Liverpool and Hamburg repertory of covers as a sign of fatigue. Indeed, it often seems the cover versions that bring a measure of energy to the record: For Chuck Berry's 'Rock and Roll Music' and in the unaccompanied vocal introduction to Dr Feelgood's 'Mr Moonlight', Lennon revived the aggressive blues shout that had enlivened 'Twist and Shout'. McCartney does not quite recapture the electricity of 'Long Tall Sally' in his cover of another Little Richard favourite, 'Kansas City/Hey Hey Hey Hey', but the track is not without vocal fireworks. And a pair of Carl Perkins tunes, 'Everybody's Trying to Be My Baby' and 'Honey Don't', give Harrison and Starr their customary solo spots.

The covers do, however, complement the originals in an almost thematic way. The new songs are a tug of war between the rock and roll leanings of the previous albums, and newly emerging country and folk influences. There had been a hint of this on *A Hard Day's Night*: in a sense, the expanded use of acoustic guitars, the wistful mood of 'I'll Be Back' and the country roots of 'I'll Cry Instead' are harbingers of a style change. Now that tendency is formalized, with the covers standing as icons at each pole: Chuck Berry, Little Richard and Dr Feelgood hold the fort for rock; the Carl Perkins numbers argue the case for rockabilly, and Buddy Holly's 'Words of Love', kitted out in Everly Brothers' style harmonies, holds the middle ground.

The originals, of course, are the key to the state of the Beatles creativity. Harrison, anxious as he was to compete with Lennon and McCartney as a songwriter, nevertheless arrived empty-handed again, although he did record a demonstration tape of a song called 'You'll Know What to Do', which seems not to have won encouragement from Lennon and McCartney.

McCartney, too, was having a dry spell. He contributed only three songs, and one of them – 'I'll Follow the Sun' – dates back to the Quarry Men days. It had evolved, however. Originally a bouncy, slightly vaudevillian song, here it is a full-fledged country and western

Beatlemania as viewed from the stage in 1964 – or at least as re-created for Richard Lester's cameras in the closing concert sequence of *A Hard Day's Night.*

ballad. One can almost hear the clip-clop of horse hooves in the acoustic guitar strumming and light percussion accompaniment. And McCartney replaced the original clichéd bridge section with a more plangent minor key melody, harmonized with Lennon. Still, it is a peculiar song, so self-possessed as to be egomaniacal. The singer, after all, is cheerfully abandoning his love, with no stated provocation, and no excuse except that it's time to go.

McCartney's 'What You're Doing' was uncharacteristic and almost Lennonesque, as though McCartney wanted to offer his own take on the relationship Lennon had described in 'Tell Me Why'. As in Lennon's song, the protagonist accuses his girlfriend of lying and causing him grief, but instead of begging her to reform, or threatening to leave, he hectors her. Musically, the song's heart is a repeating twelve-string guitar riff that runs through much of the song. The 'riff song' was not entirely new for the Beatles: 'You Can't Do That' used a similar device. 'I Feel Fine', the single recorded at these same sessions, uses a central riff more ambitiously, having it follow the chord progression around the fretboard. There would be sequels in 'Ticket to Ride' and 'Day Tripper', in 1965, but generally, this was an approach the Beatles rarely used.

McCartney's other new offering, 'She's a Woman', though musically and lyrically slight – and to some degree improvised in the studio – was catchy, danceable and diverting enough to rate its position as the B-side of 'I Feel Fine'. At heart, it is a straightforward blues progression, except that the verse is built on a series of unresolving seventh chords, and its bridge is a short minor-key excursion. In a BBC interview soon after the song was released, Lennon offhandedly described the lyrics as 'rubbishy' and McCartney did not bother to argue.

The Lennon–McCartney collaborations afford some interesting moments. 'Eight Days a Week' begins with a new twist: an alluringly harmonized fade-in introduction. Harrison and Lennon play an ascending chord progression in which the guitar's top E string is left open and allowed to ring out over each of the chords. Harrison embellishes his progression slightly, while McCartney underpins it with a D, in rapid-fire repeating triplets. There is so much going on in this short figure that one hardly notices the clash between McCartney's D's and the guitars' open E's. All that registers is the changing tension of the progression.

The song proper is something of a stylistic throwback, a burst of untroubled popsiness. Its lyric is simply a declaration of near-obsessive desire. And its verse melody winds gracefully around the chord progression, which is identical to that of the opening, but without the ringing E's, and with a walking bass line replacing the quickly repeated notes of the introduction. The verses end in a figure lifted in spirit from 'From Me To You' and 'Please Mister Postman'. The melodic momentum stops, replaced by two-syllable bursts ('hold me, love me'), harmonized in thirds by Lennon and McCartney, and punctuated with handclapping. And in the chorus Lennon and McCartney harmonize in fourths and fifths, reprising a quintessential Beatles touch from the days of 'Love Me Do'.

'Every Little Thing', though little more than an exercise in craftsmanship, is notable for a minor textural refinement: Starr touches up the chorus with a timpani, interposing a two-note burst between the lines 'Every little thing she does' and 'she does for me'.

But if the McCartney songs and the collaborations were thin, Lennon was reaching for something new in his songwriting. Until now, his songs were fairly straightforward declarations: you lied, I'm hurt, I'm going to leave you. But in 'No Reply', as in 'You Can't Do

That', he sings about jealousy, but provides a narrative structure, painting a picture of a spurned lover who begins spying on his girlfriend after she refuses to see him or take his telephone calls.

Lennon's melody, when describing his attempts to make contact, is an attractive, plaintive tune. But his discoveries are presented as old-fashioned melodrama. Shifting from C major into A minor, with a supporting harmony from McCartney and cymbal crashes from Starr, the tone changes from observational to pained. 'I saw the light,' he sings twice for emphasis before reporting: 'I know that you saw me, 'cos I looked up to see your face.' The next time, the stakes are higher: 'I nearly died, I nearly died, 'cos you walked hand in hand with another man in my place.' Yet the bridge, rather than promising retribution, switches back to the brightness of C major and offers forgiveness – predicated, of course, on a reconciliation.

Lennon also uses a condensed narrative form in 'Baby's In Black', a peculiar lament in three-quarter time. Here the object of his desire is pining fruitlessly for someone else, to the point of wearing black. The music is well matched to the text: even before the plaintive melody begins, Harrison opens the song with a solo guitar fill, leaning heavily on his tremolo bar to give the notes a twisted, slightly sour edge. He uses the same technique to spice up the song with a wonderfully rubbery guitar solo.

The move from generic expressions of emotion to picturesque storytelling was an important step for Lennon, but it was not something he chose to develop on its own terms. Shrouding his feelings in narrative was one thing; spinning entirely fictional tales was another, and he later said that it made him uneasy. He retained the option of returning to the raw expressivity of his earlier songs, while also heading toward a combination of abstract imagery and social comment. McCartney, in time, would far surpass him as a weaver of tales, developing an ability to spin entirely impersonal fantasies about, for example, Hollywood starlets ('Honey Pie'), gunslingers of the American West ('Rocky Racoon') and even sociopathic medical students ('Maxwell's Silver Hammer').

The use of narrative was not Lennon's only innovation on *Beatles For Sale*. Perhaps more crucial is the self-analysis of 'I'm a Loser'. Its closest predecessor among Lennon's songs is 'There's a Place', but that was merely about escaping pain. 'I'm a Loser' is more revealing,

Opposite, Lennon walks off the set of *A Hard Day's Night* with a souvenir, the personalized seatback from his dressing room.

John Lennon

despite Lennon's attempt to disguise its autobiographical aspect in a country texture, complete with Harrison's Perkins-style guitar texturing. The second verse is telling: 'Although I laugh and I act like a clown, beneath this mask I am wearing a frown', as is the chorus, which declares: 'I'm a loser, and I'm not what I appear to be.'

Tears-of-a-clown songs are plentiful in the pop repertory. But Lennon later said that these lines in 'I'm a Loser' summed up his state of mind in late 1964. He was beginning to tire of a life that he sometimes describes as that of a performing flea. He had perfected the public persona that stardom required. But he considered his life to be a mess. Now established in Weybridge, a London suburb, he had a wife he rarely saw and from whom he was growing estranged, and a young son he hardly knew. He had thrown himself enthusiastically into the orgiastic circus that the Beatles' touring life had become. Yet he resented the physical and psychic demands of that life.

'I'm a Loser' was the first cry from the heart during what he later called his 'fat Beatle period'. A more direct amplification of this message would be found in the title song of the Beatles' second film, and their first major project of 1965: *Help!*

6

Help! and *Rubber Soul* 1965

Harrison, Lennon, Starr and McCartney between takes on the *Help!* set, 1965.

Up till then, we had been making albums rather like a collection of singles. Now we were really beginning to think about albums as a bit of art on their own, as entities of their own. And Rubber Soul *was the first to emerge that way.*

George Martin, 1980

Help! and *Rubber Soul* 1965

The end of 1964 brought a respite of sorts. Although the Beatles were booked for their second annual Christmas show, from 24 December to 16 January, the endeavour – in which they played a concert set and participated in comedy skits – at least kept them in London. After a year that saw two visits each to Europe and North America, a film, an Australasian tour, two albums and assorted singles, a long residency at the Hammersmith Odeon seemed easy, if dull, work.

A month-long holiday followed. Starr married his eighteen-year-old Liverpudlian fiancée, Maureen Cox, on 11 February. Lennon, McCartney and Harrison, meanwhile, faced the task of composing songs for the fifth album. Like *A Hard Day's Night*, it would double as the soundtrack for the film known provisionally as *Beatles No. 2* or *Eight Arms to Hold You*, and eventually called *Help!* Shooting was scheduled to begin in the Bahamas on 23 February, and some of the soundtrack music had to be in hand so that mimed musical numbers could be choreographed.

So on the afternoon of 15 February, the Beatles took over Studio No. 2 at Abbey Road. Eight hours later they emerged with three songs virtually finished: Lennon's 'Ticket to Ride', which would be the next single, McCartney's 'Another Girl', and Harrison's first contribution since 1963, 'I Need You'. By the time they set out for the Bahamas, a week later, they had recorded eight more songs, including another Harrison effort. The sessions would resume at the end of March, and would stretch, with filming interruptions, through to mid-June. All told, they recorded twenty songs, of which only three – the Buck Owens classic 'Act Naturally' and two Larry Williams songs, 'Bad Boy' and 'Dizzy Miss Lizzy' – were covers. Although 'Dizzy Miss Lizzy' ended up as the raucous finale to the *Help!* album, the Williams covers were actually recorded specifically for the American market, to help Capitol pad out its *Beatles VI* album, a patchwork of *Beatles For*

The Beatles wave to fans at London airport in February 1965 as they leave to start work on *Help!* in the Bahamas.

Sale leftovers and material from the *Help!* sessions that was not destined for the film soundtrack.

The amount of new material the Beatles brought to the *Help!* sessions showed that they had moved past the compositional dry spell of late 1964. Nor was there any reaching back for material from the Quarry Men era. Yet the new originals were not of uniformly top quality. A few – 'The Night Before' and 'Tell Me What You See,' for example – are little more than pleasant filler. The Beatles themselves were not content with everything they had recorded; in fact, three of the originals from the February sessions were left on the shelf. One, a Lennon–McCartney collaboration, 'Wait', was revived and completed later in the year. Two others, 'If You've Got Trouble' and 'That Means a Lot', were left unissued.

Lennon and McCartney had composed 'If You've Got Trouble' as Starr's vocal showcase. Starr had, actually, been trying to come up with a song of his own, and in published interviews as early as 1963, one finds references to a song in progress called 'Don't Pass Me By', the song with which he made his compositional debut in 1968. For the present, though, he had to rely either on covers or on what Lennon and McCartney dreamed up for him. And in this case, it was not top-drawer material. Its music was little more than a six-note lead guitar riff with the accent of Stax-Volt, the American soul label, set against a steely, steadily repeated, single bell-like guitar tone and a chunky rhythm track. Starr was given a slim melody to sing, and even less impressive lyrics. In the end, the song was scrapped, and Starr settled on 'Act Naturally', which, given its film references and his own central role in *Help!*, seemed a thoroughly appropriate choice.

McCartney's 'That Means a Lot', the other reject, was not such a bad song. It has a lilting melody, and a bitter-sweet lyric about the tentative early stages of a romance. They completed a version of it early in the sessions, and perhaps one count against it was that it used exactly the same kind of accompaniment as 'Ticket to Ride' – a rolling snare and steady, crackling rhythm guitars. In view of their disinclination to repeat gestures without significant alteration, they may have decided to choose between the two, giving preference to 'Ticket to Ride'.

They tried to remake 'That Means a Lot' with a different arrangement in March, but were unable to sustain interest in it. But it was by no means wasted. McCartney passed it on to the American singer P. J. Proby, who recorded it in early April. They were, in fact, still giving away songs that they did not see fit to record themselves. McCartney in particular had become a hit factory for friends. Most notably, he contributed the tuneful 'World Without Love', 'I Don't Want to See You Again', 'Nobody I Know' and 'Woman' (the last under the pen-name Bernard Webb, in 1966) to the folk duo Peter and Gordon, Peter being the brother of McCartney's girlfriend, Jane Asher.

There was one notable change in the way the Beatles and Martin used the studio's four-track facilities this time. Until now, they had worked largely as they had during the two-track days, singing and playing their songs as if they were live performances. When they had an acceptable basic recording, they would refine and embellish it with overdubbed instrumental and vocal lines. But near the end of the *Beatles For Sale* sessions, they tried a new approach that involved building a performance in layers. First they recorded a rhythm track, with basic guitars, bass and drums. Other instrumental touches were then added, and then, once the complete backing was recorded, the vocals would be added. Lennon in particular preferred this method: not having to play while he was singing left him free to concentrate on his vocals. Another peculiar aspect to the the *Help!* sessions was that for the first time, instrumental duties within the band were blurred. For the very first song taped, 'Ticket to Ride', McCartney played not only the bass, but the lead guitar as well. He is also said to have suggested the distinctive rolling drum figure that Starr plays. Later in the session, Harrison resumed his usual position, playing lead guitar on 'Another Girl'. Yet, the next day McCartney dubbed a new lead guitar line on the song.

In the first batch of songs recorded for the album, Lennon and McCartney continued in some of the directions that *Beatles For Sale* had taken them, although for the most part they backed away from that album's country leanings. Lennon's 'Ticket to Ride', like 'I Feel Fine', grows out of an opening guitar riff, this one with a slight syncopation and a sharper edge. Of course, the text is just the opposite of the one put forth in 'I Feel Fine'. The earlier song is a paean to a woman who appreciates her man and treats him right. The woman in 'Ticket to Ride' is more independent. 'She said that living with me is bringing her down. She would never be free when I was around.' And so she's off without a second thought, leaving the singer to muse that this isn't right, despite the lyric's implication that he has only himself to blame. The chord progression is slightly quirky. The entire verse melody hovers over an A major chord, but there is so much going on – the guitar riff, Starr's ear-catching drumming, and intermittent vocal harmonies in fourths and thirds, used mostly as a kind of tension-building accenting – that the unchanging harmony does not seem monotonous in the least. It is not until the refrain that Lennon changes chords.

McCartney's offering at the first session, 'Another Girl', seemed almost a direct response to Lennon's song, but in his version he has a trump card, namely, a replacement to whom he could happily flee. She has great credentials: 'She's sweeter than all the girls, and I've met quite a few,' McCartney crows, 'nobody in all the world can do what she can do.' Which explains why a song built around a modified blues progression, with a slinky blues guitar line running through it, sounds so remarkably cheerful.

Harrison must have argued strongly on behalf of his songwriting this time around, because the group recorded two of his compositions during the first three sessions. The songs, 'I Need You', which was used in the film, and 'You Like Me Too Much', which was not, are both naïve declarations of love, with neither the conflict nor the dimension that Lennon and McCartney were weaving into their best work. Yet, there are traces of Harrison's later style in these. They are, for instance, more the work of a guitarist than of a songwriter, in the sense that they seem driven by their chord sequences rather than their melodies. Those sequences dart freely between major and minor keys, and yield melodies with the slightly exotic and sometimes mournful character typical of Harrison's work through the Beatles years and well into his solo work.

Harrison brought a new toy to the sessions, a volume pedal, which allowed him to fade in on a guitar note after it had been plucked. He used it to embellish 'I Need You', doubling the acoustic guitar chords at strategic points and accenting the opening chord sequence, which plays with variants of an A major chord. He used it again on Lennon's 'Yes It Is', a song that was left out of the film and off the album, but was released as the B-side of 'Ticket to Ride'.

Lennon later spoke disparagingly of the song, saying it was little more than an unsuccessful rewrite of 'This Boy'. There are similarities: both are slow ballads and rely on three-voice harmonies, with Lennon taking a solo moment in an arching bridge section. But where 'This Boy' was built on a common 1950s' chord progression, with entirely triadic harmonies, 'Yes It Is' is actually more original and adventurous. Its vocal harmonies, for example, are spiced with dissonances, particularly major seconds (two adjacent whole steps of the scale). Moreover, these dissonances are functional: they highlight the rather gloomy mood of the lyric.

In the opening line, 'if you wear red tonight', Lennon, McCartney and Harrison begin on an E major chord, but when they reach 'red' – a colour which, the song goes on to explain, has painful associations – the vocal harmony changes to a major second. The word 'tonight', coming as it does at the end of the line, might be expected to resolve into a comfortably settled harmony. But it too is set to a dissonance. The tension is increased just when it would normally be dissipated. The next line, 'remember what I said tonight', has a similar effect, with 'said' and 'tonight' emphasized.

As ever, the Beatles were after new textures, and besides Harrison's volume pedal, they began using an electric piano, sometimes in

Opposite, an exotic fantasy shot in the Bahamas, London and the Swiss Alps, *Help!* did not engage the Beatles as fully as *A Hard Day's Night*. Often stoned during the filming, and not particularly interested in the script, they later complained that they were treated as extras in their own film.

produced by WALTER SHENSON *screenplay by* MARC BEHM & CHARLES WOOD *story by* MARC BEHM *directed by* RICHARD LESTER

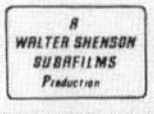

EASTMAN COLOUR

ROYAL WORLD PREMIERE

in the gracious presence of
HER ROYAL HIGHNESS THE PRINCESS MARGARET, COUNTESS OF SNOWDON
and THE EARL OF SNOWDON
Sponsored by The Variety Club of Great Britain
to aid THE DOCKLAND SETTLEMENTS and THE VARIETY CLUB HEART FUND
on
THURSDAY 29th JULY 1965
at the
LONDON PAVILION
PICCADILLY CIRCUS

combination with the studio's concert grand. The sessions would also see the introduction of more exotic percussion, including a South American guiro, on 'Tell Me What You See'. But the biggest departure was the use of outside musicians on two songs, Lennon's 'You've Got to Hide Your Love Away' and McCartney's 'Yesterday'.

'You've Got to Hide Your Love Away', a poignant ballad, follows the introspective line started with 'I'm a Loser'. Its subject has been a matter of active speculation. It may simply be a coded description of an extramarital relationship, of which Lennon's experience was by now considerable. Another current theory is that it refers to Epstein's closeted homosexuality. Both songs show Lennon's fascination with Bob Dylan's music. On 'I'm a Loser', that influence can be heard in the distinctly Dylanesque harmonica line – quite different in spirit and technique from anything Lennon had played before – and the barbed lyric. But there the Dylan influence was tempered by a country and western strain. 'You've Got to Hide Your Love Away' is more folkishly direct. Still, there are expressive touches similar to those heard in the more harmonically complex 'Yes It Is'. In the chorus, for example, the word 'hide' – the source of pain and conflict in the song – is not given the high note in the melody, an emphasis sharpened by the fact that the note clashes with the chord that accompanies it.

It was clear to Lennon and Martin that the basic recording – a simple affair on which the vocal was supported by soft-focus acoustic guitar strumming, maraccas and tambourine – lacked something. Martin brought in John Scott, a flautist, who played a lightly ornamented version of the melody on tenor and alto flutes, overdubbed in tandem, in the song's closing seconds.

Having taken the plunge, the Beatles brought in outside musicians again four months later when McCartney recorded 'Yesterday', a song that immediately became a pop standard. McCartney has often described 'Yesterday' as his most perfect song, but perhaps the most startling thing about it is that it came to him in a burst of pure, unconscious inspiration. As he tells it, he simply woke up one morning and had the tune in his head. His first thought was that it was a melody he had heard somewhere and could not place, and for several weeks he sang it to people, asking them if they knew what it was. Finding the lyrics was not as easy. 'Scrambled eggs, oh baby how I love your legs' was its provisional opening, but once McCartney realized that the melody was his own, he fitted it out as a sweet ballad about romantic loss, and the desire to turn back the clock.

When he brought the song to Abbey Road, Martin first saw what it was not – that is, a song that would lend itself to a treatment like anything the Beatles had done hitherto. McCartney and the others agreed, although they did fashion an electric guitar, bass and drums arrangement for concert use in 1966. While considering how to treat the song, Martin had McCartney record a simple version, accompanying himself on an acoustic guitar. The more he listened

Harrison looks on as director Dick Lester, with megaphone, calls the shots during the filming of *Help!*

Between shots once again, the Beatles barely make the effort of looking interested during one of the frequent lulls in the shooting of *Help!*

In one of the more interesting sequences in *Help!* the Beatles perform McCartney's 'The Night Before' on Salisbury Plain, surrounded by British troops and tanks.

Ludwig
THE
BEATLES

to the tape, the clearer the solution seemed: the song needed a string accompaniment.

McCartney resisted at first: in the Beatles' musical universe, strings on rock records were considered extraneous at best, lugubrious at worst. Martin argued that a quartet, rather than a full string section, would provide an elegant backing, and McCartney agreed to try it. Although it is often assumed that Martin wrote the arrangement, he and McCartney actually worked collaboratively at the piano, and Martin has said that some of the most distinctive touches in the quartet writing – the cello counterpoint, for example – were McCartney's ideas.

Interestingly, at the same session on 14 June that produced 'Yesterday', the Beatles recorded 'I'm Down', another McCartney song that was the polar opposite of 'Yesterday'. A blatant Little Richard knock-off, it seemed tailor-made as a concert closer, and indeed, through most of the group's 1965 and 1966 touring, it displaced 'Long Tall Sally' as the set finale.

If 'Yesterday' was McCartney's defining moment this time out, Lennon's was certainly 'Help!', a song he later called one of few honest – by which he meant emotionally revealing – songs he wrote for the Beatles. But its genesis was not auspicious. As was the case with *A Hard Day's Night*, the title of the second film was not settled upon until filming was nearly complete, whereupon Lennon and McCartney were dispatched to compose a song to fit it.

Help! was a chase film, or a parody of one. Dick Lester returned as director, and was given a grander budget. This time the film would be in colour, and it would be shot in the Bahamas, the Austrian Alps and various locations in England, with a supporting cast that included Leo McKern and Eleanor Bron. Marc Behm and Charles Wood provided a script in which Starr, the unwitting owner of a sacrificial ring, is pursued by the priests of an Eastern cult. Hence the title. For the Beatles, this scenario and the peripatetic filming schedule presented a number of problems. Lennon later complained that Lester never told them what the film was about, and since the filming was done out of continuity – the Bahamas sequences, shot first, end the film – the Beatles had no idea where they were in the story. They were also not disciplined actors, and tended to stay out all night, even when filming was scheduled to begin at dawn. Moreover, having been introduced

In this scene from *Help!*, the Beatles seek peace and protection at Buckingham Palace (actually Cliveden House, a Victorian country house near Maidenhead), but are nevertheless pursued by a sacrificial cult whose sacred ring has been sent to Ringo.

to marijuana by Bob Dylan only six months earlier, they were high through much of the filming.

The finished film shows them in good comic form, if not quite as fresh as they were in *A Hard Day's Night*. But fundamentally, the project did not interest them, and left them feeling like extras in their own film. They owed United Artists a third film, but after their experience in *Help!* they rejected one script after another, even one by the talented and then-fashionable British playwright, Joe Orton.

When Lennon turned to the task of composing 'Help!' in April, he was disinclined to produce a lightweight song that would reflect the zany shenanigans of the film. Instead, he produced another self-critical reflection. In the introduction, McCartney and Harrison call for help four times – the last in falsetto – punctuated by a descending guitar figure and Lennon's explicatory lead vocal. So far, it could be a musical lonely hearts advertisement: the singer is looking for someone

In one of their most famous concerts, the Beatles perform for an audience of 55,600 at Shea Stadium in New York on 15 August 1965. The show was filmed for television.

special. But when Lennon sings the first verse, we get a glimpse of a 24-year-old who is completely adrift:

When I was younger, so much younger than today
I never needed anybody's help in any way.
And now these days are gone, I'm not so self assured.
Now I find I've changed my mind,
I've opened up the door.

The bright, bouncy production that Martin and the group gave the recording disguised the song's confessional nature and make it perfect for use in the film. Few listeners at the time read the song as an autobiographical cry of pain; even Lennon said that it took him some time to realize that this is what the song was.

The productive sessions came to an end on 17 June. Three days later, the Beatles were back on the road, where they remained until early September. They had plenty to discuss in the press conferences that had become part of their touring ritual. Apart from the film and the new album, a second collection of Lennon's writings, *A Spaniard in the Works*, had just been published. And on 12 June they appeared on Queen Elizabeth's Birthday Honours List: they would be awarded Membership in the Most Excellent Order of the British Empire.

The 1965 summer tour took them to France, Italy, Spain and North America, the final leg starting with a concert for 55,600 listeners at Shea Stadium in New York. By now Lennon and Harrison were finding the road a depressing, stifling place. Their fans seemed not to have changed a bit in the year since the last world tour. They continued to shriek through the concerts, and the Beatles' movements were surrounded by a pandemonium that had grown oppressive.

The Beatles themselves had changed a great deal. They were experimenting by then not only with marijuana but with hallucinogenic drugs, particularly LSD. They had become increasingly interested in world politics, and chafed against Epstein's prohibition against discussing the Vietnam war or civil rights in their press conferences. They were also beginning to rebel against Epstein's control. They had rejected Epstein's suggestion that they accept an invitation to play

The Beatles display their MBE's, conferred upon them by Queen Elizabeth II on 26 October 1965. Lennon later returned his in protest at Britain's support of the American war in Vietnam, the situation in Biafra, and the lack of chart success of his single 'Cold Turkey'.

Ludwig
THE
BEATLES
VOX Continental
VOX Continental

Left, during the 1965 tours, Lennon played electric piano as well as guitar, often sliding his elbows up and down the keyboard to give their set an extra measure of ebullience. As the group sets up, Brian Epstein confers with Lennon.

another Royal Command Performance, and they refused to consider another season of London Christmas shows. They agreed to tour Britain in December, but they told Epstein that their touring days were numbered.

When the tour ended, they took a month-long break before returning to the studio to work on their sixth album. The Beatles had established a pattern of producing two albums every year, with the second out in time for the holiday market. Their scheduling in 1965 cut close to the second deadline. But by working into the early hours of the morning – and in one case, until dawn – between 12 October and 12 November, they had the album finished and in the shops by 3 December. This pressure yielded *Rubber Soul*, one of the most consistent and satisfying of all their albums. With *Rubber Soul* they finally turned their backs on cover versions. All the songs are originals, as they would be for the rest of their recording career. Of the fourteen on the album, Harrison composed two, and Starr gets his first collaborative credit, with Lennon and McCartney, on 'What Goes On', a revamped version of a song that dates back to the Quarry Men days.

There was another revival in the set too: the first traces of McCartney's 'Michelle' are heard on a practice tape from 1963, when McCartney used its bright chord progression to accompany a Maurice Chevalier imitation, apparently a favourite party trick. Now he finished it, referring to its original use by including a line in French, but otherwise making it an amorous ballad nearly as pretty as 'Yesterday'.

In George Martin's estimation, *Rubber Soul* 'presented a new Beatles to the world'. Yet it was not entirely out of the blue. In some ways, the real stylistic break had occurred in mid-June, near the end of the *Help!* sessions. In terms of sophistication, spirit and complexity of texture, the songs recorded then – particularly 'I've Just Seen a Face', 'Yesterday' and 'It's Only Love' – have much more in common with *Rubber Soul* than with the rest of *Help!* And of course, one of the the new album's tracks, 'Wait', was actually started during *Help!* What changed with *Rubber Soul* was the way the Beatles regarded a record album. Through *Help!* they saw their albums as collections of unrelated songs, any of which should be good enough to release as a single. With *Rubber Soul*, they began to toy with the idea of an album as a kind of song cycle, in which each piece was part of a bigger picture, even if the connections were never overt.

Can *Rubber Soul* really be regarded as a cycle? In a way, it shows greater thematic unity than *Sgt. Pepper's Lonely Hearts Club Band*, which is usually called the first 'concept album'. Nearly all the songs are love songs, and although that is hardly uncommon on a pop album, each song here looks at love from a distinct perspective. One of Lennon's songs, 'The Word', prefigures 'All You Need Is Love' as a celebration of love in the abstract – not as an interpersonal emotion, but as a universal concept. McCartney's 'Michelle' takes a more traditional look at purely romantic love, and is virtually alone in that regard. His 'You Won't See Me', by contrast, looks at a frustrating inability to connect. Later, in 'I'm Looking Through You', he presents a mirror image, the same relationship, but from the perspective of the disengaged partner.

Servility and sexuality mingle in McCartney's 'Drive My Car', the album's opening track, in which a would-be starlet hires a driver, dangling the prospect of love. Fidelity is declared and demanded in McCartney's 'Wait', while Lennon's 'Norwegian Wood' cryptically describes a one-night stand. Its title has never been adequately explained: the lyrics suggest that the furnishings in the woman's flat were Norwegian, although an alternate explanation is that the title is a corruption of the phrase 'knowing she would'.

Lennon also turns his attention to dysfunctional relationships. Singing 'Girl', he sounds like a fly in a spider-web: he would love to leave the icy, manipulative woman he describes, but cannot. She could almost be the same woman described in the track just before it on the record, 'What Goes On', Starr's vocal vehicle. For good measure, Lennon recalls both the jealousy of 'You Can't Do That' and the threats of 'I'll Cry Instead' in the album's biting finale, 'Run For Your Life'. Yet Lennon also contributes one of the album's most touchingly lyrical songs, 'In My Life', a reflective song in which the power of a new love is set against affection for the places, lovers and friends in his past. Even 'Nowhere Man', though not overtly a love song, and more than likely another instalment in Lennon's self-examination series, is at least about acceptance: the subject of the song may not know what he's about, but Lennon sings, 'isn't he a bit like you and me?'

Harrison's 'Think for Yourself' is less about love than its absence: angry and impatient, he tells the song's object (perhaps a friend rather than a lover) that there is time for change – but that he isn't waiting around to see it. His other contribution, 'If I Needed Someone', is a study in romantic aloofness. He is not in the market for a lover, he says, but he'll take down the phone number just in case.

The two songs released as a single fit the album's 'aspects of love' theme as well. Lennon's 'Day Tripper', another guitar-riff song, is superficially about being led on, but could equally be about drugs. Lennon would not have used the 'trip' reference without realizing its drug-culture meaning. And 'We Can Work It Out' is a classic collaboration, along the lines of 'A Hard Day's Night'. In this case, McCartney's verses, set to a bright major key melody, are about trying to save a relationship through negotiation. Lennon's bridge shifts into the minor mode and sweeps away the give and take: life is too short for that. There is one musical quirk worth noting in 'We Can Work It Out.' For the first time, the group attempts a metre change. For the most part, the song is solidly in quarter time, and although it never abandons that metre entirely, at the end of the bridge a triplet figure gives the feeling that for two bars the song has moved into triple time.

If *Rubber Soul* was a song cycle of sorts, what did the title have to do with the theme? Nothing, it seems. But it had plenty to do with the music, or at least some of it. Its origin was in a phrase McCartney heard from black American musicians, who were describing British rhythm and blues bands (specifically, the Rolling Stones) as 'plastic soul'. The Beatles turned that into a pun, changing plastic to rubber and printing the title in the shape of a shoe. The 'rubber' aspect was emphasized by the cover photo, a distorted fish-eye lens shot of the group.

One track that the title could particularly have referred to was '12-Bar Original', a slinky instrumental in the style of Booker T. and the MG's, which was recorded during these sessions but left off the album. But there were other tracks with decided Motown, Stax, and even muted Gospel influences. McCartney's 'You Won't See Me' and Lennon's 'The Word' borrow textures and chord voicings from soul records. And both the chord progression and the winding guitar and the bass riff that propels 'Drive My Car' are borrowed from Otis Redding's version of 'Respect'. The riff would continue its travels: in

In November 1965, Granada Television produced *The Music of Lennon and McCartney*, an hour-long programme devoted to the thriving songwriting partnership, with performances by the Beatles and other musicians. Between scenes the composers consult with a technician as orchestral musicians and stylish London models wait for filming to resume.

1968 Jimi Hendrix used almost exactly the same figure as the basis of his 'Crosstown Traffic', a song with an automotive motif that hinted at ties to the McCartney song rather than the Redding original.

But the album is by no means limited to or even dominated by soul moves. It offers interesting textural touches of all kinds. On 'Drive My Car', vocal harmonies in fifths give way, in the line leading into the chorus, to three-voice harmonies in which a minor second, just under the top line, creates a picturesque impression of a blaring car horn. And ever open to new sounds, the group brings in a wheezing harmonium (played by Martin) for the solo in 'The Word', and as part of the backing for Harrison's twangy, Byrds-inspired 'If I Needed Someone'. McCartney's increasingly proficient piano playing is heard on several songs, and a distorted fuzz-bass takes centre stage in 'Think for Yourself'. Slide guitars, common on blues and country records, but not previously used by the Beatles, make appearances in 'Drive My Car' and 'Run for Your Life'. And 'Girl' features elegant counterpoint between a guitar and a bouzouki, a mandolin-like instrument that Martin brought them after a visit to Greece.

The newest instrumental colour here, of course, is the sitar, the 800-year-old Indian classical instrument that Harrison became fascinated with after encountering one on the set of *Help!* Harrison began studying with the sitar master Ravi Shankar, and eventually would work Indian motifs into Beatles songs. At the *Rubber Soul* sessions, though, he was still clearly a beginner, and his sitar playing is limited to doubling the melody line and adding slight embellishments to Lennon's Dylanesque 'Norwegian Wood'.

Lennon is not often thought of as a great melodist, at least not when McCartney is close at hand. But 'Norwegian Wood' is one of several Lennon songs here notable for their easily flowing melodic grace. 'Girl' and 'Nowhere Man' also have lovely melodies, the latter abetted by lush vocal harmonies. But certainly among Lennon's finest ballads is 'In My Life'. Its recording, too, is masterful, and one of the first examples of the electronic tinkering that would become an increasingly important part of the group's studio technique. For the most part the instrumental configuration is the early Beatles set-up of guitars, bass and drums. But this is not the Beatles of the dance hall or the stadium. A gentle, relaxed rising guitar figure opens the song, supported by an almost motionless, atmospheric bass and rhythm guitar, and a drum part full of subtle touches.

The surprise is in the instrumental solo. An attractive burst of neo-Baroque counterpoint, played by Martin, it is listed on the album jacket as a piano solo, but sounds peculiar – punchier than a piano, but not sharp-edged enough to be a harpsichord. In fact, Martin recorded the solo with the tapes running at half speed, a trick that not only let him play more speedily than he might have done in real time, but which gave the piano its odd timbre when the tape was played at full speed.

When the Beatles first entered Abbey Road's portals three years earlier, there was a distinct division of labour at a recording session. The musicians played; the engineers saw to the sound. But with the *Rubber Soul* sessions, the technicians found themselves – and EMI's guidelines for proper recording – challenged by the Beatles' demands. In 'Girl', for example, they wanted to emphasize the breathing sound that Lennon made in the the refrain. Their idea was for the treble to be emphasized, and when EMI's equipment did not emphasize it sufficiently, they demanded that a way be found to filter it further. The same thing was done with the guitar solo in 'Nowhere Man'. They could now get away with some slight naughtiness as well. In 'Girl', instead of the 'oohs', 'ahs' and repeated lyrics on which they typically harmonized, Harrison and McCartney sang 'tit-tit-tit-tit' against Lennon's lead vocal in the bridge. Who would suspect such subversion in a song so beautiful?

When the Beatles and Martin filed out of the studio just past dawn on 12 November, they knew that the album they had just finished was a definite leap forward. Yet it was nothing compared with the leap they would make in 1966, when backwards tapes, electronically manipulated vocal and instrumental sounds, a more ambitious use of Indian instruments and motifs, and contributions from outside string and brass players figured into the mix.

In the meantime, they ended 1965 playing what turned out to be their last British tour, starting in Glasgow on 3 December, the day *Rubber Soul* was released, stopping in Liverpool two days later, and ending in Cardiff on 12 December.

7

Towards *Sgt. Pepper* 1966–7

John Lennon ceded the musical direction of the Beatles to Paul McCartney during the *Sgt. Pepper's Lonely Hearts Club Band* sessions, in early 1967, but the spirit of the time did not elude him: this was his psychedelic caravan, complete with the *Sgt. Pepper* drumhead.

We were getting a little bit fed up of being The Beatles … It was all getting so bloody predictable. I said, why don't we pretend that we're another band. Make up a name for it and make up an identity, make up alter egos, just pretend, so we can make a whole album from the point of view of this other band.

Paul McCartney on *Sgt. Pepper*, 1989

Towards *Sgt. Pepper* 1966–7

In 1966, the Beatles seemed to go out of their way to court trouble. They were the cause of riots in Japan and the Philippines, and at the centre of a religious controversy in the USA. They had decided it was time to speak out against the war in Vietnam, and although they couched their comments in broadly pacifist terms, their criticism was not universally well received. There was further consternation when, pressed by reporters, McCartney admitted that the band had experimented with drugs. And to top it all off, reports that they would no longer tour gave rise to rumours that they were breaking up. But 1966 was also the year of *Revolver*, an album with which they would increase the creative distance between themselves and everyone else in pop. It was the year that saw the recording of 'Strawberry Fields Forever', and the beginning of *Sgt. Pepper's Lonely Hearts Club Band*, the defining album of the summer of 1967.

Because of a scheduling fluke, the Beatles had a virtually clear calendar for the first four months of the year. Epstein had hoped that they would spend these months making a film, as they had done the previous two years. But he had not counted on the Beatles' increasing wilfulness. After *Help!*, they demanded script approval, and then refused to approve any.

During this break, Lennon and Starr flew to Trinidad with their wives. Harrison married Pattie Boyd on 21 January and flew off for a honeymoon. And McCartney stayed in London, voraciously soaking up new influences. He attended concerts of new works by Luciano Berio and Karlheinz Stockhausen, and became interested in electronic music. He developed a taste for the visual avant garde to match his new listening habits, and started collecting works by Henri Magritte and other twentieth-century Surrealists. And he helped start the *International Times*, a London underground newspaper.

All the Beatles set up home studios where they could tinker with sounds, record ideas that came to them, and make demonstration tapes to play to the others in the studio. And when they gathered at

George Harrison after his wedding to Pattie Boyd, a model he had met on the set of *A Hard Day's Night*. They were divorced in 1977 (Pattie had left Harrison for the guitarist Eric Clapton in 1974), and Harrison married Olivia Arias on 2 September 1978.

Abbey Road on 6 April, they brought with them some outlandish ideas. In fact the song they began work on that first night, Lennon's 'Tomorrow Never Knows' (the title was another Starr malapropism), was a harbinger of the experimentation to come. Lennon's lyric was far stranger and more imagistic than anything he had previously brought to the studio. Inspired by *The Psychedelic Experience*, a reinterpretation of the *Tibetan Book of the Dead*, by the LSD proponents Timothy Leary and Richard Albert, the lyric recommends:

Turn off your mind, relax and float downstream
It is not dying, it is not dying.
Lay down all thought, surrender to the void
It is shining, it is shining.

In 1965, Lennon had included cagey references to being high in his lyrics; here, only the most naïve listener could have doubted the song's provenance in the world of hallucinogenic drugs.

Reduced to its melodic and harmonic essentials, 'Tomorrow Never Knows' has very little in it. Its simple melody floats over a single chord, with a momentary fluctuation rather than a full-fledged chord change at the end of each verse. But what an extraordinary sound sculpture it is. The unchanging harmony invited a drone from Harrison's sitar and a sustained organ tone. McCartney and Starr collaborate on an almost ritualistic bass and drum figure, steady, pounding and repetitive, with the drums closely miked and electronically compressed to give them a more visceral feel. There are splashes of piano and backward guitars, and a chaotic overlay of electronic sounds, drawn from the bags of tape loops – bits of recording tape joined end to end so that their sounds keep repeating – that Lennon and McCartney had made at home. And there is Lennon's hauntingly disembodied lead vocal.

Two new techniques were used to create the peculiar vocal sound. One was Artificial Double Tracking, invented by Ken Townsend, an Abbey Road engineer, to address Lennon's desire to double his vocals without bothering to sing them twice. Townsend realized that he could create the illusion of double-tracking by taking the vocal, delaying it about thirty milliseconds, and combining the delayed version with the original. Doing this meant modifying the tape machines so that their speeds could be varied gradually – an effect for which the Beatles soon found other uses.

Lennon during the filming of a promotional video clip for 'Rain'.

The second technique was more radical. Lennon had described the sound he wanted as that of 'thousands of monks chanting', or 'like the Dalai Lama singing on a hilltop'. Failing those, he wanted to put his voice through the rotating Leslie speaker that gives the Hammond organ its characteristic oscillating sound. Doing so meant dissecting the organ and rewiring the speaker. But at that point, the Beatles' wishes were the engineers' commands.

In fact for the next two and a half months Abbey Road became an electronic wonderland for the Beatles, with virtually every session yielding new techniques. The use of backward guitar sounds in 'Tomorrow Never Knows' led to further experiments. Some may have been serendipitous: Lennon always said that he decided to add a backward vocal to the coda of 'Rain' after taking home a tape of the song-in-progress, accidentally threading it backwards on his tape recorder, and liking what he heard. But in interviews from the time, Martin said that the backward vocal was his idea.

Other uses of backward sounds were carefully planned. To produce the backward guitar solos in Lennon's gloriously lethargic 'I'm Only Sleeping', Harrison worked out the solos he wanted them to play, wrote them down in reverse order, and then overdubbed them onto a tape running backwards. Complicating matters, Harrison wanted to combine a distorted fuzz guitar and a straight guitar sound, and so recorded two sets of backward solos. The operation took a full six hours.

'I'm Only Sleeping' was also one of several recordings in which the Beatles tinkered with tape speeds. When Martin recorded his piano solo for 'In My Life', the facilities offered only full and half-speed recording. But now, after Townsend's innovations, tape speed was flexible. Fascinated with the subtle timbre changes that toying with tape speeds yielded, they began recording songs with machines running slightly slow, so that they sounded faster when played back at normal speed, or vice versa. That explains the sped-up quality of Lennon's vocal on 'I'm Only Sleeping' and McCartney's on 'For No One'.

For 'Yellow Submarine', the charming fantasy song that Lennon and McCartney composed for Starr to sing, the Beatles raided EMI's cupboards in search of sound effects. With the technical staff taking part, they dragged chains through a bathtub filled with water, blew

Starting in 1965, McCartney (*left*) sometimes played lead guitar on Beatles recordings, and he is heard in that capacity on several of the *Sgt. Pepper* tracks. Harrison, (*below*) of course, retained the lead guitarist position officially, and indeed his playing had grown considerably: during these sessions he contributed an unusually expansive solo to McCartney's 'Fixing a Hole'.

As the Beatles' music grew more complicated, so did Lennon's and McCartney's demands on Starr's percussion talents. Starr once complained that they seemed to want a drummer with four arms, and indeed, at this 1967 session, McCartney loaned his two to the task in hand.

bubbles in a bucket and tried out noises of all sorts. And there were more overdubs: a brass band was brought in to play a circusy figure, and a crowd of friends and spouses turned up to sing the chorus.

Although the taboo against outside musicians had fallen during the *Help!* sessions, no outsiders played on *Rubber Soul*. But now any inhibitions about that fell away. Two weeks before the brass was added to 'Yellow Submarine', McCartney requested that trumpets and saxophones be added to his soulful 'Got to Get You Into My Life'. Alan Civil, a French horn soloist well known in classical circles, was brought in to play the agile solo on 'For No One'. Harrison invited the tabla player Anil Bhagwat to add an improvisatory percussion part to his sitar-centred 'Love You To'. And no longer needing to be persuaded that strings could work on a Beatles recording, McCartney asked Martin to write a string score (an octet this time) for 'Eleanor Rigby'.

Some of the songs demanded more traditional rock instrumentation. Harrison's 'Taxman', which opens the record, is a plain rocker, with a sizzlingly virtuosic guitar solo – not by Harrison, but by McCartney, whose facility had clearly outstripped that of the band's lead guitarist. Lennon's 'Doctor Robert' and 'And Your Bird Can Sing' are also straightforward guitar, bass and drums pieces, the latter distinguished by a fabulous electric guitar obbligato multitracked in thirds by Harrison to create a running chordal effect. McCartney's lighter, bouncier, piano-based 'Good Day Sunshine', and the gorgeous 'Here, There and Everywhere' are also free of fancy effects and orchestral overdubs.

McCartney's 'Paperback Writer' and Lennon's 'Rain', the songs chosen for release as a single, also kept largely to the classic Beatles instrumentation, although they are notably punchier than anything the Beatles had released so far. On first hearing, 'Paperback Writer' was a knock-out. Its introduction has Lennon, McCartney and Harrison announcing the song's title in a brisk, *a cappella* choral flourish, out of which spills an energetic guitar riff. This is, for once, not a love song, but a piece of epistolary fiction – a letter from an author anxious to hawk his 1,000-page novel. It has some structural oddities. There is no bridge, merely two verses, a reprise of the introductory *a cappella* section, two more verses, another *a cappella* section and a coda.

Like 'Tomorrow Never Knows', the song rests on a single chord, with a brief change at the chorus. This harmonic minimalism is not accidental. At the end of 1965, McCartney told an interviewer that one of his goals was 'to write a song with just one note', something he thought Lennon had come close to doing in 'The Word'. McCartney is too much of a melodist to accomplish that, but by reducing the harmonic movement, he has kept his melody constricted. Moreover, he disguises this simplicity with a driving, melodic bass line, tactile layered percussion and intermittent vocal harmonies, all of which distract the ear from the song's lack of harmonic variety.

'Rain' has elements in common with 'Paperback Writer', although it is more virtuosic all around. Starr opens the song with two quick snare bursts, and then continues with one of the most energetic, complex and unceasingly fascinating drum parts he ever recorded. Paralleling McCartney's song, there is an introductory guitar riff that runs, in various guises, through the song, surrounded by a bagpipe-like drone.

McCartney's bass, placed out front in the mix, is an ingenious counterpoint that takes him all over the fretboard. Yet even when it does comparatively little, it can be the most interesting element of the performance. At the chorus, for example, while Lennon and McCartney harmonize in fourths on a melody with a slightly Middle Eastern tinge, McCartney first points up the song's droning character by hammering on a high G (approached with a quick slide from the F natural just below it), playing it steadily on the beat for twenty successive beats. The next time the chorus comes around, though, he plays something entirely different, a slightly syncopated descending three-note pattern that almost seems to evoke the falling rain.

'Rain' is not about much. Lennon simply observes that people seek shelter from both rain and shine, but that he doesn't mind either way. The remarkable thing, of course, is that after six albums and eleven singles, all packed with songs about love, or the lack of it, Lennon and McCartney had discovered that there were other things to sing about, and both *Revolver* and this, their twelfth single, were enlivened by that discovery. *Revolver* opens with Harrison's complaint about England's tax system, which was siphoning off ninety-five per cent of his earnings. Images of loneliness and alienation – an old woman picking up the rice after a wedding, a minister writing sermons that no one hears – haunt 'Eleanor Rigby'. And Lennon's 'And Your Bird Can Sing' is a message of sheer defiance. Drugs weave their way through much of *Revolver*. In his searing 'She Said She Said', a work nearly as vivid as 'Tomorrow Never Knows', Lennon describes a moment during the 1965 tour when the Beatles and the actor Peter Fonda were sitting around a pool, having taken some LSD, and Fonda mused about knowing what it was like to be dead. His claim became the song's opening line. And 'Doctor Robert' is about a physician who supplied drugs to a starry clientele.

Love songs were not completely abandoned. In 'Good Day Sunshine', McCartney blithely chirps about how wonderful it is to be in love. But in 'Here, There and Everywhere' and 'For No One', McCartney is working at a higher level, producing songs that are articulate and picturesque. The first is a tender, descriptive ballad, sung in pristine triadic harmonies. Its lyrics – 'There, running my hands through her hair, both of us thinking how good it can be; someone is speaking and she doesn't know he's there' – are a perfect evocation of idyllic, idealized romance. The second is a dual-focus portrait of abandonment: we see the spurned lover refusing to believe that the romance is over, as well as the woman, off with someone else and declaring her freedom.

Harrison, too, had come a long way as a composer. He has three songs on *Revolver*, each quite different. Besides 'Taxman', the stinging rocker, there is the laid back, slightly quirky 'I Want to Tell You', with its mildly dissonant piano part and its lyric about the frustration of being tongue-tied in the presence of someone he hopes to seduce. And in 'Love You To', he breaks new ground by melding Indian timbres and traditional melodies with an otherwise conventional pop song form.

For the album's cover, the Beatles commissioned their old Hamburg friend Klaus Voorman, who was then playing bass with the British singer Manfred Mann. Voorman provided a telling collage that contrasted the 1966 Beatles with the Moptops of the past. The current Beatles are captured in spare line drawings, with photographs of their eyes inset. Their hair is long and shaggy, and poking out of it, standing and lying in it and crawling through it, are the early Beatles, represented by photographs taken between 1962 and 1965.

During their summer world tour in 1966, the Beatles returned to Germany for the first time since 1962, and spent some time with the Rattles, a Hamburg band inspired by the Mersey Sound (and style).

As soon as the album was completed, the Beatles packed their instruments and headed to Germany for the first part of the 1966 tour. So little did they care about live performances by then that they did not bother to rehearse, nor did they attempt to produce stage versions of any of the material they had just recorded, apart from a tepid facsimile of 'Paperback Writer'. They did not pretend that their show was worth seeing: in interviews, they said quite frankly that they had become terrible performers, and that with all the screaming they could neither hear themselves nor make themselves heard.

Their doubts about their performance standard turned out to be the least of their worries. In Japan, they had been booked to play at the Budokan Hall in Tokyo, and Japanese martial arts devotees, who regarded the hall as a shrine, rioted to protest at its desecration by a Western pop group. The security provided kept the Beatles safe but stifled: they were not allowed to leave their hotel rooms. They soon came to appreciate that level of protection. In Manila, they played to

After the 1966 world tour, Lennon flew to Almeria, Spain, to portray Private Gripweed in Richard Lester's anti-war film, *How I Won the War*. It was there that Lennon began one of his most complex and beautiful songs, 'Strawberry Fields Forever'.

an audience of 100,000, the largest crowd of their career. A scheduling mix-up, however, resulted in their failing to turn up at a party hosted by Imelda Marcos, the wife of the country's President. The media worked itself into a frenzy, security was withdrawn, and the Beatles and their entourage were made to run a gauntlet at the airport, where they were further harassed by government officials before being allowed to leave.

There was more trouble in store in the USA. Some of it was harmless: on 15 June Capitol released *Yesterday and Today*, a compilation of tracks left off the American editions of *Help!* and *Rubber Soul*, plus 'We Can Work It Out', 'Day Tripper' and three tracks from the *Revolver* sessions, then still in progress. For the cover, the Beatles sent along an arty photograph taken by Robert Whittaker. In the photo, they are dressed in butcher smocks, and strewn across them are slabs of raw meat and the separate bodies and bloodied heads of decapitated baby dolls. The Beatles are beaming. The photograph had occasioned no comment in Britain, where it was used in advertisements for 'Paperback Writer'. Nor was it widely criticized in America. But as soon as it was issued, Capitol had a change of heart and withdrew it, asserting a desire to 'avoid any possible controversy or undeserved harm to the Beatles' reputation.' Instead, they issued the album with an innocuous and rather glum portrait. Asked what the relevance of the cover was, McCartney replied, 'it's as relevant as Vietnam.'

A few weeks later, *Datebook* magazine printed an excerpt from an interview with John Lennon that had been published in the Evening Standard on 4 March, in which Lennon said: 'Christianity will go. It will vanish and shrink. I needn't argue about that; I'm right and will be proved right. We're more popular than Jesus now; I don't know which will go first, rock and roll or Christianity. Jesus was alright, but his disciples were thick and ordinary. It's them that ruin it for me.'

As with the butcher photo, the observation caused no controversy when it was published in England. Nor was there any fuss when the first part of the same quote was included in a *New York Times Magazine* article on 3 July. But when the *Datebook* article was published on 29 July, an anguished outcry was raised, particularly in the South. Radio stations sponsored bonfires at which listeners could burn their Beatles records and memorabilia, and members of the Ku Klux Klan marched outside the Beatles' concerts. The Beatles and Epstein, though concerned about this, decided to go on with the tour, and to address the controversy at their first press conference. Lennon explained that he he was actually deploring the fact that popular culture carried more weight with young people than religion, adding, 'I wasn't saying that the Beatles are bigger, or better than Jesus Christ as a person, or God as a thing, or whatever it is. I just said what I said and it was wrong, or it was taken wrong, and now it's all this.' And, more or less, he apologized.

The tour had its tense moments, including a concert in Memphis when a firecracker exploded during the performance. Each of the Beatles looked around to see if one of the others had been shot. But they made it through the tour without incident. By the time they took the stage at Candlestick Park in San Francisco on 29 August – the final concert of the tour – they had resolved not to tour again, and when the tour ended they went their separate ways. Lennon had accepted Richard Lester's invitation to star with Michael Crawford in *How I Won the War*, an anti-war film he was shooting in Germany and Spain. McCartney, with Martin's help, composed a filmscore for *The Family Way*, an attractive if broadly derivative collection of short pieces scored mostly for classical brass and string ensembles. Harrison flew to India to learn more about the sitar. And Starr flew to Spain to visit Lennon.

They reconvened at Abbey Road to begin their next run of sessions on 24 November. For the occasion, Lennon brought along 'Strawberry Fields Forever', an exceptional collection of images he had pieced together in Spain. In sessions that stretched over five weeks, the Beatles recorded three very different versions of 'Strawberry Fields'. The version that was released was a composite of two arrangements, and is one of the most brilliant collaborations between the four Beatles and George Martin. Lennon's earliest demonstration tapes, recorded in Spain, capture a graceful but unusual chord progression and a melody close to that of the song's second section – the section that begins with the lines, 'living is easy with eyes closed, misunderstanding all you see.' He seems to have written the music first: on these early tapes, he mumbles and hums, starting and discarding ideas. On the first pass, in fact, the only complete lines were the third and fourth in the verse: 'That is you can't, you know, tune in but it's alright; I mean, it's not too bad.' The third line made it to the finished version, but the last was expanded to 'that is, I think it's not too bad.'

By the time Lennon returned to London, the song had two verses built around the original chord progression, plus a second progression, which functioned as a bridge, accompanying the lines 'Let me take you down, 'cause I'm going to Strawberry Fields, nothing is real, and nothing to get hung about.' He would add another verse before the formal sessions began, but in the meantime, he experimented with arrangements, trying out different kinds of accompanying styles, and even adding spacey sounds from a mellotron, an electronic instrument that uses tapes of standard instrumental sounds to produce semi-orchestral timbres.

The Beatles' first attempt, though clearly unpolished, is a beauty, and has a change of texture on every verse. There is no introduction: the song begins with Lennon singing the 'Living is easy' verse, accompanied by an eerie, slightly reedy mellotron. On the second verse, the mellotron gives way to Lennon's acoustic guitar, a gorgeously slinky bass line from McCartney and light drumming from Starr. When they reach the 'Let me take you down' section, Lennon's vocal is double-tracked, and Harrison brings in a stridently trebly slide guitar.

And then, in the most alluring moment of this version, the verse beginning, 'Always, no sometimes think it's me', is accompanied by the exquisite three-part vocal harmonies the Beatles had used so effectively in 'Here, There and Everywhere'. The bridge returns again, and the mellotron, playing a compressed version of the verse chords, brings the recording to a close.

Inventive though this version was, Lennon was unhappy with it. Four days later, they began again, this time using their traditional instrumentation, plus mellotron. In this tighter, heavier, more electric version, the textural changes between verses were dropped. Gone too were the vocal harmonies and the slinkiness of the bass line. And Starr's drumming was more complex. More crucially, the song itself was radically reconfigured. The mellotron finale was turned into an introduction, its reedy timbre exchanged for a flutey sound. And now the 'Let me take you down' section was moved up to its logical place at the start of the song. Two days' work yielded a finished version.

But after mulling it over for about a week, Lennon decided to approach the song from yet another direction. He asked Martin to write an arrangement for orchestral instruments, and on 8 and 9 December the Beatles produced a new basic track, this time including cymbals recorded backwards, a hefty array of percussion, and the exotic sound of a swordmandel, a harp-like Indian instrument. A week later, Martin brought in four trumpets and three cellos to play an arrangement in which the cellos offer an arching counterpoint to the vocal melody. When Lennon overdubbed his forceful, nuanced lead vocal, the recording was finished.

Or so Martin believed. On reflection, Lennon thought it might be a good idea to have the song begin in its rock version and end in its orchestral guise. He was not about to start anew; his suggestion to Martin was that he prepare an edit of versions two and three. Martin doubted it could be done: the two recordings were in different keys and tempos. By sheer luck, the orchestral version was both faster and higher in pitch than the electric version. By slowing it down and speeding up the other, Martin matched both key and tempo. The point where the rock band texture metamorphoses into the tapestry of brass, strings, backwards sounds and unusual timbres takes place exactly sixty seconds into the song.

'Strawberry Fields Forever', like 'Rain', is more an expression of attitude ('nothing to get hung about') than anything else, but its title refers to a Salvation Army hostel in Liverpool, near Lennon's childhood home. Lennon uses the name purely for its imagery. 'Tomorrow Never Knows' and 'She Said She Said' played with imagery too, but with 'Strawberry Fields Forever', Lennon has sighted a new goal: lyrics that have greater emotional resonance than literary sense, and music that seems to spring naturally from the wordplay (even though, in this case, the music came first).

A few days after 'Strawberry Fields Forever' was completed, McCartney brought in another song with a Liverpool connection, 'Penny Lane', a lighter song which, unlike its counterpart, describes in picturesque detail the Liverpool street for which it is named. Though more conventional on the surface, 'Penny Lane' began even more experimentally than 'Strawberry Fields'. McCartney, working alone, made a basic track that brought together three piano parts – one recorded at half speed, one with amplification and reverberation, one plain – a harmonium and various percussion effects. In a working method that would become typical in the months to come, the four tracks on which McCartney laboured were mixed down to a single tape track, opening up the rest for overdubs.

Before the song was finished, there would be more piano, guitar and bass, lead and harmony vocals, sound effects and winds and brass. The most distinctive touch, however, was the piccolo trumpet, played by David Mason. McCartney had seen Mason use the Baroque instrument in a televised performance of Bach's Brandenburg Concerto No. 2, and captivated by the sound, he had Martin invite Mason to play on his song.

'Strawberry Fields', 'Penny Lane' and 'When I'm Sixty-Four', a vaudeville-style song McCartney revived from his catalogue of teenage compositions, were all complete at the start of 1967, and looked like the beginning of a fascinating album. But EMI reminded the group that new material was overdue, so 'Penny Lane' and 'Strawberry Fields' were released as a single, removing them from consideration as album tracks.

They would be amply replaced, but progress was slow at first. In early January, Lennon came in with 'A Day in the Life', an unfinished song with lyrics that touched on a friend's recent death in a car acci-

Opposite, McCartney barely played keyboards when the Beatles began recording; by 1967, he had become quite adept. Here he plays through a new song for George Martin.

dent, a news report about potholes in Lancashire, and on Lennon's recent film, *How I Won the War*. It was a slow, hauntingly beautiful song, but it lacked a bridge. But McCartney also had a fragment – a song about waking up, catching a bus and slipping into dream – that was easily joined to Lennon's spacier song. There was a druggy undercurrent too. In the McCartney song, the dreaming begins immediately after a cigarette is smoked. And Lennon's sections before and after the McCartney contribution end with the line, 'I'd love to turn you on'. They wanted something unusual to follow that line, but in the absence of specific ideas, they played a twenty-four-bar vamp that could be overlaid later. Meanwhile, they tailored what they had. Starr's drum parts were carefully orchestrated and re-recorded, and McCartney replaced both his vocal and his original 'provisional' bassline with one that was more flowingly discursive.

McCartney tried his hand at conducting several times during the sessions for *Sgt. Pepper's Lonely Hearts Club Band*. Here, with Martin at his side, he explains his requirements to the horn players hired to play on the album's title track.

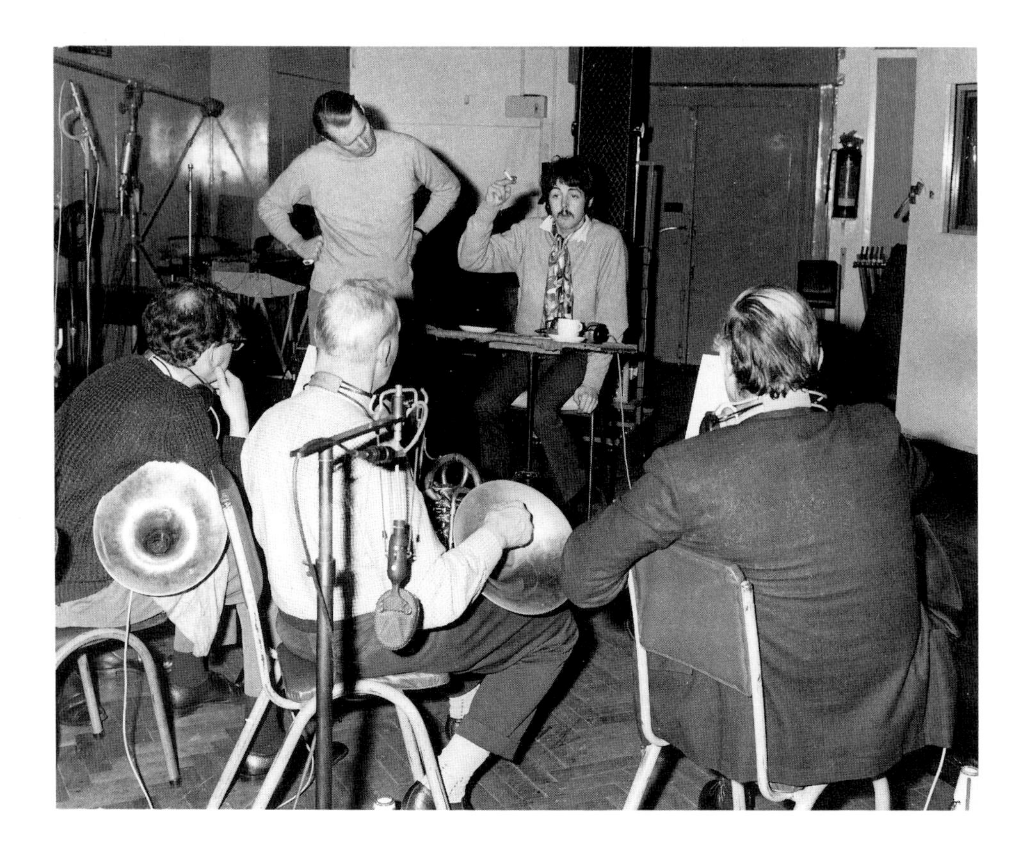

Early in February, McCartney hit upon the idea of filling the song's empty space with a cacophonous orchestral crescendo. His idea was that each musician would play from his lowest to his highest note (ideally not at the same speed as his neighbour), getting louder along the way. Martin hired forty musicians from London orchestras, who were given props – false noses, masks, bits of a gorilla costume – to create a circus-like atmosphere. With Martin and McCartney taking turns conducting, the orchestra recorded one crescendo for the middle of the work, and another for the end.

Martin has said that the musicians, drawn mostly from the Royal Philharmonic and London Philharmonic, had never before been asked to play music in which only their lowest and highest notes were given, and in which they were to play independently of other musicians. Yet in classical music circles, the idea was hardly new. The American composer John Cage had already been labouring in the fields of indeterminacy for years, and McCartney has listed Cage among the composers he was listening to at the time. And Krzysztof Penderecki, a leader of the Polish avant garde, had won considerable attention in Europe in the early 1960s for chamber and orchestral works that used indeterminate scoring.

For a pop record, though, this was distinctly radical. But the orchestral session raised another problem – how to resolve the final crescendo, which cuts off abruptly on its top note and seems to demand a follow-up. The Beatles' first solution was to hum the final E major chord. But a few days later they decided they wanted something more powerful, and replaced the hummed version with the same chord played on three pianos and a harmonium. This configuration was overdubbed on all four tracks of the tape, and the mixing board faders were slowly raised so that the sound would be sustained as the chord faded away. In the end, the chord lasted fifty-three seconds – a fifth the length of 'A Day in the Life' and nearly half the running time of 'Please Please Me'.

Several other songs were in the works by the time 'A Day in the Life' was finished, and one of them, McCartney's 'Sgt. Pepper's Lonely Hearts Club Band', gave the album its focus. The song introduces an old-time concert band, in its twentieth year and about to give a concert. It had occurred to McCartney that for this album the Beatles could step back from their Fab Four image by pretending to *be* the Sgt. Pepper band. This song would introduce the album, and the rest would be the band's stage show. Later it occurred to him that the show concept could be sharpened if the song were reprised near the end of the record.

McCartney had a model of sorts in the Beach Boys' *Pet Sounds*, the album on which Brian Wilson, the group's principal composer, distanced the band from its surf music image. Its lyrics, for the most part, had the emotional depth that the Beatles had been working toward, and its quirkily-structured songs boasted colourful instrumentation and sound effects, to say nothing of the Beach Boys' magnificent vocal harmonies, which rivalled the Beatles' own. When McCartney heard the album at the time of its release in 1966, his reaction was, 'how are we going to top this?'

As it turned out, Wilson later said that he was inspired to make *Pet Sounds* after hearing the Beatles' *Rubber Soul*. But *Sgt. Pepper* brought this creative give-and-take to an end. Wilson's plan was to respond with *Smile*, a collection of material lyrically and musically more complex than *Pet Sounds*, and meant to be as daring as *Sgt. Pepper*. But Wilson's excessive drug use (among other personal problems) caught up with him during the sessions, which ground to a halt when he had a nervous breakdown. Nevertheless, for as long as it lasted, the competitive interaction between the Beatles, the Beach Boys, the Byrds, Bob Dylan and a handful of other rock musicians unquestionably helped transform the best pop music of this time from teenage ephemera into durable art.

For the Beatles themselves, *Sgt. Pepper* was the moment when McCartney eclipsed Lennon as the dominant force in the band. Lennon had thought long and hard about the Beatles during his film break in Spain. The last tour had been an ordeal, and there were aspects of studio work that he found tedious as well. To a great extent he was content to sit around Weybridge smoking marijuana, watching television and reading. If nothing else, a residual sense of competition with McCartney drove him on.

He was, in fact, at a turning point in his songwriting. The early Beatles' songs of love and jealousy now seemed pointless to him. 'Tomorrow Never Knows' was the beginning of a new direction, and during the current sessions he had already come up with two masterpieces. The question he wrestled with was this: what was worth writing about? The stream-of-consciousness imagery in 'Strawberry Fields Forever' worked nicely as a song lyric, but there was no counting on that, or forcing it. 'A Day in the Life' provided a more practical model. Some of it had been suggested, as the song's first line says, by reading the newspaper. If news items could be filtered, toyed with and transformed, so could other things.

Thus, Lennon's three remaining non-collaborative contributions to *Sgt. Pepper* were all inspired by seemingly mundane items. The lyric for 'Being for the Benefit of Mr Kite!' was lifted almost verbatim from a Victorian circus poster that Lennon found in an antique shop. 'Good Morning Good Morning' was inspired by an advertisement for Corn Flakes. And 'Lucy in the Sky with Diamonds' took its title from a drawing by Lennon's son Julian, and some of its imagery from a scene in *Alice's Adventures in Wonderland*, augmented, clearly, by Lennon's experiences with psychedelic drugs.

What Lennon did with these modest inspirations was stunning. His music for 'Mr Kite!' turned the two-dimensional poster copy into a sonic circus. To produce the song's unusually festive sound, Martin and his engineer, Geoff Emerick, took a tape of calliope music, snipped it into pieces, threw the pieces in the air, reassembled them at random, and played the resulting tape backwards. Again, John Cage was a predecessor, having used a similar technique to produce his 'Williams Mix' in 1952, although in the Beatles case, the resulting band of tape was not the work itself, but merely embellishment. A theatre organ, added by Martin, provided a perfect finishing touch.

'Lucy in the Sky with Diamonds' is also an ideal match of text and musical texture. Its imagery is remarkably rich: 'Picture yourself in a boat on a river, with tangerine trees and marmalade skies'. On the journey, one encounters rocking horse people, cellophane flowers, newspaper taxis and most importantly, a girl with kaleidoscope eyes, who appears at the beginning and the end of the song. Lennon later described the girl with kaleidoscope eyes as a kind of female saviour, the kindred spirit he had by then determined that his wife Cynthia was not.

The song's other-worldly atmosphere is created in the opening bars by McCartney, who plays an angular, chromatic figure on a Hammond organ, electronically enhanced so that it sounds like a cross between a harpsichord and an electric guitar. Like the first version of 'Strawberry Fields', the texture builds slowly: first the organ, then Lennon's lead vocal (altered by using both Artificial Double Tracking and speed variation) and McCartney's bass. Starr, initially using only brushes on cymbals, turns up only at the end of the first verse.

Normally, the Beatles would have repeated the first verse melody here, but instead they move into a new key and present a second melody, in which Lennon again approaches McCartney's 'single note' ideal. Both these sections are in three-quarter time, but as the second melody ends, three tom-tom and bass drum beats from Starr lead into something entirely new – a change in metre (from three to four beats in a bar) and yet another key change. Suddenly, the hazy world of the first two verses gives way to the bright sunlight of the refrain, in which the song's title is sung as a celebratory proclamation.

McCartney's songs here show the penchant for imaginative storytelling that he had pursued so effectively on *Revolver*, and like Lennon, he was looking in the newspapers for his subjects. A story about a young runaway suggested 'She's Leaving Home', the next in McCartney's line of string-accompanied ballads. The theme of alienation in 'Eleanor Rigby' is repeated, but in place of that song's stark imagery, 'She's Leaving Home' presents a complete narrative. McCartney flirts with compassion for the parents here. In parenthetical lines, sung by Lennon and Harrison, they explain that they have struggled all their lives to give their daughter whatever she wanted, and are left asking themselves what they did wrong. To which McCartney, Lennon and Harrison respond, at the end of the song, that the young woman has left home simply to have fun, itself regarded as a higher value in those rebellious days.

His other efforts are generally lighter in spirit. 'Fixing a Hole' is a bright-textured bit of introspection, almost Lennonesque in character. 'Lovely Rita' describes a date with a meter maid. 'Getting Better' is a collaboration in which McCartney celebrates his independence from school and his mellowing with age, while Lennon, interestingly, confesses to wife-beating and claims to be over it. Lennon and McCartney also collaborated on 'With a Little Help From My Friends', for Starr to sing.

Harrison brought two songs to the *Sgt. Pepper* sessions. One, the dark-textured 'Only a Northern Song', was recorded and set aside,

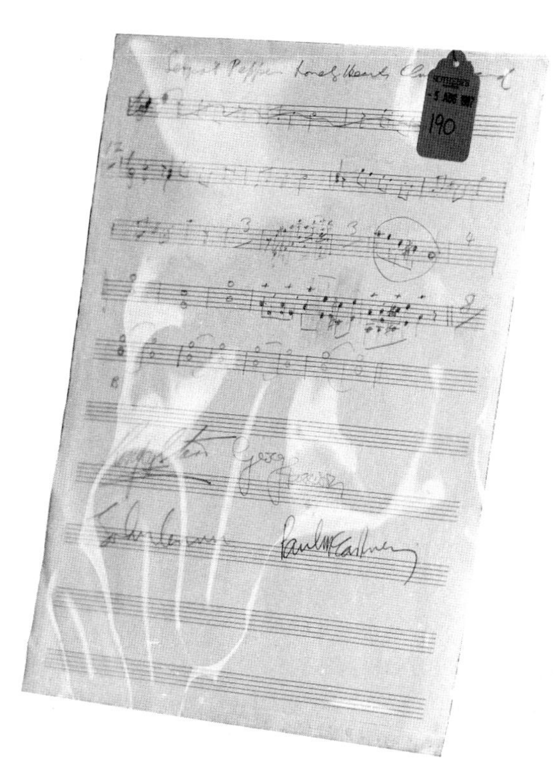

The Beatles did not write musical notation, but George Martin did. This sheet of manuscript paper, autographed by all four Beatles, contains Martin's score – dictated by McCartney – for the compact French horn break in 'Sgt. Pepper's Lonely Hearts Club Band'.

to be revived a year later for inclusion in *Yellow Submarine*, the full-length cartoon for which the Beatles half-heartedly agreed to provide a few new songs. Hidden on the soundtrack album, it is often overlooked, but in fact, it features a fabulously tactile layer of electronic effects that make the song as alluring in its own way as 'Being for the Benefit of Mr Kite!'

Harrison's more significant effort was 'Within You Without You', a lengthy meditation on the Indian philosophy that had lately captured his imagination. Its backing combines Indian instruments in dialogue with a vibrant string score by Martin. At the time the album was released, this five-minute apotheosis of raga-rock seemed an indulgence; even Harrison hinted as much by including a self-deprecating patch of laughter at the end of the song. Yet it has aged well, and in hindsight, it seems one of the most sophisticated compositions on this extraordinary collection.

At a party to introduce *Sgt. Pepper's Lonely Hearts Club Band* to the press, the Beatles – no longer sporting the matching suits and hairstyles that had been their trademark through their last public outing, the previous year – unveil the new album's gatefold sleeve.

Early in the album's running order – in the third song, 'Lucy in the Sky with Diamonds' – the Beatles use a word that perfectly sums up the feeling of *Sgt. Pepper*: kaleidoscope. In terms of technical trickery and instrumental colour, they were at their most adventurous. Just about everything is sped up, slowed down or compressed. Harrison's Indian instruments are used both as background timbre and as centre-pieces. A harpsichord holds the middle ground in 'Fixing a Hole'. There are strings on 'She's Leaving Home', brass on both the title cut and 'Good Morning Good Morning', and a chamber orchestra on 'A Day in the Life'.

The tape effects are ambitious too. Besides the collage in 'Being for the Benefit of Mr Kite!' the Beatles and Martin fashioned an amazing electronic menagerie to stampede across the soundstage at the end of 'Good Morning Good Morning'. Out of the stampede jumps a cat's miaow, edited onto a dog's bark. The sound of an orchestra tuning opens the record, and on both the title song and its reprise, applause and crowd noise create the illusion of a concert. There was also a final quirky touch. After the long final chord of 'A Day in the Life', the Beatles appended a high-pitched (fifteen kilocycle) tone, leading to a few seconds of noise, laughter and chatter. On the vinyl LP, this explosion of noise was cut into a continuous groove around the label, so that the Beatles could be heard chortling continuously until the listener lifted the stylus from the disc.

Since *Rubber Soul*, the Beatles had overseen their cover art, and it was clear that the cover of *Sgt. Pepper* had to be an exceptional production. Lennon and McCartney told the artist Peter Blake about the album's concept, and suggested the notion of an old-fashioned group portrait of the fictional Pepper band as they might appear after playing a concert in a park. Blake's idea was that the band should be surrounded by its audience, which should include people the Beatles considered important or influential. They came up with a list of musicians, gurus, writers, visual artists, comedians and sport and film celebrities, and Blake made a life-size cardboard representation of each. The celebrity crowd was assembled behind a bass drum with the ornate Sgt. Pepper logo. Immediately behind the drum stood the 1967 Beatles, in colourful, silk military band uniforms, sporting moustaches and holding orchestral instruments. To their left were wax figures of the Beatles circa 1965.

Released on 1 June 1967, *Sgt. Pepper* immediately became the focus of microscopic analysis, not only by observers of popular culture, but also by writers and musicians whose home turf was classical music. In truth, its concept album status was only skin-deep: there was no real connection between the songs, other than their supposed place in the Pepper band's stage set. Still, the concept album idea quickly took root with the most inventive bands. The Who, for example, used a radio programme format, complete with parody advertisements between songs, as the structure for *The Who Sell Out*, recorded in October. A year later the group would record *Tommy*, the first of two 'rock operas' by its guitarist and composer, Pete Townshend. And the Kinks, who rode the British Invasion wave with a run of simple, catchy hit singles from 1964 to 1966, had also matured, and were about to start a run of concept projects that began with *The Village Green Perservation Society* in 1968 and included a rock opera, *Arthur*, and several operettas.

Sgt. Pepper quickly became all things to all people. To the budding counterculture, it was a manifesto of drug consciousness, an advance report from some magical plane of existence – a place one could find by taking Lennon's advice in 'Tomorrow Never Knows', to 'turn off your mind, relax and float downstream'. But it was also something less fanciful: tangible proof that the Beatles had come of age as poets and composers.

8

Mystery Tours and Discord 1967–8

In August 1967, the Beatles and entourage set out for Bangor, Wales, to meet with the Maharishi Mahesh Yogi, a master of Transcendental Meditation who promised to show them an untapped fount of inner creative potential.

The White Album was a funny one, because at the time they came back from abroad and they all had a huge collection of songs they wanted to record. And they wanted them done all at the same time. By this time they were four individuals with their individual songs, wanting to record them with the assistance of the other people rather than being a group.

George Martin, 1993

Mystery Tours and Discord 1967–8

Even at their peak, the Beatles used to refer to 'the downfall' that they believed would eventually come. No one could accuse them of staving it off by playing it safe in their music or, lately, in their public pronouncements. And indeed, when 'the downfall' did come, it was not because the group had lost its following, but because the band's collective will had shattered. Ironically, the seeds of 'the downfall' were planted virtually at the moment of the Beatles' greatest artistic success.

Early on, when they packed into a van night after night and travelled between performances, they became a cohesive unit, not just a band but a brotherhood. But that was when they were nineteen, twenty, twenty-one years old. Their lives, public and personal, were tied up in the band. There was nothing else. But by 1967 there was plenty else. They each had interests of their own. Lennon, Starr and Harrison had families and lived outside London. McCartney, still single, lived in London and was a man about town.

Harrison, drawn to Indian music, culture and philosophy, was able to interest the others in his new obsession to some extent, but he was still testing the degree to which he could integrate this interest into his Beatles work. He had also cultivated friendships among other rock musicians, and while at the Beatles' sessions he felt like Lennon's and McCartney's water boy, outside the group he commanded considerable respect.

For Lennon this was a particularly unsettling time. Having grown bored with live performance in 1966, a year later he was bored with the routine of making recordings. Increasingly estranged from Cynthia and enamoured of drug experimentation, he withdrew into a world of his own. Still, he could rouse himself to moments of brillance when pressed. 'All You Need is Love' is a perfect example: asked to come up with a song the Beatles could sing on a live global telecast just three weeks after the release of *Sgt. Pepper*, he tapped into the *Zeitgeist* and came up with the perfect anthem for the flower-power summer.

Starr had no particular ambitions outside the group, although having been singled out for praise in the Beatles' two movies, he put the word out that he would be interested in an acting role. By the end of 1967 he agreed to play a cameo role in *Candy.* Within the group, his drumming provided a distinctive and essential element, but he suggested little, demanded less, and was content to serve as required.

McCartney, by contrast, had come into his own on the last few albums, and he was eager to continue the explorations that the Beatles had started. At this point, he was the one who came up with new ideas. And over the next two years, he would find it increasingly difficult to get Lennon and Harrison to share his vision of the Beatles' future. One of his ideas in 1967 was Apple, a company meant to oversee all the Beatles activities, including not only their musical endeavours, but everything from merchandising to sponsoring projects by other musicians and artists. A hint of the concept could be found in the small-print credits on the back cover of *Sgt. Pepper.* The company was incorporated in May, and by early 1969 it was running a fashion boutique, a film production company and a record label.

Epstein opposed the idea of Apple for understandable reasons. His management contract with the Beatles would expire on 30 September, and he was not sure on what basis – or even whether – the relationship would be renewed. Now that the Beatles had stopped touring, his primary managerial function was irrelevant. His influence on their creative work was nil: early on, when he made a suggestion during a recording session, Lennon told him to see to the percentages and leave the music to them. Most recently, he objected to the ornate *Sgt. Pepper* cover, making it clear that he was not on their wavelength.

Apple's first endeavour would be a new project of McCartney's. During a trip to America in April 1967, just after the *Sgt. Pepper* sessions, McCartney dreamed up an hour-long television film. The Beatles could hire a bus, fill it with actors and extras, and tour around England with a camera crew. They would each write short episodes, with plenty of room for improvisation. And of course, some of the film would be devoted to performances of their latest songs. His original notes, jotted on the plane trip back to England, were quite detailed. He had already settled on *Magical Mystery Tour* as the title, and had the theme song written by the time he presented the idea to the others on 25 April. His notes also specified a scene with a stripper, a sequence at an army recruiting station, a marathon, and a laboratory scene. His cast list included a courier, a driver, a busty hostess, a fat woman and a small man. All these things were included in the film.

For their self-produced *Magical Mystery Tour* television film, the Beatles rented a tour bus, filled it with actors, and cruised around England with a sketchy script, hoping that spontaneous adventure would unfold before their cameras. It didn't.

Agreeing to the plan, the Beatles began working on the title song – complete with highway sound effects and elegant brass flourishes – five weeks before *Sgt. Pepper* reached the shops. They were juggling another project too: the soundtrack for the *Yellow Submarine* animated film, which would go into production late in the year. Apart from McCartney, who read the script and offered suggestions, the Beatles were not particularly interested in this cartoon. Their obligation involved providing a few new songs and allowing some of their

For part of the 'I Am the Walrus' sequence, the Beatles donned animal costumes: left to right: McCartney, Harrison and Starr, with Lennon, as the walrus, front and centre.

recent recordings to be used on the soundtrack. When the production was complete, they agreed to make a screen appearance at the end.

So after taping the title song for *Magical Mystery Tour*, they set that project aside and turned their attention to *Yellow Submarine*. Harrison's 'Only a Northern Song', left over from the *Sgt. Pepper* sessions, would be used. Also taped in May and early June were 'Baby You're a Rich Man', a Lennon–McCartney collaboration; McCartney's popsy 'All Together Now', and another Harrison song, a magnificently dense, heavy metal precursor, 'It's All Too Much'. They also began work on one of Lennon's quirkier songs, 'You Know My Name (Look Up the Number)', an evocation of a lounge show gone haywire. Whether or not this was intended for *Yellow Submarine*, it ended up on hold – but with periodic touch-ups – until 1970, when it was released on a single with 'Let It Be'.

The Beatles devoted the last two weeks of June to preparing 'All You Need is Love', the most rhythmically complex song the group had worked on to date, and one that demanded great delicacy of texture. Considerable care was lavished on the backing track against which the Beatles and studio musicians performed live during the global broadcast on 25 June. And taking advantage of the exposure, the song was rush-released as a single. Needing a B-side, they

The Maharishi Mahesh Yogi, right, holds court, with the Beatles sitting at his feet. But their brief stay at his retreat in Rishikesh, India, in February 1968, proved a failure. By May, Lennon and McCartney announced that the Beatles and their guru had gone their separate ways.

raided their *Yellow Submarine* file, and included 'Baby You're a Rich Man'.

It had been a hectic year, and all four of the Beatles wanted a break. So in July they left both *Magical Mystery Tour* and *Yellow Submarine* hanging and did not return to work until 22 August. Even then, their activities were scattered. They spent two days working on McCartney's old-timey 'Your Mother Should Know', for *Magical Mystery Tour*, and then followed Harrison to Bangor, Wales, for a seminar on Transcendental Meditation given by the Maharishi Mahesh Yogi. The Maharishi taught that by using Eastern meditation techniques – mainly, focusing one's thoughts on a mantra, or a repeated chant – practitioners could have the same kind of insights and visions they were currently getting from drugs.

Their spiritual quest was interrupted, however, by the news that Brian Epstein had been found dead in his London home on 27 August, having taken what the coroner ruled was an accidental overdose of barbiturates. Lennon and Harrison, interviewed by television reporters in Bangor, were stunned: with glazed eyes, they repeated what the Maharishi had told them about the Hindu concept of soul transmigration. Putting off the question of whether or how to replace Epstein, the Beatles threw themselves fully into *Magical Mystery Tour*, for which they had only recorded two songs. Filming was set to begin on 11 September, and in the preceding week they began work on all the other songs that would be used in the show. The first in the new batch was another *tour de force* of nonsense verse from Lennon, 'I Am the Walrus'.

Lennon's lyric was deliberately incomprehensible, partly because after all the analysis recent Beatles recordings were given, the prankster in him wanted to give analysts something truly meaningless to ponder. The opening line, 'I am he as you are he as you are me and we are all together', could be rationalized as a philosophical insight, and 'Crabalocker fishwife pornographic priestess boy you been a naughty girl, you let your knickers down' actually seemed fairly clear. But what to make of 'Semolina pilchard climbing up the Eiffel Tower'?

Lennon's verse melody wavers chromatically, like the sound of a European police siren, and builds to an almost cathartic declaration, 'I am the eggman, they are the eggmen, I am the walrus'. And once again, the combination of the Beatles' experimentation and Martin's ear for orchestration yielded the perfect setting. Over a fairly bland basic track, Martin overlaid winds and strings, plus a choir which was asked to produce a variety of effects, ranging from carefully orchestrated sardonic laughter to chanting 'oompah, oompah, stick it up your jumper' and 'got one, got one, everybody's got one'. As a final touch, the Beatles decided, during the mixing sessions, to bring in the sound of a radio being tuned across frequencies, and stumbled upon a BBC performance of Shakespeare's *King Lear*. Thus, after four and a half minutes of bizarre lyrics and unusual noises, the record ends with Gloucester's question, 'What, is he dead?' and Edgar's immediate, 'Sit you down, father; rest you.'

McCartney and his longtime girlfriend, the actress Jane Asher, leave their rendezvous with the Maharishi in Bangor after learning of Brian Epstein's death on 27 August 1967

The other songs recorded for the show include McCartney's melancholy but typically melodic 'Fool on the Hill', an easygoing instrumental credited to all four Beatles, called 'Flying', and Harrison's 'Blue Jay Way', a deliciously gloomy evocation (abetted by organ, cellos and backwards tape) of waiting late into the night for friends who have lost their way to his house (or actually to one he was renting during a visit to Los Angeles).

The filming of *Magical Mystery Tour* was fraught with the problems one might anticipate when a bus full of actors sets off on an improvisatory journey, led by four musicians without directorial experience and varying levels of interest. When the BBC aired it on 26 December, it failed disastrously. It was, for one thing, entirely inappropriate holiday fare. But the BBC stacked the cards against it by screening it in black and white, thereby negating its vivid hues and rendering meaningless the stretches of film that depend on altered colour registration to make their effect. The recording, released as a double EP in England and as an LP in the USA (the first side was devoted to songs from the show, the second to recent singles) was snapped up enthusiastically. So was the group's new single, 'Hello Goodbye', an upbeat McCartney song recorded during the filming but not included in the show.

Near the end of the year, Harrison was commissioned to compose a score for the film *Wonderwall*. He responded with a collection of instrumentals, split between Western and Indian music. In January 1968 he flew to Bombay to complete his soundtrack, and while he was there, he recorded his Indian musicians (he did not play himself) in some short pieces, based on traditional ragas, with the idea of writing lyrics for these and proposing them as Beatles songs.

This may seem a dubious, perhaps even piratical approach to composition; indeed, for the one that was used, 'The Inner Light', Harrison's approach to the text was similarly freehanded. In November 1967 Juan Mascaró, a Cambridge scholar of Eastern religion, sent Harrison a letter praising 'Within You Without You', and a copy of his book, *Lamps of Fire*, which included ancient texts from various sources. Mascaró suggested that Harrison set some of these to music, and specifically pointed out 'The Inner Light', a poem about wisdom, from the *Tao Te Ching*. With only slight changes, Harrison fitted this text to a serene melody his Indian musicians recorded in Bombay. The other Beatles were taken with it, and released it as the B-side of the next single, 'Lady Madonna'. The first Harrison composition to be released on a Beatles single, therefore, was a combination of a traditional Indian melody and an ancient Chinese text.

McCartney gives the double thumbs up, his sign of exceptional approval, while watching a sequence from the Beatles' animated film *Yellow Submarine*.

In February, all four Beatles flew to Rishikesh, India, to continue their studies with the Maharishi. But before they left, they filed into Abbey Road once more, adding vocals to 'The Inner Light' and completing three other new songs. McCartney's 'Lady Madonna' was a rollicking, Fats Domino-inspired track, driven by McCartney's energetic piano playing and overlaid with saxophones and some wild scatsinging by Lennon, McCartney and Harrison. Another song taped during these sessions was 'Hey Bulldog', destined for *Yellow Submarine* and essentially a riff-based throw-away.

The real gem, however, was 'Across the Universe', another of Lennon's musical diary entries. Curiously, this recording lay unreleased for nearly two years. 'Across the Universe', like McCartney's 'Yesterday', was composed in a sudden burst of inspiration. As Lennon explained it, he had spent an exasperating evening arguing with Cynthia, and after she fell asleep, the lyrics came to him all at once. The first lines perfectly evoke the argument from Lennon's point of view, yet to a listener ignorant of the song's provenance, they stand as a stream of lovely images:

APPLE FILMS present
a KING FEATURES production
The Beatles
Yellow Submarine
'NOTHING IS REAL'
Based upon a song by
JOHN LENNON and PAUL McCARTNEY
Starring SGT. PEPPERS LONELY HEARTS CLUB BAND
Screenplay by LEE MINOFF and AL BRODAX JACK MENDELSOHN and ERIC
From an original story by LEE MINOFF · Design HEINZ EDELMANN · Produced by AL BRODAX · Directed by GEORGE DUNN

A theatrical poster for *Yellow Submarine* shows the entire cast of animated characters, with the good guys (Young Fred, Jeremy Boob, the Beatles and Old Fred) on the left, and the bad guys (various species of Blue Meanie) on the right.

Words are flowing out
like endless rain into a paper cup,
They slither while they pass,
they slip away across the universe.

To accommodate the odd metres of the poem, Lennon uses a gently lyrical melody, as beautiful and wrenching in its way as the best of McCartney's ballads. But he was dissatisfied with the recording, so with 'Lady Madonna' and 'The Inner Light' sharing the single and 'Hey Bulldog' reserved for *Yellow Submarine*, 'Across the Universe' was shelved.

There was another autobiographical clue buried in the lyric. 'Thoughts meander like a restless wind inside a letterbox,' Lennon sang, using an image – wind in a letterbox – similar to those used by the Japanese avant-garde artist Yoko Ono in her writings and 'instruction' pieces. Ono had come to London from New York, where she was a member of Fluxus, an underground collective of conceptual artists that included the composers La Monte Young, Jackson Mac Low and Dick Higgins, the artists George Maciunas, Takako Saito and Geoffrey Hendricks, and at least a dozen others who were influenced by the music of John Cage and the art of Marcel Duchamp. Lennon had attended a preview of Ono's show at the Indica Gallery a few months earlier, and had been taken with Ono's deliberately outrageous sculptures and performance pieces. Their paths crossed several more times, whereupon they began a peculiar correspondence, sending each other aphoristic postcards. They continued their correspondence while Lennon and the other Beatles sat at the Maharishi's feet in Rishikesh.

The Beatles had gamely followed Harrison on his spiritual quest, but the Rishikesh expedition brought their interest to an end. Starr left after eleven days, complaining about the food. The others lasted a few more weeks, but abandoned Rishikesh precipitately after the Maharishi came under suspicion of making advances to one of the women in the class, the actress Mia Farrow. They announced their break with the Maharishi, but continued to say – though with muted enthusiasm – that they considered meditation beneficial. Indeed, they had ample proof of that. During and immediately after their Indian sojourn, Lennon, McCartney and Harrison were unusually prolific, and even Starr finished a song that the others considered acceptable. This bumper crop would yield *The Beatles* – the double-disc set popularly known as the 'White Album' because of its blank cover, the antithesis of *Sgt. Pepper* – and the single 'Hey Jude'.

Work began in May, when the Beatles gathered at Kinfauns, Harrison's bungalow in Esher, to rehearse and make test recordings of twenty-three new Lennon, McCartney and Harrison songs. Four of these were dropped before the official sessions began at Abbey Road later that month, and of the nineteen that were formally recorded, two were left unreleased. That left seventeen of the Esher songs, more than enough for a conventional album. But the Beatles continued to write during the sessions, which lasted from May to October, and by the time they were finished they had recorded thirty-three new songs.

Most of the Esher surplus eventually turned up in other forms. Lennon's lyrical 'Child of Nature' was later rewritten as 'Jealous Guy', and appeared on his *Imagine* album in 1971. McCartney's 'Junk' was included on his eponymous solo début in 1970. Harrison, having brought seven songs to the sessions, ended up with three leftovers. He gave 'Sour Milk Sea' to Jackie Lomax, one of the first artists signed by Apple Records. His 'Not Guilty' turned up on *George Harrison* in 1979, and 'Circles' was included on *Gone Troppo* in 1982. Only a quirky avant-garde piece by Lennon, 'What's the New Mary Jane?', was never released commercially.

A few notable changes occurred in the Beatles' lives just before the sessions began. Back from India, they began transforming Apple from an amorphous concept into a real production company. Offices were set up, and plans were announced. Lennon and McCartney flew to New York to talk about the venture in a series of television interviews, where they described Apple as 'Western Communism' – a company that would share the Beatles' wealth by offering opportunities for artists to develop their potential. This magnanimity was short-lived, but it lasted long enough to turn Apple into a money drain, as its largesse was tapped by both sincere hopefuls and outright con artists.

Apple Records turned out to be a remarkably eclectic enterprise. There were early hits with the Welsh folk-singer Mary Hopkin, the Beatlesque rock band Badfinger and the American folk-rock singer James Taylor. The organist and singer Billy Preston and the soul-singer Doris Troy filled out the rhythm and blues end of the

One of the first public ventures of Apple, the production and merchandising company that the Beatles formed in 1967, was a London boutique. It was disastrous from the start: neighbouring businesses complained about the psychedelic mural, and the shop haemorrhaged money until the Beatles gave away its custom-designed stock and closed its doors.

Harrison had introduced the Beatles to Indian culture, and although for the others it proved to be a fad, Harrison continued his studies of Indian music for some years with Ravi Shankar, right, one of the world's master sitarists.

spectrum. The Modern Jazz Quartet, one of the premier American jazz ensembles, recorded two Apple albums. So did John Tavener, a young British composer whose music would come into vogue in the late 1980s. Harrison brought in the sitar virtuoso Ravi Shankar, as well as the Radha Krishna Temple, which sang in praise of the Hindu pantheon. What other label could boast this stylistic breadth within its first two years?

Meanwhile, in mid-May Lennon and Ono decided that they were fated for each other, and after spending a night together, while Cynthia was away on holiday, they recorded their first avant-garde collaboration, *Unfinished Music No. 1: Two Virgins*, a collection of atmospheric, seemingly improvisatory instrumental and vocal pieces. This too would find an outlet on Apple, in a jacket showing the collaborators entirely nude, front and back.

Lennon and Cynthia separated forthwith, and they were divorced by November. From late May, Lennon and Ono were inseparable, and were frequently in the news. *Two Virgins*, or its cover art, was naturally the focus of controversy when it was released soon after Lennon's divorce was final. A month earlier Lennon and Ono were arrested for possession of cannabis resin while staying in a London apartment owned by Starr. And when Ono had a miscarriage in November, Lennon documented her hospital stay with a portable cassette recorder and released the results (including a tape of the dying baby's heartbeat) as part of *Unfinished Music No. 2: Life With the Lions*.

The inseparability of Lennon and Ono extended to Beatles recording sessions, to the irritation of the others, who preferred the privacy that had been part of the group's working method. It is absurd to blame Ono for the breakup of the Beatles; the reasons are far more complex. Yet her presence clearly increased the tension in the musicians' relationship. Ono stumbled into this atmosphere with the naïve belief that as she and Lennon were now collaborators, Lennon's other collaborators would happily follow Lennon's lead and avail themselves of a new artistic sensibility. Lennon also apparently thought they might see it that way, and he was deeply wounded by what he later described as McCartney's and Harrison's dismissive treatment of Ono. It became a resentment that he dwelled on in interviews for the rest of his life.

In 1968, Lennon and Yoko Ono, soon to be his second wife, declared that they had nothing to hide, and proved it by posing nude for the cover of their controversial *Two Virgins* album, a collection of avant-garde collages. Banned in many places, it was sold in a brown paper sleeve.

Still, it is likely that the 'White Album' sessions would have seen the fragmentation of the group even without Ono. The fact is, Lennon, McCartney and Harrison were by this point fully engaged only by their own songs. When the intensive session work began, the band worked together, and it continued to do so periodically, particularly when the basic tracks for a new song were started, or when a song demanded a sense of live interaction. But within the first week, a new working method had evolved. Often, one or two Beatles could be found working on a song in one of the Abbey Road studios, while another worked elsewhere in the building. Each was in charge of his own songs, with the others drifting in and out, contributing where necessary.

This seemingly chaotic approach proved quite efficient, yet the apparent insularity of the four musicians did not prevent disputes. During the sessions for McCartney's 'Hey Jude', McCartney and Harrison were at odds over Harrison's desire to add a bluesy answering figure between the vocal lines. Harrison ended up sitting out the session, spending his time in the recording booth with Martin. There was also a battle over 'Revolution', a Lennon song released as the

B-side of 'Hey Jude'. Lennon first recorded a slow, mostly acoustic version and wanted to release it as a single. But McCartney and Harrison objected that it lacked the necessary energy, and Lennon acquiesced, remaking the song as one of the most raucous of all Beatles tracks.

Other disputes erupted regularly during the sessions. Geoff Emerick, an engineer (and later producer) who had been on Martin's team since *Revolver*, resigned because the atmosphere was so poisonous. And Starr found the sessions so dispiriting that on 22 August he quit the band, convinced that he was not needed. In a way, he was right. During his nearly two week absence, McCartney did much of the drumming. Still, they coaxed him back on 4 September, in time to film promotional clips for 'Hey Jude' and 'Revolution'. The group's first single on its new Apple label, these two songs offered a glimpse of what the Beatles were up to at Abbey Road. The musical implications were clear enough: apart from comparatively subtle chamber orchestra assistance on 'Hey Jude', these songs showed the Beatles as a straightforward rock band, with no overt studio trickery, backwards tapes, exotic instruments or psychedelic sounds.

There were a few new twists. McCartney's 'Hey Jude' – his avuncular advice to the five-year-old Julian Lennon about dealing with his parents' divorce ('take a sad song and make it better') – is a tuneful piano ballad that clocks in at over seven minutes, an unusual stretch for a pop single, and longer than anything the Beatles had included on an album. Moreover, the last four minutes were simply a singalong wordless chorus ('nah nah nah nah-nah-nah naaaah') repeated over and over, with occasional scat-singing flourishes from McCartney.

'Revolution' was raw Lennon, back in form as a rock screamer and supported by aggressive, distorted guitars and a rollicking piano. Cosmic imagery and evocations of universal love are sidelined for the moment. Here Lennon expresses his uneasiness with the exhortations to revolution by militant student movements both in the USA and in Europe. Lennon felt he had common cause with these groups. He agreed with their opposition to the Vietnam war, and he was all for the empowerment of what he considered to be his audience. But in singing that 'we all want to change the world', he added a caveat. 'But when you talk about destruction, don't you know that you can count me out.'

Although he acquiesced in the decision to remake 'Revolution' as a rocker, Lennon had no intention of abandoning the original slow version. That version, renamed 'Revolution 1', was included on the album, and with the single and another recording from the album, 'Revolution 9', it made a compellingly picturesque trilogy. In the acoustic version Lennon presents his argument gently, and a little ambiguously: here, when talk turns to destruction, he is unable to make up his mind, and sings 'don't you know that you can count me out – in'. In the more furious electric version, violence seems a certainty, and Lennon has decided: count him out. But his protests do not stop the rush toward destruction. The triology's denouement, 'Revolution 9', is an extraordinary piece of electronic music that, in just over eight minutes, paints a vivid picture of revolutionary chaos. It is not a paean to revolution as a heroic endeavour, although fragments of triumphal music peek through the texture. It is a gritty look at the collapse of a society.

The basis of the work, though virtually inaudible in the finished production, is an instrumental jam, cut from the end of 'Revolution 1'. Over several days, Lennon and Ono, with help at one session from Harrison, raided EMI's archives and their own record collections, and made tape loops from sound effects recordings and from snippets of orchestral, choral and opera recordings. They used material from the 'A Day in the Life' sessions, and recorded mellotron sounds, spoken observations and off-the-cuff aphorisms, hysterical laughter, shouts and even the chanting of football crowds. All this was laid over the original Beatles recording, as was a tape loop of a clinical voice intoning the words 'number nine'. This repeating 'number nine', panned across the stereo image and fading in and out over the course of the work, became the recording's most recognizable leitmotif, but there were recurring musical motifs as well. What all this added up to was a work that was alternately comical and terrifying, an incoherent mass of sound from which a cinematic drama seemed to emerge.

Stranger still, the song that follows this nightmare on the album (and which closes the final side) is Lennon's 'Good Night', a sweet lullaby, sung by Starr and accompanied by a lush string backing that emerges from beneath the final shouts of 'Revolution 9'. The juxtaposition is brilliant in its incongruity.

Opposite, though not the Beatles' principal spokesman for peace – that was Lennon's job – Starr poses here with a dove in a 1968 portrait by Richard Avedon.

Actually, 'Revolution 9' was not the Beatles' first piece of electronic music. The group had assembled an electronic work during the early part of the *Sgt. Pepper* sessions. Directed by Paul McCartney, the untitled piece ran nearly fourteen minutes and actually had a public performance in January 1967 at a 'Carnival of Light' concert at the Roundhouse Theatre in London. But it was never released on disc. Starr, too, presided over a tape work that used percussion sounds.

Apart from 'Revolution 9', there was little on *The Beatles* that broke new ground in the way that tracks on *Revolver* or *Sgt. Pepper* had. And in fact, much the same can be said of the two albums they would record in 1969, *Let It Be* and *Abbey Road.* Lennon, McCartney, Harrison, and now Starr, were composing first-rate material. Yet if the Beatles development from 'Love Me Do' to 'I Am The Walrus' was a story of incessant forward movement and growth, this final phase was one of consolidation.

The Beatles, in fact, is a fascinating compendium of compositional and performance styles that shows how wide-ranging the Beatles' musical imaginations were, and how versatile they were as performers and arrangers. There are some marvellous parodies and tributes here, most of them by McCartney. His 'Back in the U.S.S.R.' plays off the title of Chuck Berry's 1959 'Back in the U.S.A.', but is actually a take-off on the Beach Boys' early surf music style. 'Ob-La-Di, Ob-La-Da' is calypso. 'Martha My Dear', a song about McCartney's sheepdog, has its roots in the turn-of-the-century salon song. 'Rocky Racoon' parodies the storytelling ballads of the American West, and 'Honey Pie', scored with jazzy winds, is fully in the style popularized by the crooners of the 1920s. 'Helter Skelter' was meant to show that the Beatles could rock as hard as any of the bands just coming up; in fact, McCartney has said that he was inspired by hearing an interview in which Pete Townshend of the Who says that his group had just recorded the heaviest, most firebreathing piece of rock ever committed to record. McCartney wanted to pre-empt them.

Lennon's parodies are less straightforward. 'Happiness is a Warm Gun' begins as another in Lennon's introspective series, but a dark, eerie, organ-based opening section gives way to pure blues, and then at the refrain to a highly effective skewering of the 1950s' doo-wop vocal style. He toys with the Beatles themselves in 'Glass Onion', a song that refers to lyrics in several earlier Beatles recordings, and includes the kind of red herrings (the claim that Paul was the walrus, for example) that would keep amateur Beatleologists speculating for years. And just as McCartney's 'Honey Pie' captured the sound of the 1920s, Lennon's 'Good Night' could easily pass as something from the Bing Crosby or Frank Sinatra songbooks. Otherwise, his borrowings are from current styles. He responds to the growing vogue for British blues-rock in the hard-driving 'Everybody's Got Something to Hide Except Me and My Monkey', and more stunningly in 'Yer Blues', itself another thoroughly Lennonesque study in word imagery.

Of course, not everything on *The Beatles* is referential. Of the Lennon contributions 'The Continuing Story of Bungalow Bill' is a Lennon fantasy about a safari hunter, and 'Cry Baby Cry' hints at the *Alice in Wonderland*-style imagery of 'Lucy in the Sky with Diamonds,' though without the psychedelia. 'Sexy Sadie', despite the altered name and sex of the central character, is an acidic assessment of the Maharishi, couched in a nicely arching melody, and an alluring texture based on an electronically altered piano sound. The more sensitive side of Lennon's songwriting is here too. In the graceful, plaintive 'Julia', he accompanies himself on acoustic guitar, and sings a pained ode to the memory of his mother, tinged with imagery that refers to Ono.

McCartney's non-parodic explorations take a few unusual turns. Besides such straightforwardly attractive, light-textured songs as 'Blackbird', 'Mother Nature's Son', and 'I Will', he toyed with his listeners' expectations – if only briefly – with 'Wild Honey Pie' and 'Why Don't We Do It In the Road?; two free-wheeling bursts so uncharacteristic that many listeners at first thought Lennon must have been behind them.

Starr's 'Don't Pass Me By', the song he had been tinkering with since 1963, has its roots in country music. Had the Beatles recorded it on *Beatles For Sale* or *Rubber Soul*, it undoubtedly would have come complete with twangy guitars. But they saw the song differently now. Instead, they brought in a few piano tracks on which the sound is electronically processed to imitate a Hammond organ. Also in the texture are sleigh bells, an eccentric touch for a country song. Yet the country influence comes through, not least because Martin brought in a violinist to play a fiddle solo appropriate to a barn dance.

Of the seven new songs that Harrison brought to the sessions, five were recorded and four made it onto the album, each entirely different in character and none showing any trace of Harrison's Indian dabblings. 'Piggies', for example, is social satire in the style of the day, dressed in a faux-Baroque setting built around harpsichord and strings. The contrast between the civilized veneer of the music, and the imagery of the lyrics, in which nattily dressed pigs are shown to be cannibalistic, was what made the song seem sardonic rather than heavy-handed. 'Savoy Truffle', a tribute to a friend's sweet tooth (and a tongue-in-cheek warning about the consequences) is basically a good-natured throwaway in a hard rock style. And 'Long, Long, Long' is an introspective love song so dark in texture as to seem ready to implode.

The best of Harrison's new songs, and one of the album's most inviting moments, is 'While My Guitar Gently Weeps'. Both the Esher rehearsal tape and the first formal recording of the song at Abbey Road show that Harrison originally conceived it as a gentle,

As members of Cream, Eric Clapton (seated) and Jack Bruce (left) were heroes of the nascent British blues rock movement. Clapton had been friendly with Harrison since 1965 when, as a member of the Yardbirds, he performed on the Beatles' Christmas Show. In 1968, he contributed an exquisitely doleful lead guitar line to Harrison's 'While My Guitar Gently Weeps'; Harrison returned the favour the following year, co-writing and playing on Cream's 'Badge'.

minor key folk-song, slightly mournful but not lugubrious. But his ideas expanded during the sessions, and the finished version thrives on textural details. Its introduction, originally a simple walk through the song's chord progression, ended up featuring a piano repeating a single note in a varied rhythm for three bars before escaping into a gloss of the song's melody. Set against this is a strummed acoustic guitar and a drum pattern punctuated by a quickly closing high hat. But the most striking aspect of the recording is the lead guitar part, played by Eric Clapton. Using a wah-wah pedal (which lets a guitarist pivot between extreme treble and extreme bass timbres), Clapton added a line that wove around Harrison's vocal, perfectly conveying the image of a weeping guitar.

Clapton, once a member of the Yardbirds and John Mayall's Bluesbreakers, was by this time a star of the blues-rock power trio Cream, and was revered in the rock world as a virtuoso soloist. For the Beatles and other pop bands of the 1960s, virtuosity in its showiest form was never a principal concern. Obviously, one had to come through with solos where required, and the right kinds of accompaniments; and McCartney's bass lines were certainly virtuosic. But the extended jamming that Clapton and Cream were known for – as were musicians like Jimi Hendrix, a black American guitarist who had moved to London – took instrumental virtuosity in rock to a new level. The Beatles themselves never took up the challenge, although they alluded to it in 1969, in a jam at the end of *Abbey Road*.

The one Harrison song that was recorded but not included on the album, 'Not Guilty', was nearly as interesting. In it, Harrison sings about the tensions within the band in terms that barely disguised the subject. He worked hard on it, recording more than a hundred takes before he had an acceptable backing track, and then adding aggressive, layered guitars and double-tracked percussion. Perhaps the lyrics doomed it: it was one thing for Lennon to criticize the Maharishi or for Harrison to skewer bourgeois society, but 'Not Guilty' aired the band's own dirty laundry.

There was a certain irony in calling this collection of solo projects *The Beatles*, a title that asserts the band's unity. But then, this was the Beatles as they were: four musicians whose musical personalities had been forged in the same crucible, but who were now intent on exploring different terrain. And in any case, it was not until Lennon began publicly airing the group's internal battles, in 1970, that anyone outside the group and EMI's engineers knew how fractious things were. To all appearances, life was still fine in Beatle-land, and *The Beatles*, far from exploding that myth, seemed to support it.

The Final Year 1969

9

By 1969, Lennon was less interested in the Beatles' projects than in promoting tongue-in-cheek philosophies such as Bagism – the notion that if people climbed into bags so that they could be heard but not seen, racism and other prejudices could be overcome.

The Dick Lester version of our lives in Hard Day's Night *and* Help! *made it look fun and games: a good romp? That was fair in the films but in the real world there was never any doubt. The Beatles were doomed. Your own space, man, it's so important. That's why we were doomed because we didn't have any.*

George Harrison, in *I Me Mine*, 1980

The Final Year 1969

For the most part, Harrison, Lennon and Starr were content with the state the Beatles had reached. In the eyes of the world, the group remained untouchable and untoppleable as pop music royalty. Yet at the same time, Apple gave them outlets for projects that did not fall comfortably under the Beatles banner.

Lennon quickly began making use of this freedom, recording and releasing his experimental collaborations with Ono. Harrison had brought out *Wonderwall* and would soon make *Electronic Sound*, a collection of Moog synthesizer practice tapes, recorded with the electronic music composer Bernie Krause (whose name, to his consternation, was hidden under a wash of silver paint on the album cover) and other collaborators. Starr's interests, for the moment, were in film. After his cameo in *Candy*, he would take on a more extensive role in *The Magic Christian*, with Peter Sellers, in February 1969.

McCartney, however, missed the collective spirit of the group's early days, and he was convinced that giving a few concerts – perhaps in a controlled environment – would revive that spirit. The recording studio, he believed, had liberated their imaginations, but had also fostered an unfortunate insularity, for which the discipline of rehearsing and playing for an audience was the logical antidote. The others had their doubts, although in September 1968 Harrison mused in interviews about taking over a concert hall and giving performances for a few months. The next month, McCartney announced that once *The Beatles* was finished, the group would work up some of the new songs for a television taping, and would then perform them live. Soon there was talk of a three-day booking in mid-December at the Roundhouse, with proceeds from the sale of 4,500 tickets going to charity.

But true consensus within the Beatles was a slippery concept by the end of 1968. As the concert date approached with no sign that rehearsals might begin, the booking was scrapped, and a new date (but no venue) was announced for mid-January. In fact, the plan had

Ever since his walkabout in *A Hard Day's Night* Starr had been considered the most natural actor among the Beatles, and during the group's final months he turned to film for a solo outlet. After a bit-part in *Candy*, he co-starred with Peter Sellers, right, in *The Magic Christian*, 1969.

changed yet again. Now, still with an eye towards giving a concert, the Beatles would get together just after the New Year and begin preparing new material. The rehearsals would be filmed for a television special, and then they would go to some exotic location – a Roman amphitheatre in North Africa, the Sahara desert and even a big ship in the Mediterranean were mentioned – to play a single concert, which would also be filmed. They hired Michael Lindsay-Hogg, the director who had made their promotional films for 'Paperback Writer', 'Rain', 'Hey Jude' and 'Revolution', to film this endeavour from start to finish. To an extent they carried out their plan, except that the exotic concert venue turned out to be the roof of their new Apple offices and recording studio in Savile Row, London, on a cold January afternoon.

With the tensions of the 'White Album' sessions still fresh in their minds, and with the added pressure of a camera crew following them around, the Beatles began their rehearsals at Twickenham Film Studios on 2 January. Because these were not proper recording sessions, there were no real studio facilities. But the cameras, and a portable tape recorder used to make reference recordings, captured an extraordinary amount of detail about the Beatles' working methods and interaction. We hear them, for example, limbering up on countless oldies. Songs by Chuck Berry, Buddy Holly, Little Richard, the Drifters, Bob Dylan, Carl Perkins, Smokey Robinson, the Rolling Stones, the Temptations and even a few of their own hits are touched upon. Mostly, these are unbuttoned, unpolished performances.

The real work at hand, of course, was the new material, of which there was plenty, with contributions from all four Beatles. In fact, if every new song tried out at these sessions had gone through to completion, the group could easily have filled another double album. Besides the songs included on the *Let It Be* album, these sessions yielded the first workouts of more than half the songs that would be recorded later in the year for *Abbey Road* – including Starr's 'Octopus's Garden', McCartney's 'Maxwell's Silver Hammer', 'Oh! Darling', 'She Came In Through the Bathroom Window' and 'Her Majesty', and Lennon's 'Sun King', 'Mean Mr Mustard' and 'Polythene Pam', and Harrison's 'Something' – as well as quite a few songs that found homes on their post-Beatles solo albums.

The reference tapes made by the film crew capture the complete development of several of the new songs, from the moment the composer played it to the others through to the finished production. McCartney is heard sitting at the piano or with his bass, singing out the chords to his songs while the others follow along, or scat-singing sections that lack lyrics, and sometimes adding vocal harmonies even before the lyrics are finished. Songs are tried slow and fast, in electric and acoustic versions, and with different kinds of introductions and solos.

Often, the lyrics come together gradually while the band is churning through the chords. 'Get Back', for example, began life as 'No Pakistanis', a parody – one of several recorded during these sessions –

of the 'Britain for the British' stance taken by various right wing groups. The Pakistani notion was soon dropped, but the refrain – 'get back to where you once belonged' – became the peg around which two scant unconnected fantasies were spun. And at one point, the tapes capture McCartney coming up with the line 'Jo Jo left his home in Tucson, Arizona'. Lennon asks, 'Is Tucson *in* Arizona?' 'Yeah,' McCartney tells him, 'it's where they make *High Chapparal*'.

There is also plenty of chat, which runs the gamut from hilarious monologues by Lennon, to serious discussions of the feasibility of various concert proposals. And there are fights. Harrison, at this point, had the longest list of grievances. He objected to McCartney's telling him when and how to play. And having become a more prolific composer, he wanted his songs better represented on the Beatles' albums. After a particularly tense session on 10 January, he walked out, clearly with the intention of not returning. The others continued without him; Lennon went as far as to suggest that they invite Eric Clapton to sit in. Five days later, when all four met to negotiate their future, Harrison made it clear that he would no longer consider the prospect of a live performance, but would return if they would leave Twickenham and begin work on an album. The film was summarily redefined as a television programme about the making of a new Beatles album, and the musicians and film crew moved to the group's new Apple Studios, where most of the material on the *Let It Be* album was recorded in ten days of sessions. Eventually, the television idea was scrapped in favour of a theatrical film.

All that makes the production of the album sound much more clear-cut than it was. In fact, it was a disaster, although in concept, it should have been quite easy. By the time the sessions moved to Apple, the Beatles had announced that they were getting back to their roots – that their new album would be recorded live in the studio, without overdubbing or fancy technology. Since they would not, after all, perform live, this was the next best thing. And the album's title, at this stage, was to be *Get Back*.

To make sure that the group's textural demands could be met without multitracking (they later did some slight touch-up overdubbing), Harrison brought in Billy Preston, an American organist who the Beatles had met at the Star Club in 1962, when he was part of Little Richard's band. Preston would soon become an Apple artist in

Will it be a live concert? A television special? A film? McCartney, at the piano, leads his fractious colleagues in a rehearsal during the filming of *Let It Be* in January 1969.

his own right, but for now he was almost a fifth Beatle. He played on most of the sessions, took a few prominent solos (on 'Get Back' for instance), and was given a label credit for his performance.

The formal sessions were as unruly as those at Twickenham: jams and oldies performances punctuated attempts to record new material, and the Beatles decided that some of these off-the-cuff performances should be included on the record. By 29 January, they had completed several new songs, and the next day, in the hope of getting versions that really did sound live, they clambered up to the windswept Apple roof-top and gave a concert for the cameras while crowds gathered on the street and on adjacent roof-tops. The police eventually stopped the performance, but the Beatles did get forty-two minutes of taping done, which yielded the last twenty minutes of the *Let It Be* film.

Back in their basement studio, on 31 January, they finished off three more songs, and then, considering their work done, they washed their hands of the project, leaving George Martin and Glyn Johns to sort out the audio recordings, and Michael Lindsay-Hogg to make his way through a month's worth of film. The outcome was a confusing mess. In early March, Lennon and McCartney asked Johns to compile the *Get Back* album. He produced a sequence that fulfilled the group's wish to mix impromptu material and between-songs chatter with finished recordings of the new songs. Or so he thought. In the end, they refused to sign off on it, and his sequence was shelved. Except for some minor tinkering, the tapes were untouched for the rest of the year.

A few of his selections, dropped from the finished album, are worth noting, since they represent the free-wheeling atmosphere of the project. One was an instrumental jam, provisionally titled 'Rocker', which fades in on its final thirty seconds and then, after a breakdown and some discussion, goes into the Drifter's classic 'Save the Last Dance for Me', which pivots briefly into one of Lennon's new songs, 'Don't Let Me Down'. In the discussion that follows, one can hear that they actually were thinking in terms of a concert set. At least, Lennon goes through the order that the songs are to be played.

Also dropped was McCartney's 'Teddy Boy', and understandably: clearly unfinished, it meanders, with the others following McCartney as he hums his way through it. And then there is Lennon's 'Dig It', one of several jams in which the band played a slowly evolving vamp while Lennon ad libbed lyrics. Although part of the version Johns included on *Get Back* was shown in the film, only a few seconds of the song made it onto the final album – a pity, because unpolished as it was, its word-play and name associations were amusing, and it showed that the band and Preston could cook when the mood was right. Otherwise, Johns had only eight new songs to work with, plus a quick rendering of a Liverpool skiffle classic, 'Maggie Mae', which was also retained in the final sequence. He opened the album with 'One After 909', a Lennon antiquity, composed in the 1950s and untouched since the abortive attempt to record it in 1963.

Lennon's other contributions were 'Dig a Pony', a page of stream-of-consciousness lyrics set to a bluesy melody in three-quarter time, and 'Don't Let Me Down', a more sophisticated look at the concerns and insecurities he had explored in 'If I Fell'. 'Don't Let Me Down' has some interesting musical touches. Its verses are built around a vacillating E major and F sharp minor chord sequence – a representation, one could argue, of the lyric's principal concern, the mixture of joyous optimism (E major) and doubt, fear and caution (F sharp minor) that a new relationship brings. And as in 'All You Need is Love', the metre is governed by the shape of the lyric, not by conventional verse concerns. Thus, each stanza begins with a single five-beat bar, which leads immediately back to quarter time, a lopsided arrangement by conventional pop songwriting standards.

Harrison came to these sessions with a cart-load of songs, but the sessions yielded only one finished one, 'For You Blue', a straight twelve-bar blues, embellished by a slide guitar solo by Lennon and an atmospherically tinkly piano accompaniment by McCartney.

McCartney dominated the rest of the set. Along with the unfinished 'Teddy Boy', there was 'Get Back', which after all its transformations ended up as a pleasant mid-tempo rocker. The image McCartney used to describe it – 'music to rollercoast by' – captures its spirit. There was the more hard-driving 'I've Got a Feeling', to which a late 1968 Lennon fragment, 'Everybody Had a Hard Year', was grafted as a secondary melody, and 'Two of Us', a folksy tune that hearkened back to 'I'll Follow the Sun'. And McCartney sang two piano-based ballads with lilting melodies that helped make them immediate standards, 'Let It Be' and 'The Long and Winding Road'.

As the first glimpse of the widely publicized and long-awaited *Get Back* project, 'Get Back' and 'Don't Let Me Down' were released as a single with due fanfare on 11 April. In its advertisements, Apple emphasized the live-in-the-studio aspect, declaring the recordings to be 'The Beatles as Nature Intended'. The album, it was announced, would be available in the summer.

Test pressings of the Glyn Johns sequence were made and widely distributed. And in May a cover photo was taken. Angus McBean, the photographer who had shot the cover of *Please Please Me*, was called back to recreate that photo, with the 1969 Beatles standing in exactly the same positions (leaning over a balcony at EMI's headquarters in Manchester Square) as in 1963. Yet, the Beatles were uneasy about *Get Back*, and refused to approve its release. A revamped version fared no better, and the summer release date came and went.

Complications thwarted Lennon's original idea of marrying Yoko Ono in Paris, but eventually they found a registry they could call home in Gibraltar. They were wed there on 20 March 1969, and flew to Amsterdam for their 'Bed-In for Peace' honeymoon. Lennon catalogued their travails in 'The Ballad of John and Yoko'.

Long the only unmarried Beatle, Paul McCartney is flanked by Linda Eastman and her daughter Heather after their wedding at the Marylebone Registry Office in London, 12 March 1969.

Lennon and Ono believed that they should use their celebrity – and its immediate media access – to campaign for peace. They held a second 'Bed-In' in Montreal from 26 May to 2 June, during which 'Give Peace a Chance' was written and recorded.

The Beatles, actually, were on to other things. In February, they began a series of sporadic sessions, producing material that would find its way onto the *Abbey Road* album. On 12 March, McCartney married Linda Eastman, an American photographer whom he had met in 1967. Eight days later, Lennon and Ono married too. The Lennons had undertaken an aggressive campaign for world peace, and decided to use the natural publicity that a Beatle wedding was likely to draw as a platform for their new mission. After marrying in Gibraltar, they flew to Amsterdam for their honeymoon, which they staged as a week-long 'Bed-In for Peace', inviting journalists to a series of bedside interviews. They repeated this in Montreal in late May.

Lennon documented the wedding and all the events surrounding it in 'The Ballad of John and Yoko'. Perhaps as an offshoot of his peace campaigning, Lennon began thinking of songwriting as a kind of journalism: he could write and produce recordings about whatever was on his mind, and get them immediately into the stores. This was to be his first try at that, although as it turned out, six weeks elapsed between the recording session and the release of the disc. 'Give Peace a Chance', similarly, was recorded in his Montreal hotel room and released five weeks later. The process wasn't really perfected until early

1970, when he wrote and recorded 'Instant Karma!' in a day, and had it in the stores eleven days later.

Only McCartney was available when Lennon was ready to record 'Ballad', so on 14 April they divided the instruments between them (Lennon played all the guitar lines, McCartney played bass, drums, piano and maracas) and completed the recording themselves. The song's salient feature was its refrain. Surely still mindful of the commotion his 'bigger than Jesus' statement had caused in 1966, Lennon mischievously ended each verse with the lines, 'Christ you know it ain't easy, you know how hard it can be. The way things are going, they're going to crucify me.' Sure enough, some radio stations played an edited version.

For the flip side of the single, Harrison was again given an opportunity to shine, and supplied 'Old Brown Shoe', a song that had a workout during the January sessions. Two days after the 'Ballad' recording, the full group gathered to record this, with McCartney providing a jangly piano part and an unusually rapid tandem bass and guitar line.

'Ballad' and 'Old Brown Shoe' were recorded specifically for release as a single. What the group thought it was up to at its other early 1969 sessions is not clear. *Get Back* was finished but in limbo, and it was not until later in the year that they definitively decided to pull together for another album. Yet on 22 February, the Beatles and Billy Preston reconvened to work on Lennon's 'I Want You (She's So Heavy)'. They worked on it more in April, and finally finished it in August.

Hardly the most popular song on *Abbey Road*, it is nevertheless one of the most innovative. Something of a Minimalist experiment, it owed something to 'Hey Jude', but went far beyond it. It is, in a way, two musically disparate ideas: an introductory section and refrain in triple metre, and a verse in quarter time. This shift from three to four beat measures, as well as an accompanying shift from a kind of icy, driving severity to a warm blues style, creates an interesting tension and keeps the listener slightly off balance.

The introductory figure is a rising and falling guitar arpeggio, supported by an almost Tchaikovskyesque bass line and an expanding organ chord. It does not quite lead into the song proper: it simply stops, and from the silence Lennon's voice emerges. The verse is an expansion of the title line, sung to a blues melody with the lead guitar following in tandem, McCartney's bass weaving around it with increasing virtuosity, and Preston's organ providing Stax-flavoured, texture-filling figuration. Yet after a few repetitions, Lennon shifts gears again. Singing a dangling 'She's so – ', he leads the group back into the music of the introduction, finishing the lyric ('She's so heavy') in two- and then three-part harmony with a passing dissonant touch.

The song moves back and forth between these two ideas for just over four and a half minutes, eventually leaving the final 'She's so' unresolved and heading into an instrumental rendering of the introductory music. This time the opening chord progression is repeated over and over, unchanging except in two details. McCartney's bass line darts freely around the chords, exploring different harmonic and rhythmic possibilities each time. And progressive layers of synthesized white noise create the sound of arctic winds. After three minutes, Lennon had an engineer snip the tape, making for an abrupt ending. The implication is that the guitar arpeggios and white noise would otherwise have kept repeating forever.

Also in the works by the end of April were McCartney's 'Oh! Darling', a love song in a raucous, updated 1950s' style, and Starr's new children's song about an aquatic utopia, 'Octopus's Garden'. Lennon's 'You Know My Name (Look Up the Number)', on the shelf since 1967, was taken down for some vocal overdubbing, but was still considered unfinished. The final touches were added seven months later, and it was released in 1970 as the B-side of the 'Let It Be' single. Sessions for Harrison's graceful 'Something' got under way in May. It was his most conventional love song, and his most successful, being not only his first (and only) A-side of a Beatles single, but a song widely covered by other musicians. These early sessions ended on 6 May, and work would not resume until July. But before the hiatus, one more song was taped, a gently plaintive McCartney melody with what under normal circumstances might have seemed a peculiar title, 'You Never Give Me Your Money'.

The circumstances were anything but normal, though. Since February, the group's finances had been precarious. Lennon told the press that Apple was almost bankrupt – that it had become an open house for freeloaders, and that money was pouring out of it more quickly than even the Beatles could coin it. McCartney insisted that

Although the Beatles signed countless autographs over the years, complete sets with special characteristics – for instance, the individual caricatures here – are especially prized by collectors.

things were not so dire, but proposed hiring the New York law firm of Eastman and Eastman to sort things out. Eastman and Eastman was a prestigious firm that had contacts in music and publishing stretching back decades. The catch, from the other Beatles' point of view, was that Lee Eastman and his son John were about to become McCartney's father-in-law and brother-in-law.

Nevertheless, in early February, all four signed an agreement appointing Eastman and Eastman as general counsel for Apple. But Lennon, Harrison and eventually Starr, had doubts about the arrangement. Lennon had a competing proposal. Allen Klein, a New York music manager who had negotiated a fortune in royalties for the Rolling Stones, had flown to London to offer his services as soon as Lennon's assessment of Apple's finances hit the papers. Brusque and down to earth, exactly the opposite of the Eastmans, Klein impressed Lennon, who signed him on as his personal representative after a single meeting. Harrison and Starr backed Klein too. McCartney did not. So the others, with typical naïvety, decided that both John Eastman and Allen Klein could look after the group's interests.

Their first joint endeavour should have been to buy NEMS Enterprises, Epstein's management firm, which took a twenty-five per cent commission on the Beatles' record royalties, and was now

for sale. Epstein's family said it would rather sell the company to the Beatles than to the highest bidder, the Triumph Investment Group. Yet just as NEMS was within their grasp, managerial infighting at Apple scared the Epsteins into the arms of Triumph.

Eventually Klein managed to buy the Beatles out of the NEMS contract. But another disappointment loomed. Dick James, the publisher who signed Lennon and McCartney in 1963, and was the principal shareholder of Northern Songs, the company he created to handle their catalogue, was alarmed by Lennon's avant gardism and had staunchly opposed their involvement with Klein. He had also had enough of the group's increasingly high-handed treatment of him. So when Lennon and McCartney were on their honeymoons, in March, he sold his shares in the company to Lew Grade's ATV Music.

Klein sought to seize control of the company for the Beatles. Complicated negotiations were undertaken with a consortium that controlled the decisive shares, and which was inclined toward the Beatles. But at the last minute, Lennon publicly proclaimed his disinclination to deal with businessmen, and by late May, Grade had won control of the company. It was around the same time that Klein was formally installed as manager. He began dismantling Apple's staff forthwith.

All these battles, to say nothing of the widening creative gulf between the musicians, made the dissolution of the Beatles inevitable. Starr and Harrison had already quit and come back. Lennon was making it clear that he saw his destiny elsewhere. McCartney, who had been the *de facto* director of the band since *Sgt. Pepper*, had been rebuffed in his choice of manager. And so they went their separate ways in May. When they reconvened in July, it was to record what they and everyone around them knew would be their final album.

It was, at first, to be called *Everest*. The name came from the brand of cigarettes that one of the engineers smoked, but the Beatles soon seized on the idea that calling their final album *Everest* was in itself a statement. They had confounded everyone who had thought them a passing fad in 1963 and 1964, and who thought they would be destroyed by controversy in 1966. Now they were walking away from the Beatle myth while they were at their peak, towering over all their competitors both creatively and as a popular phenomenon.

They even agreed to be flown to Mount Everest to shoot a cover photo. But when the time came to make arrangements for the trip, none of them could be bothered. In the end, one of them suggested going out into the road to shoot the cover. McCartney sketched out a cover design, the photographer Iain Macmillan was commissioned to shoot the Beatles traversing the Abbey Road zebra crossing, and suddenly the album became *Abbey Road*. Actually, the album was not even recorded entirely at EMI's Abbey Road studios. After the *Get Back* sessions at Apple, the Beatles were eager to assert their independence from EMI, so from February to May they visited other London studios. Mostly, they did so without George Martin, who had found the tense January sessions unbearable. He returned for the July sessions only after McCartney promised him that the Beatles would work as they had in years past, and that they would treat him as a producer, not as a lackey.

Abbey Road was by no means a return to the experimentation of *Sgt. Pepper* and *Revolver*, but every track was laboured over in great detail. EMI had upgraded to eight-track facilities, which again doubled the Beatles' overdubbing and balancing flexibility. Yet even this relative opulence was insufficient, and in several cases they filled eight tracks, mixed them down to two and then filled the tape again. Orchestras sweeten several songs and sound effects were used freely, among them bubble-blowing on Starr's 'Octopus's Garden' and a blacksmith's anvil in 'Maxwell's Silver Hammer'. And heard for the first time on a Beatle record was the Moog synthesizer, the latest electronic instrument, newly famous as the instrument on which the American composer Walter (now Wendy) Carlos had produced *Switched-On Bach*.

The sessions began, fittingly, with McCartney alone in the studio, adding vocals to 'You Never Give Me Your Money'. He also recorded the twenty-three-second 'Her Majesty', really just a throw-away, although it had been germinating at least since the January sessions. Early July also saw work on McCartney's 'Golden Slumbers/Carry That Weight', a setting of a poem by the sixteenth-century playwright Thomas Dekker. There was an immediate philosophical disagreement on how to proceed. McCartney, with encouragement from Martin, wanted to link several songs together in a huge suite, with stretches in which individual songs were inseparable from those around them. There was reason to think in bigger terms. Around the time 'Get Back' hit the charts, the Who had wrested the spotlight from the Beatles with *Tommy*, a rock opera in the truest sense of the term, a unified, dramatic whole in which each song advances the narrative.

Lennon thought the McCartney–Martin suite idea was nonsense. The main motivation, he argued, was to disguise the fact that so many of the songs they were considering for inclusion – his own 'Mean Mr Mustard' and 'Polythene Pam', and McCartney's 'She Came in Through the Bathroom Window', for example – were merely fragments tried at the January sessions and never developed further. They were obviously not promising enough to merit full-length development, and by Lennon's lights, weaving them together as a suite was a pretentious cheat.

This was, in truth, a peculiar objection for Lennon, who had not minded joining disparate fragments to produce 'A Day in the Life' or 'Happiness is a Warm Gun'. In any case, Martin mediated a compromise. The first side of the album, and the start of side two, would have full-length, independent songs, as Lennon wanted. But the album would end with the suite McCartney proposed. Other than this structural disagreement, the sessions went smoothly through July and August. The final touches were put on the album on 25 August,

John Lennon/bag one

John Lennon

Left, the cover of Lennon's *Bag One* collection of erotic lithographs, a project which, like the *Two Virgins* album, celebrated Lennon's love for Ono in a way that courted controversy.

and it was released thirty-one days later. The compromise, it turned out, was a good thing.

Lennon's contributions to the effort were few, but first rate. Besides 'I Want You (She's So Heavy)', there was 'Because', a stunningly harmonized melody woven around a lyric filled with naturalistic imagery and light puns. Lennon always maintained the the chord sequence was derived from Beethoven's 'Moonlight' Sonata, which he heard Ono play and asked her to play backwards. If the story is true, other harmonic alterations took place along the way, but certainly the accompaniment owes something to the Beethoven work.

Lennon's other full-length offering, 'Come Together', began life as a gift to Timothy Leary, the American LSD guru. Visiting Lennon during the Montreal Bed-In at the end of May, Leary said that he was planning to run for political office and asked Lennon to write a song around his campaign slogan, 'Come Together'. Lennon ended up keeping the song himself, bringing it to the Beatles' session in late July. 'Come Together' makes a superb opening track: it launches the album with Lennon hissing the word 'shoot', followed by a rising guitar figure that obscures what he is actually saying – 'shoot me'.

The song landed him in legal hot water. A typical Lennon lyric, it interspersed nonsense phrases, outlandish wordplay and utopian sentiment. But as was Lennon's wont while composing, he used another song as a template. This time it was Chuck Berry's 'You Can't Catch Me', and unfortunately, he retained a line of Berry's lyric with only slight alterations. Berry's publisher sued, and the case dragged on to the mid-1970s, when Lennon agreed to record 'You Can't Catch Me' and a few more songs from the publisher's catalogue on *Rock 'n' Roll*, his 1975 oldies collection.

Also among the free-standing songs were Starr's 'Octopus's Garden' and McCartney's 'Oh! Darling' and 'Maxwell's Silver Hammer', an oddity with a lyric about a cranium-smashing, psychopathic medical student, set to an incongruously singsongy melody. The second side began with a second Harrison offering, 'Here Comes the Sun', in which a gracefully lilting melody supports a lyric about the arrival of spring after a dismal winter. Harrison's introduction is based on variations of a D major chord fingering, a trick he last used on 'If I Needed Someone'. The acoustic guitar holds centre stage, with drums, bass, and delicate synthesizer tracery added, all making for a beautifully transparent sound. The melody is accented with judiciously applied three-part vocal harmonies. The two Harrison compositions included here, together with the earlier 'While My Guitar Gently Weeps', show that Harrison had at last found his voice, and could write songs easily on a par with those Lennon and McCartney were producing. For that matter, 'Here Comes the Sun' is far more substantial than 'Maxwell's Silver Hammer'.

There is something to Lennon's complaint that the album's closing suite is an easy way of sweeping together the shards of unfinished songs. Yet the construction was hardly slapdash. In some cases ('Sun King' and 'Mean Mr Mustard,' 'Polythene Pam', and 'She Came in Through the Bathroom Window', and 'Golden Slumbers' and 'Carry That Weight') fragments were fashioned into medleys before they were recorded. Others were fitted together like pieces of a jigsaw puzzle. Experiments were tried and abandoned: 'Her Majesty' had been inserted between 'Mean Mr Mustard' and 'Polythene Pam', but was sliced out when McCartney realized that the suite flowed better without it. And where the joins were rough, orchestrations smoothed out the connections.

Granted, the fragments yoked together bear no relation to each other. But what a colourful cast of characters they present. The set begins with McCartney rooted firmly in the real world, complaining about business in 'You Never Give Me Your Money'. But it quickly drifts into the free-floating fantasy world of Lennon's 'Sun King', a land of three- and four-part harmony with only a mildly dissonant sheen, where everybody is said to be laughing and happy.

A drum fill from Starr introduces 'Mean Mr Mustard', a harmless eccentric, and 'Polythene Pam', with her curious sartorial specialities (a polythene bag, and jackboots and a kilt). A guitar solo leads into 'She Came in Through the Bathroom Window', written by McCartney after a souvenir-hunting fan broke into his house. This brings the first part of the suite to a close. And just as that section began with McCartney's gentle piano chording, so does the continuation, 'Golden Slumbers' and its extension, 'Carry That Weight', which reprises the melody of 'You Never Give Me Your Money', this time with more abstract lyrics.

The final section, 'The End', is the Beatles' self-conscious valedictory. As such, it includes something unusual for the Beatles, a jam in which each takes the spotlight for a moment. McCartney, Harrison and Lennon alternate brief lead guitar solos in a dialogue that highlights their individual styles: McCartney's playing is fleet and virtuosic, Harrison's is simpler, slinkier and more bluesy, and Lennon's is a chunky, chordal growl. Even Starr takes a solo. And as the song comes to a close, McCartney, Lennon and Harrison harmonize on a single line that would seem to embody the experience the Beatles had come through since 1962, and a sentiment they had promoted since 1965:

And in the end
The love you take
Is equal to the love you make

It was the perfect ending for the Beatles' recording career. Or, it would have been. But real life is not so tidy. The Beatles' recognition of this is clear from the way the album actually ends: after a long silence, the brief 'Her Majesty' suddenly pops out of the speakers. Its appearance was an accident: after lopping it out of the medley, an engineer affixed it to the end of the reel. When McCartney heard it on a playback of the finished suite, he decided to leave it there.

It also creates a circular effect that the Beatles cannot have intended, but which is interesting harmonically. Because of the way it was cut from the medley, 'Her Majesty' lacks its final note, and so ends in the middle of a chord sequence. As it turns out, it is is the same key as 'Come Together', so if the album is played again immediately after 'Her Majesty' ends, the progression is resolved. Similarly, the sudden tape cut at the end of 'I Want You (She's So Heavy)' leaves the song, and side one of the album, unresolved. But side two begins with 'Here Comes the Sun', which starts with exactly the chord needed to finish the sequence.

When the Beatles finished *Abbey Road*, Lennon reasserted his need for what he called a divorce from the Beatles. The others, and Klein, persuaded him not to discuss these feelings publicly: EMI and Klein were negotiating a revision of their contract, which would provide them with greater royalties on earlier albums. It would not do for EMI to know that the Beatles might no longer be a going concern.

Lennon's interviews from the time left the impression that he was more interested in his own projects than Beatles endeavours, but

The Beatles in the spring of 1969, in one of their last publicity photos as a band.

that the door to future collaborations was always open. In the meantime, despite his objection to performing live when McCartney suggested it, he accepted an invitation, on the spur of the moment, to perform at a rock and roll oldies show in Toronto on 13 September. He brought the Plastic Ono Band, which in this case included Eric Clapton on guitar, Klaus Voorman on bass and Alan White on drums. The set included oldies ('Blue Suede Shoes', 'Money', and 'Dizzy Miss Lizzy'), Lennon's 1968 'Yer Blues', a new, as yet unreleased song, 'Cold Turkey', and the anthemic 'Give Peace a Chance', along with two of Ono's extended avant-garde feedback-and-wailing pieces. All this was recorded, and released before the year's end as *Live Peace in Toronto*.

Meanwhile, it was time to settle the fate of *Get Back*. Lindsay-Hogg had produced a cut of the film, which was now called *Let It Be*. When the Beatles saw it, they realized that they had never completed two of the songs they are seen working on – Harrison's 'I Me Mine' and Lennon's 'Across the Universe' – and that recordings would be needed for the soundtrack album. For the Lennon song, the 1968 recording was taken off the shelf. And on 3 January 1970, all but Lennon gathered at Abbey Road to record 'I Me Mine'. This was the last session devoted to recording new Beatles material.

Johns produced another sequence using these new elements, but like his earlier effort, it failed to please the Beatles. The album was loose, as they wanted it; but it was also sloppy. Lennon and Harrison had recently renewed an old friendship with Phil Spector, the American producer known for his grandiose yet tightly controlled 'wall of sound' production style. In late March, Spector was handed the tapes and given a tall order: the finished *Let It Be* album had to reflect the contents of the film, and it had to at least allude to the original 'as nature intended' idea, although Spector was free to use standard post-production techniques. Lennon and Harrison reckoned that whatever Spector did would be an improvement.

For the most part, they were wrong, although it is an overstatement to call Spector's *Let It Be* a disaster from start to finish. Spector wisely left 'Get Back', 'For You Blue', 'Two of Us' and 'One After 909' alone, simply creating clean, crisp mixes from the eight-track sessions tapes. Like Glyn Johns, he included dialogue, count-ins and the off-the-cuff version of 'Maggie Mae'. And by doing some judicious editing and restructuring, he transformed the 3 January version of 'I Me Mine', which lasted only a minute and a half, into a full-length song.

On the other hand, 'Dig It' was reduced to a snippet that scarcely hinted at the free-wheeling spirit of the original. And several songs were severely overproduced. The fact that 'Let It Be' had already been released as a single, for example, did not stop him from entirely recasting it. He added echo to Starr's simple high hat taps, making for a cascading effect foreign to the feel of the song. With two guitar solos to choose from, he suppressed the one heard on the single and used the other. And he restructured the song, editing in a repetition of one of the verses.

Far more egregious was his treatment of 'The Long and Winding Road' and 'Across the Universe'. Calling in the orchestrator Richard Hewson to create new arrangements, Spector layered an orchestra and choir on both songs, transforming them into pompous goo. And 'Across the Universe', sped up in 1968 to create the other-worldly vocal effect that Lennon liked, was now brought down to normal speed, and sounded slow and draggy. 'I Me Mine' was given the orchestral treatment too, but survived it better than the others.

Lennon thought Spector's work was fine. McCartney was outraged when he heard it, and was particularly incensed by what had become of 'The Long and Winding Road'. Whether he nevertheless approved it for release is an open question: McCartney claimed that he did not hear the album until its release, but Spector claimed that McCartney sent his approval by telegram.

In any case, when the album was released on 8 May 1970, it was disappointingly anticlimactic. The material on it was already well known, thanks to bootlegs of the Glyn Johns mixes, and most listeners agreed with McCartney that Spector's transformations were appallingly un-Beatles-like. And in fact, by the time the album was released, the breakup had been made official. On 10 April, McCartney said as much while promoting his début solo album, *McCartney*. He had played all the instruments on this record, and as an added display of independence, he included a self-interview with press copies.

Asking himself if there were plans for new Beatles recordings, or whether he missed the other Beatles and Martin while recording *McCartney*, his blunt answer was no. He gave the same response to a question about whether the Lennon–McCartney partnership might be revived. To a question about whether the album represented a split with the Beatles or merely a rest, he said, 'time will tell'. And he characterized his reasons for breaking with the Beatles as 'personal differences, business differences, musical differences, but most of all because I have a better time with my family. Temporary or permanent? I don't know.'

The hopeful clung for a while to that 'I don't know' and 'time will tell', abbetted by interviews in which the others suggested that the breach might not be irreparable. Yet, listening to *Let It Be* alongside *McCartney* and *Live Peace in Toronto* – or by the end of the year, Harrison's *All Things Must Pass* and Lennon's *Plastic Ono Band* – the real answer was clear.

Only eight years earlier, the Beatles had ventured forth from Liverpool and quickly conquered the music world with an original amalgam of rock, rhythm and blues, country, English folk and traditional music, a touch of avant gardism and a healthy measure of imagination. They logged tens of thousands of miles on tour, and recorded thirteen albums and twenty-two singles for EMI – more than 200 songs, mostly their own compositions. They had broken the barriers between high and low art, and between different pop genres, in ways that no rock band before them had done. And now, because they felt that their individual musical destinies lay in different directions, the Beatles era was over.

Epilogue

The rock world has produced many genuinely inventive, technically advanced composers, and it has produced superstars who have sold more records than the Beatles did at their height. Yet no group or solo performer has attained the stature – the almost universal acceptance across musical boundaries, and the sense of being the standard against which others are measured – that the Beatles achieved.

By the time of the breakup, Lennon, Harrison and McCartney had all produced musical works outside the group. McCartney had composed the soundtrack music for *The Family Way*, and Harrison produced the *Wonderwall* soundtrack and *Electronic Sound*. In October 1969, Starr began recording a collection of cabaret standards, and by the end of the year, McCartney was working on his first collection of post-Beatles rock songs.

John Lennon, of course, was by then an experienced hand at solo projects – or really, collaborations with Ono. Their first joint project actually predated their romantic involvement. Fascinated with Ono's conceptual art projects after seeing her *Unfinished Paintings and Drawings* exhibition in November 1966, he sponsored a London show called *Yoko Plus Me* in October 1967. Half a year later they recorded *Unfinished Music No. 1: Two Virgins*, and released it around the time of the 'White Album'.

In spring 1968, now demanding recognition as soul mates, they began their campaign for world peace, staging events of various kinds. *Acorns for Peace* was unveiled (or planted) at Coventry Cathedral in June, and in July, 365 message-bearing balloons were released over London as the inaugural event in Lennon's *You Are Here* exhibition. At the end of the year, they documented Ono's hospital stay, during her miscarriage, for one side of *Unfinished Music No. 2: Life With the Lions*. The other side was a recording of Lennon's first performance as an accompanist to Ono at a concert in Cambridge in March 1969. Scenes from their first Bed-In were included on *The Wedding Album*.

Yet another avant-garde project – a recording of a studio full of people laughing wildly for half an hour – was left unissued.

Besides all this, Lennon and Ono produced numerous avant-garde films in 1969 and 1970. Some were whimsical. For *Bottoms* and *Up Your Legs Forever*, they had visitors drop their trousers to be filmed. *Fly*, with a suitable soundtrack by Ono, followed the painstakingly filmed (with help of sugar water) travels of a fly around a woman's body, and *Smile* was a study of Lennon smiling. Others were more intense. In *Rape*, a camera followed a woman through the streets and into her apartment (her sister collaborated by providing the key) chronicling her changing response, from curiosity and humour at first to extreme irritation as the camera grew more intrusive.

Yet for all this activity, the field in which Lennon was most at home remained the pop song, and he did not neglect it. 'Give Peace a Chance' emerged from the Montreal Bed-In of May and June 1969. 'Cold Turkey' was an acknowledgement of something the Beatles had been keeping quiet: the fact that Lennon and Ono had developed a heroin habit by mid-1969. 'Cold Turkey' was about the painful process of kicking that habit, and to make that pain tangible, in the record's final moments, Lennon borrowed Ono's screaming technique. Even before the Beatles had officially broken up, Lennon had released these two songs as singles, as well as 'Instant Karma' and the *Live Peace in Toronto* album.

In 1970, after months of pursuing Ono's ex-husband, Tony Cox, in the hope of gaining custody of her daughter, Kyoko, the Lennons went to Los Angeles to vent their frustrations at primal scream therapy sessions with Dr Arthur Janov, an experience that yielded the intensely personal (and often blisteringly angry) songs compiled on the *Plastic Ono Band* album. Among them was 'God', which includes his denial of a list of the world's idols, from Buddha to the Beatles.

Plastic Ono Band was spare, almost Minimalist in texture. *Imagine*, its successor in 1971, hid its harshness under a sugar coating of strings and production effects. Its title song, a utopian vision of a world without national boundaries or greed, joined 'Give Peace a Chance' as an idealist anthem. That song, along with 'Jealous Guy' and 'Oh My Love', is sweetly lyrical. But there is unvarnished anger here too. 'I Don't Want to Be a Soldier' and 'Gimme Some Truth' are shots across the bow of the establishment, and 'How Do You Sleep?' is an undisguised attack on McCartney (in response, Lennon said, to a somewhat subtler attack on McCartney's *Ram* album).

Lennon and Ono moved to New York soon after *Imagine* was finished, and forged links to the radical anti-war underground. This proved imprudent: once the Nixon administration got the idea that Lennon would be the drawing card at an anti-Nixon demonstration, it moved to have him deported, claiming his 1968 drug conviction as justification. Thus began a five-year battle to remain in the USA.

During his 'radical' phase, Lennon slipped into his songwriter-as-journalist persona, and with a New York bar band called Elephant's Memory as his backing group, he recorded *Some Time in New York City*, a collection of his positions on everything from Northern Ireland to the uprising at Attica State Prison. Musically, these folksy outpourings were the least inspired songs he had yet released, and even his most ardent fans were beginning to wonder if the creative well had run dry. Lennon no doubt sensed this. *Mind Games*, in 1973, was an attempt to return to the spirit of *Imagine*. But here too, his inspiration was inconsistent. The pressures on him could not have helped. While he fended off the American government's harassment, his relationship with Ono foundered. The two separated in 1973, and for a year and a half Lennon split his time between New York and Los Angeles.

Lennon had two albums in the works concurrently during this period. The first was *Rock 'n' Roll*, the collection of oldies he agreed to record as the cost of settling the 'Come Together' plagiarism suit. The other was *Walls and Bridges*, a collection of autobiographical and self-analytical songs that was a decided improvement on *Mind Games*. He and Ono were reconciled in January 1975, whereupon Lennon virtually dropped out of sight for five years, preferring to raise their son Sean outside the public eye. But Lennon continued to compose, and in 1980, as his fortieth birthday approached, he and Ono returned to the music world with *Double Fantasy*, a collection of songs about the joys and stresses of marital life, arranged as a dialogue.

Lennon's return to public life would have galvanized the rock world even if *Double Fantasy* had not had some of his best post-Beatles music on it. Suddenly he was available for lengthy retrospective interviews, and was already at work on a follow-up, to be called *Milk and Honey*. But at nearly 11 pm on 8 December, as he and Ono walked from their limousine to the doorway of the Dakota Apartments, Lennon was shot dead by Mark David Chapman, a demented fan for whom he had autographed a copy of *Double Fantasy* earlier in the day.

Lennon's death, and the manner of it, shocked the world. But it did not silence him, entirely. In 1984, Ono released their work-in-progress, *Milk and Honey*, the first of several posthumous projects that include *Menlove Avenue*, a collection of unreleased performances, and *Live in New York City*, a recording of a 1972 concert with Elephant's Memory. Ono also provided several hundred hours of Lennon's working tapes for use in a radio series, *The Lost Lennon Tapes*, and allowed her private film archive to be used in the making of *Imagine: John Lennon*, a 1988 documentary film.

Paul McCartney's first post-Beatles album, *McCartney*, said a lot about its maker. Its cover photo, with its spilled bowl of cherries, seemed a wistful comment on the Beatles' breakup, but then, so did the other jacket photos, which depicted domestic tranquillity. By playing all the instruments himself, he made it clear that he was prepared to stand on his own as a one-man band. Whether he could stand alone as a songwriter seemed less certain. He had, of course, done so already, with songs like 'Yesterday'. In fact, he was extraordinarily facile, able to produce songs out of thin air on demand. But this facility was a mixed blessing. Too often, his thin-air creations remained vaporous, and without Lennon's trusted critical voice, he was unable to separate the wheat from the chaff. *McCartney* points up this problem. First rate songs like 'Maybe I'm Amazed', 'Every Night' and the lilting 'Junk' sit beside throwaways like 'The Lovely Linda' and 'That Would Be Something'.

The consistency problem was more acute in his second and third albums, *Ram* and *Wild Life*, both recorded in 1971, the latter with McCartney's new band, Wings. McCartney hoped that Wings would be a stable group that could evolve from project to project. But except for his wife Linda, who was now playing keyboards, and Denny Laine, a guitarist who had been in an early line-up of the Moody Blues, Wings' personnel changed frequently

Red Rose Speedway, in 1973, was a distinct improvement, full of beautifully textured songs (but also featuring the treacly 'My Love'). And the same year saw further progress: the composition of 'Live and

Let Die', a high-energy theme song for a James Bond film, and *Band on the Run,* the album that would become a high-water mark of McCartney's solo career. *Band on the Run* was a triumph snatched from the jaws of disaster. Half of Wings resigned the day Paul and Linda McCartney and Denny Laine left for Lagos, Nigeria, to begin recording. McCartney was mugged soon after his arrival. Yet the album was McCartney's most consistent, and most spirited, since the Beatles. Its successor, *Venus and Mars*, in 1975, was cut from similar cloth.

With its release, McCartney and a newly reconstituted Wings undertook a world tour, stopping only to record *Wings at the Speed of Sound* in 1976. The tour produced a triple live album, *Wings Over America*, and a film, *Rockshow*, which included McCartney's remakes of a handful of Beatles songs, along with stage versions of his solo material.

The tour gave McCartney a creative boost; yet *Wings at the Speed of Sound* and its 1978 follow-up, *London Town*, were retreats from the bright sound of *Band on the Run* and *Venus and Mars.* Now McCartney was lightening the textures, looking at music that prized melody, character and introspection over energy and drive. There were also responses to the criticism he had earned so far: in 'Silly Love Songs', he confronts those who objected to the sappiness of 'My Love', but he is none too convincing.

As in his Beatles days, McCartney regularly released singles that did not appear on his albums. One of these, the singsongy 'Mull of Kintyre' – a paean to the environs of his Scottish farm – proved to be one of the best-selling records of all time, eclipsing even 'I Want to Hold Your Hand', though for no discernible musical reason. McCartney's luck changed for the worse with *Back to the Egg* in 1979, a collection that explores a great many styles, from hard rock to 1940s' pastiche. It deserved better than the critical thrashing it received.

McCartney undertook a tour of England, and was about to tour Japan in 1980 when he was arrested for marijuana possession at Narita International Airport in Tokyo. He spent eight days in jail, and was deported. For all practical purposes, Wings fell apart then. McCartney did what he did when the Beatles broke up: he released a one-man-band album, *McCartney II.* His instrumental arsenal had grown, as had his performing ability, yet the album had little to recommend it, and it signalled the start of an alarming desire to produce disco funk tracks, here embodied in 'Coming Up'. This would join the composition of glutinous love songs as a continuing current in McCartney's work.

The Japanese fiasco, combined with Lennon's murder at the end of 1980, cured McCartney of his desire to tour, at least for the time being. But in 1982, just as his listeners were about to write him off once again, he produced another of his better solo efforts, *Tug of War*. The album, which included some gorgeously lyrical songs and collaborations with Carl Perkins and Stevie Wonder, was the first of several projects that reunited McCartney with George Martin. *Pipes of Peace*, released in 1983, was not quite as consistent. But it too had some crossover appeal: a couple of the songs were collaborations with Michael Jackson, then at the height of his fame. The McCartney–Jackson friendship was shattered in 1985, when Jackson paid $47 million for the Lennon–McCartney publishing catalogue, outbidding McCartney and Ono.

Some of the *War* and *Peace* songs, along with a few Beatles remakes and a handful of new tunes, made up the soundtrack to *Give My Regards to Broad Street*, McCartney's unsuccessful bid to both write and star in a film. Smarting from that failure, he refashioned his sound yet again, and produced the trendy and only fleetingly satisfying *Press to Play* album in 1986.

By now the pop market had moved on to other things. A core of ageing Beatles fans continued to follow McCartney's work, and he attracted some younger listeners too; but mostly, as he approached his fifties, he seemed to lose his ability to reach the top of the pop charts, even when his work was at its best. His *Flowers in the Dirt*, released in 1989, was a solid, durable album on a par with *Band on the Run* or *Tug of War*; yet it failed to make a dent in the American pop charts. Nor did the well-crafted *Off the Ground* fare well in 1993.

Yet his 1989 and 1993 world tours proved that he could still draw big audiences, even if they mainly wanted to hear Beatles and Wings songs. Those were the centrepieces of the film and live album each tour produced – The *Get Back* film and the *Tripping the Live Fantastic* album in 1990, and the *Paul Is Live* album and video in 1993. Also of interest among McCartney's releases are *Back in the U.S.S.R.*, an album of rock oldies, recorded in 1987 and originally released only in the

Soviet Union, and *Unplugged*, an acoustic concert recorded for MTV, the American music video station in 1991.

There are several non-rock productions among McCartney's post-Beatles works. The most ambitious is a grandly-scaled classical work, *Paul McCartney's Liverpool Oratorio*, a collaboration with the London-based American filmscore composer and conductor Carl Davis. The Liverpool Philharmonic commissioned it as part of its 150th anniversary celebration, and would have been happy with a ten minute overture. But McCartney, with Davis providing technical support, composed a quasi-operatic work for full orchestra, mixed choir, boys choir and vocal soloists, in eight movements that clocks in at about ninety minutes.

It is, to be sure, a straightforwardly tonal piece, and its Achilles heel – as is so often the case in McCartney's work – is its text. Its hero is a Liverpool Everyman who wrestles with his Muse before coming to terms with it. Along the way, conservative family values are celebrated, sometimes touchingly, sometimes mawkishly. But whatever the flaws of the text, the work does include some truly beautiful choral and vocal writing. And a lengthy violin solo suggested that McCartney might have a concerto in him. The première performance at the Anglican Cathedral in Liverpool on 28 June 1991, with Davis on the podium, was recorded and released by EMI's classical arm.

A more recent non-rock project is *Strawberries Oceans Ships Forest* a 1993 collaboration with a producer known as Youth, released under the name the Fireman. Here McCartney experiments with ambient techno-pop, and presents nine pieces – or, actually, nine versions of a single piece, each using different synthesizer coloration and effects.

For George Harrison, the breakup of the Beatles was a golden opportunity. He had come of age as a songwriter, and his contributions to *Abbey Road* were among that album's highlights. He had also become quite prolific, and now he could record his songs without competition or criticism from Lennon and McCartney. His first collection, *All Things Must Pass*, was a triple album – two discs of new songs plus a collection of session jams.

Harrison began explaining his interest in Hinduism here, offering songs about the transitory nature of life and the triviality of mundane struggle compared with the quest to be one with the Godhead. Songs about more worldly matters were interspersed, and the album was rapturously received. But his first single, 'My Sweet Lord', landed him in earthly trouble: just as Lennon had been sued by Chuck Berry's publisher for lifting a line from 'You Can't Catch Me', the publisher of the old Chiffons hit, 'He's So Fine', sued Harrison on the basis of melodic similarities in the choruses of the two songs. Harrison lost the suit, which dragged on for two decades.

In 1971 Harrison helped arrange an all-star benefit concert at Madison Square Garden, in New York, to raise relief money for Bangla Desh. Bob Dylan, Eric Clapton, Ringo Starr, Billy Preston and dozens more musicians played in this precursor of Live Aid and other rock charity concerts, and the performance yielded an album and a film, *The Concert for Bangla Desh.* Disputes over everything from distribution rights to taxes kept the proceeds from being put immediately toward the relief effort.

The songs Harrison recorded for *Living in the Material World* in 1973 furthered his Eastern religious agenda, and although the album reached the top of the American charts, there was growing resistance to what many listeners considered Harrison's preachy tone. Still, as on *All Things Must Pass*, the material was by no means exclusively spiritual: 'Sue Me Sue You Blues', for example, offers a glimpse into the legal infighting among the former Beatles.

Harrison's slide from pop chart grace began with *Dark Horse*, in 1974, which was perceived as more preaching and whining. A tour of the USA, undertaken to promote the record, was disastrous: Harrison, unused to singing more than a song or two in an evening, did nothing to prepare himself vocally, and had sung himself hoarse before the show got on the road. *Extra Texture*, in 1975, was an improvement, and boasted a few appealing songs in the ruminative style that Harrison had been drawn to since his Beatles days. *Thirty-Three and a Third*, released in 1976, was notably more upbeat, the sermonizing replaced by some satirical comment on the ways of the material world. Specifically, his 'This Song' commented on the 'He's So Fine' lawsuit, and a video clip made to promote the song parodied the trial. Stylistically, Harrison's reach was fairly broad here: one hears everything from traditional blues to light jazz, along with Harrison's own recognizable style.

Harrison took a three-year break from the music world after *Thirty Three and a Third.* He had been estranged from his wife Pattie for some time; she had, in fact, become romantically involved with Eric Clapton, whom she later married. The Harrisons' divorce was finalized in 1977, and in 1978 Harrison married Olivia Arias. He also began to dabble in the film world, bailing out Monty Python's troubled *Life of Brian*. Because this first experience as a film producer proved both pleasing and lucrative, he formed his own company, HandMade Films, which made twenty-seven films before Harrison sold his interest in 1994.

Harrison's 1979 return to recording, *George Harrison*, was lighter in spirit than its predecessors, with songs about everything from automobile racing to psychotropic mushrooms, along with a reworking of 'Not Guilty', his defensive response to the inter-Beatle squabbling during the 'White Album' sessions. But his audience, like McCartney's, had dwindled by 1979, and when he submitted his next album, *Somewhere in England*, at the end of 1980, he had to face something unthinkable for a former Beatle: his record company demanded changes. He complied, defiantly adding 'Blood from a Clone', a song about record company interference in artistic endeavours, to a line-up that already included 'Unconsciousness Rules', a swat at disco. The request for a revamp did, however, afford Harrison an opportunity to add 'All Those Years Ago', a touching, upbeat tribute to Lennon, on which McCartney and Starr overdubbed instrumental contributions.

By 1982 it seemed as though Harrison was finding his battles in the music business utterly dispiriting. When he released *Gone Troppo* that year, he did nothing whatsoever to promote it, and it barely registered in the charts – a pity, really, since it was full of bright, humorous, energetic songs, rich in melodic charm. Once again, he stepped away from music, not returning until 1987, when *Cloud Nine* brought him his biggest success since *All Things Must Pass*. Recorded at his home studio, with contributions from Starr and Clapton, and co-produced by Jeff Lynne of the Beatles-influenced Electric Light Orchestra, the album was refreshingly spirited, and included a nostalgic skewering of the Beatles myth, 'When We Was Fab'. Now back in the limelight, he teamed up with Dylan, Lynne, the 1950s' legend Roy Orbison and a younger rock star, Tom Petty, to record *The Traveling Wilburys* in

1988. The album, collaboratively composed and recorded in short order, was brimming with spontaneity and humour. Orbison died soon after the record was released, but others kept the Wilburys alive, recording a second album, quirkily named *Volume 3*, in 1990.

Harrison has remained the most reclusive of the former Beatles, but in 1991 he made a tentative return to the stage, touring Japan with the support of Eric Clapton and his band, singing a combination of his Beatles-era compositions and selections from his solo work. A sampling of the performances can be heard on the *Live in Japan* album, released in 1992.

It seemed likely that Ringo Starr would devote himself to films after the breakup of the Beatles, and to an extent he did, appearing in several films and even doing some directing. Yet he had musical ambitions too. In late 1969 and early 1970 he recorded *Sentimental Journey*, a collection of cabaret standards. He worked with some starry arrangers – Quincy Jones, John Dankworth and Paul McCartney, among them – and the music was solid enough. But Starr proved no competition for Frank Sinatra or Ella Fitzgerald. He next turned his hand, without greater success, to country and western music, travelling to Nashville to record the homely *Beaucoups of Blues*.

Starr had better luck when he returned to rock and roll. As the only one of the former Beatles who enjoyed warm relations with all the others, he was able to draw on the songwriting talents of all three when he recorded *Ringo*, in 1973. The others played on the recording too, making it as close to a reunion project as the group would come. *Ringo* showed that with the right material, Starr's plaintive baritone had an appeal. He sought to create the same effect on *Goodnight Vienna* in 1974, but despite contributions from Lennon and other rock stars, the record lacked the dazzle of its predecessor.

In 1975 Starr's marriage fell apart, and he began a jet-setting lifestyle that exacerbated a drinking problem which, he later said, had developed during his years as a Beatle. Lennon, McCartney and Harrison each contributed a song to *Rotogravure*, which featured the graffiti-covered door of the former Apple offices on its cover. But by 1976, Beatles connections were not enough to buoy up a badly-sung, bored-sounding performance. *Ringo the 4th* fared no better in 1977, and although Starr participated in a likeable promotional television special co-starring Carrie Fisher and Art Carney to promote *Bad Boy* in 1978, that album too proved unsaleable.

Poor record sales were hardly the worst of Starr's problems at this time. He nearly died of an intestinal ailment in April 1979, and a few months later his house in Los Angeles burned to the ground. Lennon's death also hit him hard. By early 1981, he had recorded most of a new album, with contributions from McCartney and Harrison, but he did not have the heart to record the new songs Lennon had sent along. Nevertheless, *Stop and Smell the Roses* was surprisingly upbeat, and had something that had been missing since *Ringo*: a sense of humour.

But although Starr's wedding to the actress Barbara Bach (with whom he had starred in *Caveman*, a film about prehistoric times, in 1980) rated international news coverage, partly because McCartney and Harrison attended (and participated with Starr in a jam session), the album barely cracked the charts. His next, *Old Wave*, recorded in 1983, suffered a worse fate: it was released in only a handful of countries, the USA and Britain not among them. With his musical career seemingly over, Starr dropped out of sight, making occasional appearances on television and on stage, and recording songs for various benefit and compilation albums. Late in 1988, he recognized that alcoholism had become an impediment in both his private and professional life. He checked into a rehabilitation center in Arizona, and when he emerged he began making plans for a comeback. He assembled a solid, supportive band of ageing stars and almost-stars from the 1960s and 1970s, and undertook a tour, taking turns singing oldies with his bandmates.

He toured again in 1992, this time with a new album, *Time Takes Time*. The record was Starr's best: more consistently pleasing than *Ringo*, it showed him as an assured performer and songwriter, and set his modest voice within a Beatlesque backing. But he was unable to persuade the rock world of the 1990s that his work merited attention, and the album went largely ignored.

When the Beatles were together and at the height of their fame, the press regularly published reports saying that a breakup was imminent. Once the Beatles did separate, the press reversed polarity and began claiming, year in and year out, that they would get back together. The former Beatles themselves often fanned those rumours:

at various points in the 1970s, each of them hinted that perhaps a reconciliation might be fun. But all four never said so at the same time. The death of John Lennon should logically have ended hopes for a Beatles reunion; yet reports persisted through the 1980s, with Julian Lennon supposedly sitting in for his father.

Then suddenly, in 1989, a three-way collaboration of the surviving Beatles began to seem plausible. That November, a complex web of lawsuits – the Beatles and Apple against EMI, the Beatles against each other – was settled after twenty years of wrangling. With relations between the surviving former Beatles again amicable, Apple revived a project that had been shelved since 1970, a film documentary in which the Beatles would tell their own story. Over the next few years, McCartney, Harrison and Starr sat for interviews as Apple collected film footage from television archives around the world. From the start, McCartney spoke about getting together with his old bandmates to record soundtrack music for what was turning into a ten- or fifteen-hour series. It took him five years to persuade the others, but in February 1994, they assembled at McCartney's studio in East Sussex, and turned on the tape machines.

What they did during those sessions, and during further sessions in February 1995, was collaborate – with Lennon – on two new songs. On a visit to New York in January 1994, McCartney obtained some of Lennon's unfinished work tapes from Ono. Back in England, McCartney, Harrison and Starr listened to three or four songs before settling on two lilting ballads, 'Free as a Bird' and 'Real Love.' They added new instrumental lines and vocal harmonies, and McCartney wrote new lyrics for sections that Lennon had left unfinished, utterly transforming Lennon's rough, home-made recordings. For a few moments, if only in an electronically enhanced reality, the Beatles were back together making new music.

Further Reading

Biographies I: The Beatles as a Group

Baker, G. A. *The Beatles Downunder: The 1964 Australia and New Zealand Tour* (Glebe, Wild and Wooley, 1982)

Braun, M. *Love Me Do: The Beatles' Progress* (London, Penguin, 1964)

Davies, H. *The Beatles* (New York, McGraw-Hill, 1968, rev. 1985)

Norman, P. *Shout! The Beatles in Their Generation* (New York, Fireside, 1981)

Pawlowski, G. L. *How They Became the Beatles: A Definitive History of the Early Years 1960–1964* (New York, Dutton, 1989)

Schaffner, N. *The Beatles Forever* (Harrisburg, Pennsylvania, Cameron House, 1977)

Braun, an American journalist, followed the Beatles around England in late 1963 and to Paris in January 1964, and paints a compellingly realistic portrait of them on the eve of global success. Davies had complete access to the Beatles when he wrote this authorized biography in 1967, so although they ultimately expurgated his text, he covers their history thoroughly and offers eyewitness accounts of composing and recording sessions. Norman's book includes some controversial theories, but offers a broader, more complete and more analytical look at the group than Davies. Pawlowski and Baker look closely at specific periods in the group's history, and Schaffner offers an interesting personal overview.

Biographies II: The Beatles (and Others) Individually

Blake, J. *The Beatles after the Beatles* (New York, Perigee, 1981)

Clayson, A. *The Quiet One: A Life of George Harrison* (London, Sidgwick and Jackson, 1990)

Ringo Starr: Straight Man or Joker (New York, Paragon House, 1992)

Coleman, R. *John Lennon* (New York, McGraw Hill, 1984)

Brian Epstein (New York, McGraw Hill, 1989)

Giuliano, G. *Blackbird: The Life and Times of Paul McCartney* (New York, Dutton, 1991)

Robertson, J. *The Art and Music of John Lennon* (New York, Birch Lane, 1990)

Sutcliffe, P. and A. Clayson *Stuart Sutcliffe: The Lost Beatle* (London, Sidgwick and Jackson, 1994)

Wiener, J. *Come Together: John Lennon in His Time* (New York, Random House, 1984)

Woffinden, B. *The Beatles Apart* (New York, Proteus, 1981)

Lennon is the most vigorously chronicled of the former Beatles, and as a general biographer Coleman – who had co-operation and use of materials from both Cynthia Lennon and Yoko Ono – is the most comprehensive and accurate available. Wiener concentrates on the political aspects of his music, and Robertson offers a good overview of his works, including obscure avant-garde projects. Coleman also presents the only detailed look at the troubled life of Brian Epstein. McCartney, Harrison and Starr have guarded their privacy jealously, and lack thorough, serious biographies. These all rely heavily on news-paper, magazine and television interviews and other previously published material, but they marshal the historical facts efficiently.

Discographies, Chronologies and Reference Works

Castleman, H. and W. J. Podrazik *All Together Now* (Ann Arbor, Pierian Press, 1976)

The Beatles Again? (Ann Arbor, Pierian Press, 1977)

The End of the Beatles? (Ann Arbor, Pierian Press, 1985)

Dowdling, W. J. *Beatlesongs* (New York, Fireside, 1989)

Harry, B. *The Ultimate Beatles Encyclopedia* (New York, Hyperion, 1992)

Lewisohn, M. *The Beatles Live!* (New York, Henry Holt, 1986)

The Beatles Recording Sessions (New York, Harmony, 1988)

The Beatles Day By Day (New York, Harmony, 1990)

The Complete Beatles Chronicle (New York, Harmony, 1992)

Robertson, J. *The Complete Guide to the Music of the Beatles* (London, Omnibus, 1994)

Stannard, N. *The Long and Winding Road* (London, Virgin, 1982)

Sulpy, D. and R. Schweighardt *Drugs, Divorce and a Slipping Image: The Unauthorized Story of the Beatles' 'Get Back' Sessions* (Princeton Junction, New Jersey, The 910, 1994)

Turner, S. *A Hard Day's Write* (New York, Harper Perennial, 1994)

Wiener, A. *The Beatles: The Ultimate Recording Guide* (Holbrook, Mass., Bob Adams, Inc., 1994)

Lewisohn's books are essential. Painstakingly researched, passionately detailed and lavishly illustrated with unusual documents, news clippings and photographs, they accurately establish where the Beatles were, what they did and, in their recording sessions, how their innovations came about. *Chronicle,* the broadest overview, includes details of concerts, radio and television appearances and recording sessions; *Recording Sessions* studies the latter in much finer detail. Sulpy and Schweighardt offer a revealing analysis of the fractious *Get Back/Let It Be* sessions. The Castleman/Podrazik collaborations, though nominally discographies (group and solo), are actually far-reaching compendiums that include useful listings of all kinds, but take the story only to 1983. Wiener's more up-to-date *Ultimate Guide* offers chronologies, discographies and videographies of both group and solo work. Harry's *Encyclopedia* is handy for identifying peripheral characters in the Beatles' story. The Turner, Robertson, Stannard and Dowdling books examine the discography track by track, offering a variety of insights, and in Dowdling's case, relevant quotations from the Beatles.

Analysis

Hertsgaard, M. *A Day in the Life, The Music and Artistry of the Beatles* (New York, Delacorte, 1995)

MacDonald, I. *Revolution in the Head* (New York, Henry Holt, 1994)

Mellers, W. *Twilight of the Gods, The Music of the Beatles* (London, Faber and Faber; New York, Viking, 1973)

O'Grady, T. *The Beatles* (Boston, Twayne, 1983)

Riley, T. *Tell Me Why* (New York, Alfred A. Knopf, 1988)

The most eloquent, perceptive and historically accurate of these is Hertsgaard, who had access to working tapes unavailable to the others. Mellers approaches the Beatles' music as an older academic who seems not to fully grasp its aesthetic, yet he makes some interesting observations about how the songs work in purely structural terms. O'Grady's and Riley's historical notes are imperfect, but their observations on the music are often astute. O'Grady's is more technical, Riley's is for the general reader. MacDonald's song by song analysis is often contentious, but he includes handy charts relating the Beatles' work to the political and cultural history of the era.

Interviews and Memoirs

Best, P. with P. Doncaster *Beatle! The Pete Best Story* (New York, Dell, 1985)

DiLello, R. *The Longest Cocktail Party: An Insider's View of the Beatles* (New York, Playboy Press, 1972; Ann Arbor, Pierian Press, with additions, 1983).

Epstein, B. with D. Taylor *A Cellarful of Noise* (New York, Souvenir, 1964)

Gambaccini, P. *Paul McCartney in His Own Words* (New York and London, Quick Fox, 1976).

Harrison, G. *I Me Mine* (London, Genesis, 1980)

Editorial comments in D. Taylor. *Fifty Years Adrift* (London, Genesis, 1984)

Martin, G. with J. Hornsby *All You Need is Ears* (New York, St. Martin's Press, 1979)

Martin, G. with W. Pearson *Summer of Love: The Making of Sgt. Pepper* (London, Macmillan, 1994)

Miles *The Beatles in Their Own Words* (New York and London, Quick Fox, 1978)

John Lennon in His Own Words (New York and London, Quick Fox, 1981)

Peebles, A. *The Last Lennon Tapes* (London, BBC, 1981)

Sheff, D. and B. Golson *The Playboy Interviews with John Lennon and Yoko Ono* (New York, Playboy Press, 1981)

Taylor, D. *As Time Goes By: Living in the Sixties* (London, Davis–Poynter, 1973)

Fifty Years Adrift (London, Genesis, 1984)

Wenner, J. *Lennon Remembers* (New York, Popular Library, 1971)

Williams, A. with W. Marshall *The Man Who Gave the Beatles Away* (New York, Ballantine, 1975)

The Beatles were generally forthcoming in their interviews, and Lennon tended also to be expansive and self-analytical. The Wenner, Sheff and Peebles interviews are extensive and often cutting reflections on the Beatles (and more). In *I Me Mine*, Harrison reflects on his songwriting. Derek Taylor, who worked as an assistant to Brian Epstein and later as head of Apple's publicity department, adds context to Harrison's comments, and Harrison returned the favour in Taylor's own *Fifty Years Adrift*. Of the memoirs, Taylor's urbane recollections make the best reading, but Epstein and Martin have essential information to impart, as do Pete Best, the group's drummer during its formative years, Williams, its first manager, and DiLello, who worked at Apple from 1968 to 1970 and who paints a vivid and often humorous picture of the Beatles' troubled company.

Guides to Locations

Bacon, D. and N. Maslov *The Beatles' England* (San Francisco, 910 Press, 1982)

Forsyth, I. *The Beatles' Merseyside* (Market Drayton, Shropshire, S.B. Publications, 1991)

Jones, R. *The Beatles' Liverpool* (Wirral, Jones, 1991)

Lewisohn, M., P. Schreuders and A. Smith *The Beatles' London* (New York, St. Martin's Press, 1994)

All useful, illustrated guides to the places where the Beatles worked and lived.

Miscellaneous

The Beatles Complete Scores (New York, Hal Leonard, 1993)

This invaluable 1,138-page volume includes every song the Beatles recorded for EMI transcribed in full score – with all the guitar voicings, bass lines, drum parts, vocal harmonies and production embellishments – by Tetsuya Fujita, Yuji Hagino, Hajime Kubo and Goro Sato.

Di Franco, P. (ed.) *The Beatles in Richard Lester's A Hard Day's Night* (New York, Penguin, 1977)

Thomson, E. and D. Gutman (eds.) *The Lennon Companion* (New York, Schirmer, 1987)

Thomson and Gutman have brought together a trove of important newspaper and magazine articles, criticism and even a scholarly paper or two. Several entries are crucial: William Mann's December 1963 review of *With the Beatles*, Maureen Cleave's 1966 *Evening Standard* article, 'How Does a Beatle Live? John Lennon Lives Like This', with the observations on Christianity that caused Lennon grief in the USA, and Ned Rorem's 'The Music of the Beatles' are here, as are observations by Luciano Berio, John Tavener, Joshua Rifkin, Noel Coward, Tom Wolfe, Kenneth Tynan and others. Di Franco's book includes the script of *A Hard Day's Night*, an invaluable interview with Richard Lester and reminiscences by Walter Shenson.

Selective Discography

Part I of this discography covers the recordings the Beatles made for EMI between 1962 and 1970, and follows the sequences that were released in Great Britain and most of the world. American releases, which bore different titles and song sequences – and which went out of print when they were superseded by the compact disc reissues, which followed the international format – are noted only when pertinent.

Part II covers pre-EMI recordings of historical interest that have been released commercially in various forms, as well as archival material released by EMI after the group's breakup.

The Beatles released their material in three formats: on 45rpm singles, long-playing albums, which generally did not include the songs released as singles (although there are exceptions), and extended-play discs, which usually included songs already available on albums and singles. Because the extended-play releases were essentially samplers, they are not included here except in the two cases where they include otherwise unavailable songs. However, singles that also appeared on albums are included in the interest of presenting the sequence of singles and albums intact. Similarly, compilations and greatest hits albums are not included except where they include otherwise unavailable material.

For each release, the original catalogue numbers and release dates are given. Compact disc catalogue numbers are provided for the albums. Compact disc versions of the singles and extended-play discs are available on CD only in boxed sets: *The Beatles CD Singles Collection* (Parlophone C2 0777 7 15901 2 2), *The Beatles Compact Disc EP Collection* (Parlophone C2–15852). The non-album tracks have also been compiled on the two *Past Masters* compact discs. *Past Masters Volume 1* (Parlophone CDP 7 90043 2) covers 1962 to 1965; *Past Masters Volume 2* (Parlophone CDP 7 90044 2) includes songs released between 1965 and 1970.

Part I: EMI Recordings 1962–70

Single (5 October 1962)
Love Me Do (John Lennon/Paul McCartney), 4 September version
P.S. I Love You (John Lennon/Paul McCartney)
Parlophone R 4949

Single (11 January 1963)
Please Please Me (John Lennon/Paul McCartney)
Ask Me Why (John Lennon/Paul McCartney)
Parlophone R 4983

Please Please Me (22 March 1963)
I Saw Her Standing There (John Lennon/Paul McCartney)
Misery (John Lennon/Paul McCartney)
Anna (Go To Him) (Arthur Alexander)
Chains (Gerry Goffin/Carole King)
Boys (Luther Dixon/Wes Farrell)
Ask Me Why (John Lennon/Paul McCartney)
Please Please Me (John Lennon/Paul McCartney)
Love Me Do (John Lennon/Paul McCartney), 11 September version
P.S. I Love You (John Lennon/Paul McCartney)
Baby, It's You (Hal David/Burt Bacharach/Barney Williams)
Do You Want To Know A Secret (John Lennon/Paul McCartney)
A Taste Of Honey (Bobby Scott/Ric Marlow)
There's A Place (John Lennon/Paul McCartney)
Twist And Shout (Phil Medley/Bert Russell)
Parlophone LP: PMC 1202/PCS 3042
CD: CDP7 46435 2

Single (12 April 1963)
From Me To You (John Lennon/Paul McCartney)
Thank You Girl (John Lennon/Paul McCartney)
Parlophone R 5015

Single (23 August 1963)
She Loves You (John Lennon/Paul McCartney)
I'll Get You (John Lennon/Paul McCartney)
Parlophone R 5055

With The Beatles (22 November 1963)
It Won't Be Long (John Lennon/Paul McCartney)
All I've Got to Do (John Lennon/Paul McCartney)
All My Loving (John Lennon/Paul McCartney)
Don't Bother Me (George Harrison)
Little Child (John Lennon/Paul McCartney)
Till There Was You (Meredith Willson)
Please Mister Postman
(Holland–Bateman–Gorman–Dobbins– Garrett)
Roll Over Beethoven (Chuck Berry)
Hold Me Tight (John Lennon/Paul McCartney)
You Really Got a Hold On Me (William Robinson)
I Wanna Be Your Man (John Lennon/Paul McCartney)
Devil in Her Heart (Richard Drapkin)
Not A Second Time (John Lennon/Paul McCartney)
Money (That's What I Want) (Berry Gordy/
Janie Bradford)
Parlophone LP: PMC 1206/PCS 3045
CD: CDP7 46436 2

Single (29 November 1963)
I Want To Hold Your Hand (John Lennon/
Paul McCartney)
This Boy (John Lennon/Paul McCartney)
Parlophone R 5084

Single (Germany, 5 March 1964)
Komm, gib mir deine Hand
(Lennon–McCartney–Nicolas–Hellmer)
Sie liebt dich
(Lennon–McCartney–Nicolas–Montague)
Odeon 22 671

Single (20 March 1964)
Can't Buy Me Love (John Lennon/Paul McCartney)
You Can't Do That (John Lennon/Paul McCartney)
Parlophone R 5114

Long Tall Sally (19 June 1964)
Long Tall Sally (Entoris Johnson/
Richard Penniman/Robert Blackwell)
I Call Your Name (John Lennon/Paul McCartney)
Slow Down (Larry Williams)
Matchbox (Carl Perkins)
Parlophone EP: GEP 8913

Single (10 July 1964)
A Hard Day's Night (John Lennon/Paul McCartney)
Things We Said Today (John Lennon/Paul McCartney)
Parlophone R 5160

A Hard Day's Night (10 July 1964)
A Hard Day's Night (John Lennon/Paul McCartney)
I Should Have Known Better (John Lennon/
Paul McCartney)
If I Fell (John Lennon/Paul McCartney)
I'm Happy Just To Dance With You (John Lennon/
Paul McCartney)
And I Love Her (John Lennon/Paul McCartney)
Tell Me Why (John Lennon/Paul McCartney)
Can't Buy Me Love (John Lennon/Paul McCartney)
Any Time At All (John Lennon/Paul McCartney)
I'll Cry Instead (John Lennon/Paul McCartney)
Things We Said Today (John Lennon/Paul McCartney)
When I Get Home (John Lennon/Paul McCartney)
You Can't Do That (John Lennon/Paul McCartney)
I'll Be Back (John Lennon/Paul McCartney)
Parlophone LP: PMC 1230/PCS 3058
CD: CDP7 46437 2

Single (27 November 1964)
I Feel Fine (John Lennon/Paul McCartney)
She's a Woman (John Lennon/Paul McCartney)
Parlophone R 5200

Beatles For Sale (4 December 1964)
No Reply (John Lennon/Paul McCartney)
I'm a Loser (John Lennon/Paul McCartney)
Baby's in Black (John Lennon/Paul McCartney)
Rock and Roll Music (Chuck Berry)
I'll Follow the Sun (John Lennon/Paul McCartney)
Mr Moonlight (Roy Lee Johnson)
Kansas City/Hey, Hey, Hey, Hey (Jerry Lieber/
Mike Stoller/Richard Penniman).
Eight Days A Week (John Lennon/Paul McCartney)
Words Of Love (Buddy Holly)
Honey Don't (Carl Perkins)
Every Little Thing (John Lennon/Paul McCartney)
I Don't Want to Spoil the Party (John Lennon/
Paul McCartney)

What You're Doing (John Lennon/Paul McCartney)
Everybody's Trying to Be My Baby (Carl Perkins)
Parlophone LP: PMC 1240/PCS 3062
CD: CDP7 46438 2

Single (9 April 1965)
Ticket To Ride (John Lennon/Paul McCartney)
Yes It Is (John Lennon/Paul McCartney)
Parlophone R 5265

Beatles VI (14 June 1965), a compilation album including the release of:
Bad Boy (Larry Williams)
US, Capitol T/ST 2358

Single (23 July 1965)
Help! (John Lennon/Paul McCartney)
I'm Down (John Lennon/Paul McCartney)
Parlophone R 5305

HELP! (6 August 1965)
Help! (John Lennon/Paul McCartney)
The Night Before (John Lennon/Paul McCartney)
You've Got To Hide Your Love Away (John Lennon/Paul McCartney)
I Need You (George Harrison)
Another Girl (John Lennon/Paul McCartney)
You're Going to Lose That Girl (John Lennon/Paul McCartney)
Ticket to Ride (John Lennon/Paul McCartney)
Act Naturally (Vonie Morrison/Johnny Russell)
It's Only Love (John Lennon/Paul McCartney)
You Like Me Too Much (George Harrison)
Tell Me What You See (John Lennon/Paul McCartney)
I've Just Seen a Face (John Lennon/Paul McCartney)
Yesterday (John Lennon/Paul McCartney)
Dizzy Miss Lizzy (Larry Williams)
Parlophone LP: PMC 1255/PCS 3071
CD: CDP 7 46439 2

Single (3 December 1965)
We Can Work It Out (John Lennon/Paul McCartney)
Day Tripper (John Lennon/Paul McCartney)
Parlophone R 5389

Rubber Soul (3 December 1965)
Drive My Car (John Lennon/Paul McCartney)
Norwegian Wood (This Bird Has Flown) (John Lennon/Paul McCartney)
You Won't See Me (John Lennon/Paul McCartney)
Nowhere Man (John Lennon/Paul McCartney)
Think For Yourself (George Harrison)
The Word (John Lennon/Paul McCartney)
Michelle (John Lennon/Paul McCartney)
What Goes On (John Lennon/Paul McCartney/Richard Starkey)
Girl (John Lennon/Paul McCartney)
I'm Looking Through You (John Lennon/Paul McCartney)
In My Life (John Lennon/Paul McCartney)
Wait (John Lennon/Paul McCartney)
If I Needed Someone (George Harrison)
Run For Your Life (John Lennon/Paul McCartney)
Parlophone LP: PMC 1267/PCS 3075
CD: CDP7 46440 2

Single (10 June 1966)
Paperback Writer (John Lennon/Paul McCartney)
Rain (John Lennon/Paul McCartney)
Parlophone R 5452

Single (5 August 1966)
Yellow Submarine (John Lennon/Paul McCartney)
Eleanor Rigby (John Lennon/Paul McCartney)
Parlophone R 5493

Revolver (5 August 1966)
Taxman (George Harrison)
Eleanor Rigby (John Lennon/Paul McCartney)
I'm Only Sleeping (John Lennon/Paul McCartney)
Love You To (George Harrison)
Here, There and Everywhere (John Lennon/Paul McCartney)
Yellow Submarine (John Lennon/Paul McCartney)
She Said She Said (John Lennon/Paul McCartney)
Good Day Sunshine (John Lennon/Paul McCartney)
And Your Bird Can Sing (John Lennon/Paul McCartney)

For No One (John Lennon/Paul McCartney)
Doctor Robert (John Lennon/Paul McCartney)
I Want To Tell You (George Harrison)
Got to Get You into My Life (John Lennon/Paul McCartney)
Tomorrow Never Knows (John Lennon/Paul McCartney)
Parlophone LP: PMC/PCS 7009
CD: CDP7 46441 2

Single (17 February 1967)
Strawberry Fields Forever (John Lennon/Paul McCartney)
Penny Lane (John Lennon/Paul McCartney)
Parlophone R 5570

Sgt. Pepper's Lonely Hearts Club Band (1 June 1967)
Sgt. Pepper's Lonely Hearts Club Band (John Lennon/Paul McCartney)
With a Little Help From My Friends (John Lennon/Paul McCartney)
Lucy in The Sky With Diamonds (John Lennon/Paul McCartney)
Gettin Better (John Lennon/Paul McCartney)
Fixing a Hole (John Lennon/Paul McCartney)
She's Leaving Home (John Lennon/Paul McCartney)
Being for the Benefit of Mr Kite! (John Lennon/Paul McCartney)
Within You Without You (George Harrison)
When I'm Sixty-Four (John Lennon/Paul McCartney)
Lovely Rita (John Lennon/Paul McCartney)
Good Morning Good Morning (John Lennon/Paul McCartney)
Sgt. Pepper's Lonely Hearts Club Band (reprise) (John Lennon/Paul McCartney)
A Day in the Life (John Lennon/Paul McCartney)
Parlophone LP: PMC/PCS 7027
CD: CDP7 46442 2

Single (7 July 1967)
All You Need is Love (John Lennon/Paul McCartney)
Baby, You're a Rich Man (John Lennon/Paul McCartney)
Parlophone R 5620

Single (24 November 1967)
Hello Goodbye (John Lennon/Paul McCartney)
I Am the Walrus (John Lennon/Paul McCartney)
Parlophone R 5655

Magical Mystery Tour (8 December 1967)
Magical Mystery Tour (John Lennon/Paul McCartney)
Your Mother Should Know (John Lennon/Paul McCartney)
I Am the Walrus (John Lennon/Paul McCartney)
The Fool on the Hill (John Lennon/Paul McCartney)
Flying (John Lennon/Paul McCartney/George Harrison/Richard Starkey)
Blue Jay Way (George Harrison)
Parlophone 2–EP set: MMT/SMMT 1
[Note: In the USA, the *Magical Mystery Tour* EPs and the preceding three singles were issued as an LP, *Magical Mystery Tour* (27 November 1967, Capitol MAL/SMAL 2835). This format was later issued in Great Britain as well (19 November 1976, Parlophone PCTC 255) and on CD: CDP7 48062 2]

Single (15 March 1968)
Lady Madonna (John Lennon/Paul McCartney)
The Inner Light (George Harrison)
Parlophone R 5675

Single (30 August 1968)
Hey Jude (John Lennon/Paul McCartney)
Revolution (John Lennon/Paul McCartney)
Apple R 5722

The Beatles (known as the 'White Album') (22 November 1968)
Back in the U.S.S.R. (John Lennon/Paul McCartney)
Dear Prudence (John Lennon/Paul McCartney)
Glass Onion (John Lennon/Paul McCartney)
Ob-La-Di, Ob-La-Da (John Lennon/Paul McCartney)
Wild Honey Pie (John Lennon/Paul McCartney)
The Continuing Story of Bungalow Bill (John Lennon/Paul McCartney)
While My Guitar Gently Weeps (George Harrison)
Happiness is a Warm Gun (John Lennon/Paul McCartney)
Martha My Dear (John Lennon/Paul McCartney)

I'm So Tired (John Lennon/Paul McCartney)
Blackbird (John Lennon/Paul McCartney)
Piggies (George Harrison)
Rocky Raccoon (John Lennon/Paul McCartney)
Don't Pass Me By (Richard Starkey)
Why Don't We Do It in the Road (John Lennon/ Paul McCartney)
I Will (John Lennon/Paul McCartney)
Julia (John Lennon/Paul McCartney)
Birthday (John Lennon/Paul McCartney)
Yer Blues (John Lennon/Paul McCartney)
Mother Nature's Son (John Lennon/Paul McCartney)
Everybody's Got Something to Hide Except Me and My Monkey (John Lennon/Paul McCartney)
Sexy Sadie (John Lennon/Paul McCartney)
Helter Skelter (John Lennon/Paul McCartney)
Long, Long, Long (George Harrison)
Revolution 1 (John Lennon/Paul McCartney)
Honey Pie (John Lennon/Paul McCartney)
Savoy Truffle (George Harrison)
Cry Baby Cry (John Lennon/Paul McCartney)
Revolution 9 (John Lennon/Paul McCartney)
Good Night (John Lennon/Paul McCartney)
Apple 2–LP set: PMC/PCS 7067–8
CD: CDS7 46443 8

Yellow Submarine (17 January 1969)
Only a Northern Song (George Harrison)
All Together Now (John Lennon/Paul McCartney)
Hey Bulldog (John Lennon/Paul McCartney)
It's All Too Much (George Harrison)
All You Need is Love (John Lennon/Paul McCartney)
[The rest of the album consists of George Martin's orchestral incidental score for the *Yellow Submarine* film]
Apple LP: PMC/PCS 7070
CD: CDP7 46445 2

Single (11 April 1969)
Get Back (John Lennon/Paul McCartney)
Don't Let Me Down (John Lennon/Paul McCartney)
Apple R 5777

Single (30 May 1969)
The Ballad of John and Yoko (John Lennon/ Paul McCartney)
Old Brown Shoe (George Harrison)
Apple R 5786

Abbey Road (26 September 1969)
Come Together (John Lennon/Paul McCartney)
Something (George Harrison)
Maxwell's Silver Hammer (John Lennon/ Paul McCartney)
Oh! Darling (John Lennon/Paul McCartney)
Octopus's Garden (Richard Starkey)
I Want You (She's So Heavy) (John Lennon/ Paul McCartney)
Here Comes the Sun (George Harrison)
Because (John Lennon/Paul McCartney)
You Never Give Me Your Money (John Lennon/ Paul McCartney)
Sun King (John Lennon/Paul McCartney)
Mean Mr Mustard (John Lennon/Paul McCartney)
Polythene Pam (John Lennon/Paul McCartney)
She Came in through The Bathroom Window (John Lennon/Paul McCartney)
Golden Slumbers/Carry That Weight (John Lennon/ Paul McCartney)
The End (John Lennon/Paul McCartney)
Her Majesty (John Lennon/Paul McCartney)
Apple LP: PCS 7088
CD: CDP7 46446 2

Single (31 October 1969)
Something (George Harrison)
Come Together (John Lennon/Paul McCartney)
Apple R 5814

No One's Gonna Change Our World
(12 December 1969), a benefit album for the World Wildlife Fund including the release of:
Across the Universe (John Lennon/Paul McCartney) (original mix)
EMI Starline SRS 5013

Single (6 March 1970):
Let It Be (John Lennon/Paul McCartney)
You Know My Name (Look Up the Number) (John Lennon/Paul McCartney)
Apple R 5833

Let It Be (8 May 1970)
Two of Us (John Lennon/Paul McCartney)
Dig a Pony (John Lennon/Paul McCartney)
Across the Universe (John Lennon/Paul McCartney)
I Me Mine (George Harrison)
Dig It (John Lennon/Paul McCartney/George Harrison/Richard Starkey)
Let It Be (John Lennon/Paul McCartney)
Maggie Mae (Trad./Arr. John Lennon/Paul McCartney/George Harrison/Richard Starkey)
I've Got a Feeling (John Lennon/Paul McCartney)
One After 909 (John Lennon/Paul McCartney)
The Long and Winding Road (John Lennon/Paul McCartney)
For You Blue (George Harrison)
Get Back (John Lennon/Paul McCartney)
Apple LP: PCS 7096
CD: CDP7 46447 2

Part II: Archival Recordings

The Beatles With Tony Sheridan

In Hamburg in June 1961 and April 1962, the Beatles recorded six songs as a backing band for Tony Sheridan, and two more on their own. The recordings have been released on various labels over the years, most recently as *The Early Tapes of the Beatles* (Polydor 823 701–2, 1984, which also includes non-Beatles material). The Beatles recordings are:

Cry for a Shadow (John Lennon/George Harrison)
Ain't She Sweet (Jack Yellen/Milton Ager)
My Bonnie (Charles Pratt)
The Saints (Traditional, arr. Tony Sheridan)
Why (Tony Sheridan/Bill Crompton)
Sweet Georgia Brown (Ben Bernie/Maceo Pinkard/Kenneth Casey)
Take Out Some Insurance On Me Baby (Charles Singleton/ Waldenese Hall)
Nobody's Child (Mel Foree/Cy Cohen)

The Decca Audition

The Beatles' unsuccessful recording test for Decca, on 1 January 1962, was released by several small labels in the 1980s. The session included:

Like Dreamers Do (John Lennon/Paul McCartney)
Money (That's What I Want) (Berry Gordy/Janie Bradford)
Till There Was You (Meredith Willson)
The Sheik of Araby (Harry Smith/Ted Snyder/Frances Wheeler)
To Know Her is to Love Her (Phil Spector)
Take Good Care of My Baby (Gerry Goffin/Carole King)
Memphis (Chuck Berry)
Sure to Fall (Carl Perkins/William Cantrell/Quinton Claunch)
Hello Little Girl (John Lennon/Paul McCartney)
Three Cool Cats (Jerry Lieber/Mike Stoller)
Crying, Waiting, Hoping (Buddy Holly)
Love of the Loved (John Lennon/Paul McCartney)
September in the Rain (Al Dubin/Harry Warren)
Besame Mucho (Consuelo Velasquez/Selig Shaftel)
Searchin' (Jerry Lieber/Mike Stoller)

The Star Club Tapes

Recorded on 31 December 1962, these live recordings were first released in 1977, and have been issued by several small labels since then. The most complete CD version is *The Beatles Live at The Star Club in Hamburg Germany 1962* (Overseas 38CP–44):

I Saw Her Standing There (John Lennon/Paul McCartney)
I'm Gonna Sit Right Down And Cry Over You (Joe Thomas/Howard Biggs)
Roll Over Beethoven (Chuck Berry)
Hippy Hippy Shake (Chan Romeo)
Sweet Little Sixteen (Chuck Berry)
Lend Me Your Comb (Carl Perkins)
Your Feets Too Big (Ada Benson/Fred Fisher)

Where Have You Been All My Life (Barry Mann/Cynthia Weill)
Twist and Shout (Phil Medley/Bert Russell)
Mr Moonlight (Roy Leen Johnson)
A Taste of Honey (Bobby Scott/Rick Marlow)
Besame Mucho (Consuelo Velasquez/Selig Shaftel)
Till There Was You (Meredith Willson)
Reminiscing (King Curtis)
Kansas City/Hey, Hey, Hey, Hey (Jerry Leiber/Mike Stoller/Richard Penniman)
Nothin' Shakin' (Cirino Colacrai/Eddie Fontaine/Dianne Lampert/Jack Cleveland)
To Know Her is to Love Her (Phil Spector)
Little Queenie (Chuck Berry)
Falling in Love Again (Sammy Lerner/Frederick Hollander)
Sheila (Tommy Roe)
Ask Me Why (John Lennon/Paul McCartney)
Be-Bop-A-Lula (Gene Vincent/Tex Davis)
Hallelujah I Love Her So (Ray Charles)
Red Sails in the Sunset (Jimmy Kennedy/Will Grosz)
Everybody's Trying to Be My Baby (Carl Perkins)
Matchbox (Carl Perkins)
I'm Talking About You (Chuck Berry)
I Wish I Could Shimmy Like My Sister Kate (Piron)
Long Tall Sally (Entoris Johnson/Richard Penniman/Robert Blackwell)
I Remember You (Johnny Mercer/Victor Schertzinger)

The Beatles at the Hollywood Bowl (6 May 1977)
Concert recordings from 23 August 1964(*) and 30 August 1965(†)
Twist and Shout (Phil Medley/Bert Russell)†
She's a Woman (John Lennon/Paul McCartney)†
Dizzy Miss Lizzy (Larry Williams)†
Ticket to Ride (John Lennon/Paul McCartney)†
Can't Buy Me Love (John Lennon/Paul McCartney)†
Things We Said Today (John Lennon/Paul McCartney)*
Roll Over Beethoven (Chuck Berry)*
Boys (Luther Dixon–Wes Farrell)*
A Hard Day's Night (John Lennon/Paul McCartney)†
Help! (John Lennon/Paul McCartney)†
All My Loving (John Lennon/Paul McCartney)*
She Loves You (John Lennon/Paul McCartney)*
Long Tall Sally (Entoris Johnson/Richard Penniman/Robert Blackwell)*
LP: Parlophone EMTV 4

Live at the BBC (30 November 1994)
BBC radio performances, recorded between 1963 and 1965.
Beatle Greetings (spoken)
From Us To You (John Lennon/Paul McCartney)
Riding On a Bus (spoken)
I Got a Woman (Ray Charles)
Too Much Monkey Business (Chuck Berry)
Keep Your Hands Off My Baby (Gerry Goffin/Carole King)
I'll Be On My Way (John Lennon/Paul McCartney)
Young Blood (Jerry Leiber/Mike Stoller/Doc Pomus)
A Shot of Rhythm And Blues (Terry Thompson)
Sure to Fall (Carl Perkins/William Cantrell/Quinton Claunch)
Some Other Guy (Jerry Leiber/Mike Stoller/Ritchie Barrett)
Thank You Girl (John Lennon/Paul McCartney)
Sha La La La La! (spoken)
Baby It's You (Hal David/Burt Bacharach/Barney Williams)
That's All Right (Mama) (Arthur Crudup)
Carol (Chuck Berry)
Soldier Of Love (Cason/Moon)
A Little Rhyme (spoken)
Clarabella (Pingatore)
I'm Gonna Sit Right Down and Cry Over You (Joe Thomas/Howard Biggs)
Crying, Waiting, Hoping (Buddy Holly)
Dear Wack! (spoken)
You Really Got a Hold On Me (William Robinson)
To Know Her is to Love Her (Phil Spector)
A Taste of Honey (Bobby Scott/Ric Marlow)
Long Tall Sally (Entoris Johnson/Richard Penniman/Robert Blackwell)
I Saw Her Standing There (John Lennon/Paul McCartney)
The Honeymoon Song (Theodorakis/Sansom)
Johnny B Goode (Chuck Berry)
Memphis, Tennessee (Chuck Berry)
Lucille (A. Collins/Richard Penniman)
Can't Buy Me Love (John Lennon/Paul McCartney)
From Fluff to You (spoken)
Till There Was You (Meredith Willson)
Crinsk Dee Night (spoken)

A Hard Day's Night (John Lennon/Paul McCartney)
Have A Banana! (spoken)
I Wanna Be Your Man (John Lennon/Paul McCartney)
Just A Rumour (spoken)
Roll Over Beethoven (Chuck Berry)
All My Loving (John Lennon/Paul McCartney)
Things We Said Today (John Lennon/Paul McCartney)
She's a Woman (John Lennon/Paul McCartney)
Sweet Little Sixteen (Chuck Berry)
1822! (spoken)
Lonesome Tears in My Eyes (Johnny Burnette/Dorsey Burnette/Burlison/Mortimer)
Nothin' Shakin' (Cirino Calacari/Eddie Fontaine/Diane Lampert/Jack Cleveland)
The Hippy Hippy Shake (Chan Romero)
Glad All Over (Bennett/Tepper/Schroeder)
I Just Don't Understand (Wilkin/Westberry)
So How Come (No One Loves Me) (Boudleaux Bryant)
I Feel Fine (John Lennon/Paul McCartney)
I'm a Loser (John Lennon/Paul McCartney)
Everybody's Trying to Be My Baby (Carl Perkins)
Rock and Roll Music (Chuck Berry)
Ticket To Ride (John Lennon/Paul McCartney)
Dizzy Miss Lizzy (Larry Williams)
Kansas City/Hey, Hey, Hey, Hey (Jerry Leiber/Mike Stoller/Richard Penniman)
Set the Fire to the Lot! (spoken)
Matchbox (Carl Perkins)
I Forgot to Remember to Forget (S. Kesler/C. Feathers)
Love These Goon Shows! (spoken)
I Got to Find My Baby (Chuck Berry)
Ooh! My Soul (Richard Penniman)
Ooh! My Arms (spoken)
Don't Ever Change (Gerry Goffin/Carole King)
Slow Down (Larry Williams)
Honey Don't (Carl Perkins)
Love Me Do (John Lennon/Paul McCartney)
CDs: EMI/Apple CDP 8 31796 2

Single (20 March 1995)
Baby, It's You (Hal David/Burt Bacharach/Barney Williams)
I'll Follow the Sun (John Lennon/Paul McCartney)
Devil In Her Heart (Richard Drapkin)
Boys (Luther Dixon/Wes Farrell)
EMI/Apple 7243 8 82073 2 4

Videography

Films

A Hard Day's Night (1964), *Help!* (1965), *Magical Mystery Tour* (1967), *Yellow Submarine* (1968), *Let It Be* (1969–70)

A Hard Day's Night is also available on a CD–ROM (Voyager, 1993), which additionally includes the complete script, the theatrical trailer and an essay by Bruce Eder.

Documentaries

The Compleat Beatles (1982) – a good career overview with interesting performance clips, but with inaccuracies in the narration.

The Beatles: The First U.S. Visit (1990) – An effective Apple production that uses footage from the Maysles Brothers' 1964 documentary, *What's Happening! The Beatles in the USA* and performances from the Ed Sullivan Show and the Washington Coliseum concert.

Other Beatles performance footage is included in the commercially released instalments of *Ready, Steady, Go!*, a British television programmme. Their own performances in *Around the Beatles*, a 1964 television special that also featured other artists, has been released as *Ready, Steady Go! Special Edition.* In Japan, the group's 30 June 1966 performance at Budokan Hall has been released commercially.

Index

Page numbers in italics refer to picture captions.

Photographic Acknowledgements

Apple/Hulton Deutsch: 16, 19, 20, 23, 48b, 49, 50, 55, 57, 64–65, 73, 79, 94, 100, 102, 104–105, 113, 128, 132, 135, 137, 138, 146, 158, 165, 169, 176, 185, 194
BFI/Universal: 99, 108, 121b, 125
BFI/United Artists: 170
Rex Features: 2, 15, 37, 38–39, 40, 43, 48t, 51, 52–53, 63, 73–74, 80, 81, 83, 95, 111, 115, 119, 121t, 122–123, 127, 140–41, 151, 152, 157, 161, 166–7, 174, 179, 182, 187, 195, 198–9, 200, 206
Redferns: 26, 28–29, 32, 33, 34, 3 60, 67, 77, 84, 88–89, 91, 93, 126, 145, 164, 190–91

Quoted Lyrics